THE
GOLDEN CONDOM

ALSO BY JEANNE SAFER

THE
GOLDEN CONDOM

And Other Essays on Love Lost and Found

Jeanne Safer, Ph.D.

PICADOR

NEW YORK

picadorusa.com • picadorbookroom.tumblr.com
twitter.com/picadorusa • facebook.com/picadorusa

Picador® is a U.S. registered trademark and is used by St. Martin's Press under license from Pan Books Limited.

For book club information, please visit facebook.com/picadorbookclub or e-mail marketing@picadorusa.com.

Designed by Omar Chapa

The Library of Congress Cataloging-in-Publication Data

Names: Safer, Jeanne, author.
Title: The golden condom : and other essays on love lost and found / Jeanne Safer.
Description: New York : Picador, 2016.
Identifiers: LCCN 2015037148 | ISBN 9781250055750 (hardcover) | ISBN 9781250055767 (e-book)
Subjects: LCSH: Love—Psychological aspects. | Sex (Psychology) | Interpersonal relations. | BISAC: PSYCHOLOGY / Interpersonal Relations. | PHILOSOPHY / Social.
Classification: LCC BF575.L8 S315 2016 | DDC 152.4/1—dc23
LC record available at http://lccn.loc.gov/2015037148

Our books may be purchased in bulk for promotional, educational, or business use. Please contact your local bookseller or the Macmillan Corporate and Premium Sales Department at 1-800-221-7945, extension 5442, or by e-mail at MacmillanSpecialMarkets@macmillan.com.

First Edition: April 2016

10 9 8 7 6 5 4 3 2 1

For Terry Laughlin, my coach, my friend, my inspiration

AUTHOR'S NOTE

The names and identifying characteristics of most of the interview subjects, patients, and acquaintances described in this book have been changed.

CONTENTS

THE
GOLDEN CONDOM

INTRODUCTION

Another book on love? No emotion has transfixed, perplexed, devastated, and inspired humanity more than this one, and none has been more exhaustively dissected. Nonetheless, I believe that the lovers whose intimate voices you will hear in these pages have something unique to contribute.

I bring a special perspective to this daunting topic: forty years as a psychoanalyst, researcher, and teacher of dream interpretation, during which I have witnessed and facilitated the secret struggles of my patients to create real love in their lives by figuring out why it has eluded them. I have also spent six decades in this struggle myself; the golden condom of the title has a starring role in the story of my own passionate and tormented love affair at age nineteen.

A note about what kinds of love did and did not make the cut: I touch on adultery only in passing and masochism only in its emotional form as a key element in obsessive and unrequited passion, not in its currently trendy sadomasochistic sexual guise. I also explore relationships that are not usually included in examinations of love—friendship and its discontents, and the subtle and often underground emotions between mentors and protégés and patients and therapists—because I believe that they have more in common with classic passionate love than most people realize. In fact, it was my insight into just how closely intimate friendship and sexual passion are related that inspired me to write this book.

The dark side of love—obsession, betrayal, vengeance, and unrequited longing—gets serious attention because these excruciating experiences are so common that few people escape them, and everybody could use more insight into them. I am especially fascinated by how the past informs the present, by why we choose the beloveds we choose, and most of all, by how lovers who start out, as I did, only attracted to the "wrong" people ever manage to extricate themselves from the torments of loving those who cannot reciprocate.

I also wanted to celebrate the kinds of love that I love best: love that comes late in life, love that prevails through conflict and hardship, love that persists after the death of the beloved, and love that can be reclaimed even from the ruins of abandonment and betrayal.

You will find both cutting-edge and time-honored research on the science and the psychology of love, much of it by my favorite psychoanalytic theorists, as well as my own clinical insights and explanations of lovers' intriguing and powerful dreams.

The book's three sections follow a trajectory from love that tortures us, through love that causes as much pain as pleasure, to love that makes life worth living. The middle-aged and the old, you will find, can love as passionately as the young—and often more wisely.

What attracted me to the particular stories I've chosen to

tell? Many are quirky, against the grain, surprising. Among many others, you will meet the woman who wreaked vengeance on a rival by putting chopped-up tilapia to an off-label use; the man who had never let himself love another living thing, including his dog; the producer who found love for the first time at age fifty-six; the writer who decided to forgo friendship forever after her closest friends betrayed her when she was a teenager; the executive who revealed her youthful passion for a sexy heroin user; and the beautiful and charming Internet stalker.

A certain optimism born of my long professional experience with lovers underlies even the most devastating relationships in this book: I believe that insight is liberating and that because of it, people are not doomed to blindly repeat past hurts forever.

There is no subject in the world more thrilling, terrible, or complicated than love in all its manifestations. I hope that these essays will illuminate your experiences of love in your own life.

PART I

HOPELESS LOVE

1

LEAVING UNLOVING LOVERS AND UNFRIENDLY FRIENDS

Out of the blue, the woman who had once been my closest friend and confidante left me a message that she was in the hospital. We hadn't spoken in two years. I decided, after several days of agitated deliberation, not to call her back.

It was one of the hardest, and smartest, things I've ever done.

At first I was gratified—even thrilled—to hear her voice again, speaking my name. "Hello, Jeanne," she said, informing me of her whereabouts in the slightly stilted tone that I remembered she always used whenever she was uncomfortable. "I'm getting some tests—an MRI and some others. I think I'm all right. We'll talk over the weekend." My first impulse was to try to reach her immediately. But something about her message and the way she delivered it, both what she said and what she omitted, gave me pause.

I remembered all too clearly our last conversation, two years earlier. She had used the same tone then. I had been the one in the hospital—for an entire month, with a dangerous but curable form of leukemia—and I had asked her to come and see me when I felt desperate for her company and some edible food, and she neither came, nor called, nor sent me anything, abandoning me on one of the darkest nights of my life. It took her two days to call me back with a lame excuse (there was too much traffic, and the hospital food couldn't be *that* bad, as if that was the point). Her voice was flat, vague, slightly disembodied, and subtly defensive, and she had gotten off the phone as quickly as possible. She promised to explain later, but she never called back.

"Why on earth would you call her?" said my husband, who knew our whole history and had witnessed most of it, both our long intimacy and its abrupt demise. "Be careful." His pronouncement seemed so bald, so final, so devoid of hope. What he said disturbed and frightened me because I didn't want his verdict to be true. Here was my chance to get back the one woman in the world who spoke my language when I thought I had lost her forever.

We had been soul mates and professional colleagues for more than twenty years before she vanished, each other's bulwark in life. She understood things about me I didn't understand about myself, and I never knew anyone more generous, more delighted by a friend's success, or more consoling in adversity. She was brilliant, mordant, and astute, and I loved that she never suffered fools. Our conversations were my stimulant and my solace; "I've never talked to anybody the way I talk to you," she told me once, and I felt the same way. But even before she deserted me, the fallout from an extended marital crisis had made her increasingly self-absorbed and subtly demanding, and I found those conversations less mutual as time went on.

Her fuse also got much shorter, and I, who prided myself on addressing problems in relationships, never felt I could reveal my growing discontent without risking the fallout of her displeasure.

Despite her shocking behavior, I missed her so intensely that I wasn't ready to give up on her yet, so I made excuses for her, putting the best possible spin on that twenty-second message: clearly, I wasn't forgotten. She was seeking me out; she was turning to me in her hour of need. Maybe she felt all the things I hoped she felt, but couldn't put them into words. Being hospitalized must have brought me to mind. Maybe she identified with me, felt sorry about the way she had acted, and wanted to make amends. It must have taken a lot to make that call; after all, she risked getting me on the phone, and then she would have had to explain herself. I was glad I hadn't answered the call, because caught unawares I would certainly have followed my first instinct and engaged with her, even if all she'd wanted was advice. But shouldn't I at least give her the benefit of the doubt after two decades of intimacy, acknowledge the effort, and send her a brief e-mail asking what she wanted to talk to me about?

I couldn't immediately see the message for what it was: the presumptuous, self-absorbed expression of a person who now only thought of me to make use of me—for support, for attention, for the medical expertise I had often provided in the past. There was neither empathy nor apology in her voice or her words—no acknowledgment of how I might feel to get a call from her two years late, and then only when she needed me because she was in trouble herself. The person who left that message, regardless of what she had once been to me, was not capable of apologizing now; she could never again be a true or trustworthy friend to me. Slowly it dawned on me that the woman

I wanted back in my life didn't exist anymore and hadn't for years.

The first sensible thought I had was to do nothing, to wait and think it through. If she were sincere, if I really mattered to her still, she would certainly call again. I listened to her message twice more and asked my husband to listen as well in case I was misinterpreting. So much seemed at stake that I felt I had to be careful; one false step and she might retreat forever. The fate of the relationship seemed entirely in my hands, a thought that in itself should have tipped me off to its precariousness.

Then two songs came into my head. I found myself singing them aloud, over and over. "Cry me a river . . ." I belted repeatedly as I walked around the apartment pondering my options. Julie London's bitter torch song segued into Linda Ronstadt's "You're No Good," the unofficial anthem of all reformed masochists—and of masochists trying to reform. I hadn't thought of it since the seventies, and very satisfying it was to proclaim.

But why, I suddenly asked myself, was I singing about exorcising a tormented love affair after getting a cryptic call from a former friend? Because the state of mind that she evoked in me—the paralysis, the desperate attempts at self-control, the justifications that couldn't justify, the anxiety that a wrong move on my part could be fatal, the strangulated fury, the feeling that parting would be unendurable—was exactly the same.

I had heard that same cool and heedless tone she used from the first man I felt I couldn't live without. He was a graduate student on a time-limited fellowship from another university—graceful, sardonic, golden haired, with a motorcycle, and I was an intense, lonely, nineteen-year-old sophomore. My parents' marriage was disintegrating, and I tried, unsuccessfully, to make him my refuge. I would do anything to have him reach for me,

even though I could never count on him, even after he told me
he preferred an old girlfriend in another state. The night before
he left town forever, my darkest until the one on which my
friend forsook me, I had also waited by the phone that never
rang. When he finally came to say good-bye the next morning
just before he rode out of my life, he explained gratuitously that
he had spent the night consoling another woman who was broken up by his leaving. Unprotesting and dry eyed by force of
will, I let him kiss me good-bye and promise to stay in touch.

But even this did not break the spell of my longing for him.
To my astonishment, he actually did write and call me over the
next year, often to ask advice about other women and to tell me
about his travails with them. "You're the first person I turn to
when I want to talk," he said, and despite everything, I was
gratified to hear it because it meant I was special to him—the
same response I had when my friend said virtually the same
thing to me decades later. When he came back to see me briefly
the following summer, I welcomed him with a combination of
vengefulness and excitement—a mistake I vowed not to make
again with my friend.

My entire adult life, my long career as a psychoanalyst,
and thirty-three years of marriage to the man who showed up
every day I was in the hospital as well as every other day had
not severed the bonds of hunger, despair, and enraged humiliation over my long-lost lover that I buried in 1967. My reactions to my friend's call catapulted me back to him and exposed
a wound that had never healed, that I had not even realized I
bore. I knew the outlines of my youthful disastrous attachment, but the full meaning and impact of the experience had
lain, unmetabolized and radioactive, a long-dormant template
I thought I had destroyed long ago, until I heard her voice and
felt exactly the same way.

The parallels between these two people from opposite ends of my life were both uncanny and enlightening. The common denominator was that both seemed so essential to me that I would have done anything to keep them, to the point of ignoring information that would make a more rational person flee. Betrayal is gender blind, and sex is a sufficient, but not necessary, component; a woman can hurt you as much as a man, a friend as much as a lover. Anybody who feels indispensable has power over you, and your desperation can make you behave in equally self-damaging ways.

Masochism is an equal-opportunity destroyer, and crumbs from the table are the same, whether they are offered by a beloved who kisses your eyes and then turns away or an intimate who prizes you and then disappears when the going gets rough. Masochism can hide behind the most beguiling facades, and it can seduce you at any age if your history makes you susceptible. The bonds of empathy between friends even much later in life can be as deceptive and compelling as adolescent passion, as skin deep as beauty. And the cure is the same: walking away. It took me almost half a century to realize this and only three days to do it.

2

OF HUMAN BONDAGE
Obsessive Love

THE LURE OF THE UNATTAINABLE

He had a beautiful body (at least she thought so), and he knew—
or seemed to know—his own mind. He experimented with
shooting heroin and never called her, but toyed with whatever
woman was close at hand. All these obstacles, which would horrify and repel a less besotted person, simply made him more
fascinating and desirable to the naive, studious, and insecure
nineteen-year-old who was in thrall to him.

He still had a beautiful body and a beautiful wife, but this
fifty-five-year-old actor and former heartthrob fell for a wan-
nabe filmmaker whose body was not only beautiful but half the
age of his. After a brief affair, he continued to pursue her desperately and fruitlessly for five more years, driving hours for
even a glimpse of her, jeopardizing everything and everyone he

held dear. He put his emotional well-being in her inadequate and unwilling hands.

He was an appealing, multitalented, academic star at twenty, and he charmed myriads of young women who yearned to be his. But he spent his last two years of college as the self-proclaimed "love slave" of one who, though she had a deliciously sexy body, rarely had fewer than two other boyfriends.

She was a fortysomething executive, warm and vivacious, with devoted friends, who had caught the eye of more than one sophisticated and accomplished man. Yet for days at a time, she sat in front of her computer screen transfixed and tormented, surreptitiously scanning the Internet postings of a depressed, uneducated loser whom she found overwhelmingly desirable, even though his body was far from beautiful and his life was a shambles. For eight years, she had remained bound to him even though he continued to live with his ex-wife after they divorced and never even called to ask how she was when she had a dangerous illness.

Why?

The young are not the only ones wasting themselves on objects of desire who are unwilling or unable to reciprocate; the middle aged, and even senior citizens, fall under the same spell. This predicament is so common that it can hardly be called an aberration.* Even though it inspires some of the world's greatest literature, music, and art, obsessive love is one of the most potent and compelling of tortures and one of the most difficult to

---

* A study of 155 men and women (R. Baumeister, S. Wotman, and A. Stillwell, "Unrequited Love: On Heartbreak, Anger, Guilt, Scriptlessness, and Humiliation," *Journal of Personality and Social Psychology* 64, no. 3 [March 1993]: 377–394) found that only 2 percent of them had managed to avoid being on one side or the other of an unrequited love affair.

overcome—especially because it feels beyond conscious control. Tormented lovers try the patience even of those who truly love them, because the sufferers do not desire help extricating themselves though they claim to be seeking it; this is an illness from which nobody wants to be cured.

Obsessive love, while it creates widespread misery, only becomes cause for alarm and an indication of deeper psychopathology when it goes on for decades, involves compulsive stalking (either digital or literal), self-destructive behavior serious enough to interfere with health or the ability to function for a significant length of time, massive anxiety, depression, suicidal thoughts or actions, or delusional thinking.

The lovelorn give terrible interviews in the throes of obsessions. They all sound the same; age and circumstances make no difference. Even though unrequited passion can be spellbinding on the stage or the screen, the narratives offered by those in its immediate grip seem numbingly routine. They can talk forever about the beloved's charms or flaws, and give detailed reports of every meeting, every failure to meet, every lovemaking session, every rejection significant or petty (she didn't remember his birthday despite all the hints he'd dropped, he didn't respond to her meticulously crafted casual text message for a week), all of which is of little interest to anyone but themselves. How do they manage to turn so riveting a topic into a bore? Tunnel vision makes them lose the ability to observe or understand their experience. The world shrinks to include only two people, only one of whom—the beloved—has power. This inequitable distribution naturally breeds resentment and feelings of hopelessness that the dependent person dare not express for fear of alienating the necessary person even more. Hapless lovers are unable to analyze accurately why they feel what they feel or why they choose whom they choose and cannot seem to fathom why the object of their affection fails to respond. All they know is that he or she is indispensable, that life without this beloved has no joy or meaning to offer. Their self-absorption is paradoxical, since they believe that all they think about is the elusive other. Nobody has self-knowledge when immersed in a futile love affair; that only comes afterward—sometimes decades afterward, when the experience can finally be processed in relative tranquility.

To be consumed by unsatisfiable desire is to live in an altered state of consciousness. You are in a private realm, saturated with intense emotion, both positive and negative, that seems impossible to describe accurately to an outsider. In retrospect, when the person around whom your world revolved—who has been your world—shrinks back to human proportions, it is often difficult to imagine what you ever saw there.*

Only when the folly and pain of a doomed romance is recollected in tranquility (a state not easy to attain, because the shame, the longing, and the bitter disappointment can persist long afterward) does the constricted perspective open up and insight and awareness become possible.

Adolescence and postadolescence are the prime times for hopeless love affairs. In most cases, maturity, experience, and exposure to those actually capable of reciprocal love eventually diminish the magnetic pull of the unavailable. The services of a good therapist considerably raise the odds of recognizing people willing and able to respond, as well as understanding why they never seemed to be around before (when in fact we were

---

* She did not speak or turn away
  But saw the man she'd loved just yesterday
  And knew he was ordinary
      —"The End of Love," by seventh- and eighth-century Indian poet Amaru,
      adapted from the Sanskrit

unable to notice them). Yet there are those who persist or even succumb to obsession for the first time later in life and still struggle to extricate themselves as the years go by. Some never escape from the imprisoning conviction that a cold or unattainable lover can be persuaded to become warm or attainable if they only discover the key.

THE MAN WITH THE GOLDEN ARM

Maggie Clark is one of the most accomplished women I know. An adept public speaker at sixty-three who appears regularly in the media, she heads a major accounting firm in partnership with her husband of forty years. She has a loyal and sensitive nature as well as business savvy and good judgment. I knew that she also had an insecure side, but I had no idea of the depths of desperation and inadequacy that had engulfed her in her youth until we spoke about the college boyfriend—if he could even be called that—whom she worshipped and who treated her with appalling callousness. She described their relationship with far more contempt, clarity, and candor than she felt at the time.

To my surprise, Maggie, whose demeanor is usually demure, spoke in a tone more appropriate at a raunchy bachelorette party about this man's physical attributes and how downcast she was to discover that they were mostly for show. "He had a hot body and a little green sports car," she said, "but the action was never as good as the anticipation." This "sexy, smart" acquaintance of her brother's was a philosophy major "with a basketball player's build—tall, lean, and well muscled," she recalled, still savoring the image years later. Her condescension was a later-life corrective—an exorcism, really—of the overpowering desire she had felt for him, as well as her retribution for the humiliating treatment she had tolerated from him.

Even more compelling than his gorgeous physique was his penchant for risk taking. "He announced proudly, 'I fasted for three days to see what it would do to me,' and I was so impressed," she recalled. "I put him on a pedestal. He seemed so exciting and seductive when I was nineteen; I was smitten. I worked hard to make the reality match the fantasy."

Maggie was looking for a man to look up to, and this one seemed to fit the job description. At the time, she was trying frantically to convince herself that his inside was worthy of his outside, contrasting herself to him and finding herself wanting. Her painful awareness of her own timidity caused her to mistake foolhardiness (of which the fasting stunt was one of the early warning signals) for courage and character, and confirmed his superiority and his allure in her eyes. He was someone to idealize and to emulate, her passport to adventure and personal growth. On the surface, he seemed so bold, so strong, so in control, as narcissists often do to those less enamored of themselves.

Maggie's adoration of her Adonis and her anxiety about losing him led her to put herself at his disposal without complaint. "I wanted so desperately to be with him for an hour that I would have done anything," she said—adding that she had never told a living soul about her behavior. "He would see me when he deigned to," she said, still embarrassed and offended by the memory. "I kept thinking that if I were a little bit sexier or smarter myself, and if I were just good or adoring enough, he'd want to be more involved with me. I could never cross him or object to anything he did; I felt so tentative—I didn't have good self-esteem then." She longed to be like him, and to be chosen by him was a way to bask in reflected glory before she had any of her own.

She was not, however, the only one who had noticed his

charms. "This was the seventies—he lived in a group house, and there was another woman living there. I was annoyed because she had access." He didn't have to bestir himself; Maggie had to make all the effort in order to get even a crumb of attention from him. "I was always the one to call him," she said. The very fact that her rival had the upper hand because she was more conveniently located should have made it clear to Maggie that women were interchangeable to him, but instead, it made her work even harder to attract him.

Maggie was a psychology major, and she referred to a concept from learning theory to explain the tenacity of her own behavior and his hold on her. "He showed just enough interest in me for it to be intermittent reinforcement," she said. Intermittent reinforcement, also known as partial reinforcement, describes a paradoxical phenomenon observed in experimental subjects: they learn best and retain what they learn the longest when the rewards for correct responses are unpredictable. This principle is often applied to human motivation. It is one partial explanation for Maggie's chronic subservient behavior. She doggedly persisted in making herself available to the man she wanted when he felt like seeing her, even though she felt bad about doing so, because sometimes it worked and he seemed to respond to her.

This impassioned young woman seethed with suppressed resentment about her inconsistent beloved's insensitive behavior toward her, but she could not let herself acknowledge the selfishness and contempt that underlay it. For months, she continued to pursue and to idealize him, hoping to win his favor. Her eyes were finally opened one night when his true character was revealed in a way that even she could not justify or ignore.

"I had come to his house to stay overnight with him," she told me, "but instead of spending time alone with me, he took me downstairs where his housemates were shooting heroin and said, 'I want to try this.'" This was an experiment of his that did not seem the least bit glamorous or admirable to her, but she could not protest. As repelled and horrified as she was, she stayed riveted to the spot; she still needed to impress him. The scene was shocking and sad to hear about, even forty-four years afterward. "I sat there trying very hard to be cool, watching him put a needle in his arm. I felt I didn't matter enough. I could show up, but he would do what he felt like doing, anyway; this was always the deal. He never changed his routine for me." Mainlining heroin in her presence rather than giving her his attention went far beyond ordinary boorishness. Even in extremis, she felt inadequate in his eyes, obliged to prove to him that she was sophisticated and game for anything.

Then his behavior became even worse. When he was finally ready to go to bed—he was still high at the time—he went upstairs with her and coolly proposed yet another experiment to add to his catalog of experiences: "Let's try anal sex."

His timing and his attitude, rather than the specific request, left her aghast and brought her to her senses. "I like to think that his shooting up would have been enough to end it for me— that on reflection I would have drawn the right conclusions— but it wouldn't have been," she admitted. "I'd have excused it, talked myself into tolerating it, tried to prove my sophistication. But this was too much." The one-two punch finally jolted her out of her fantasy and showed her the ugly truth about his character. "The first round was hard drugs, but wanting to use me sexually on top of that was totally over the line. He had no consideration for me or my feelings—he was completely into himself and just wanted to try new things. That was the worst, and it put everything in perspective for me. It became so crystal clear that this guy is a shithead, a fuckhead, and a jerk."

She flatly refused; it was the first time she had refused him anything. She spent the rest of the night on the couch by herself. Then she left in the morning, never to return. True to form, he did not even bother to call her afterward, or ever again, and their affair ended abruptly.

Maggie explained what had most appalled her about how he acted on their final night together. "If he cared about me at all, he wouldn't experiment with narcotics while I was staying over, and he wouldn't treat me like garbage"—a low bar indeed. "His behavior passed beyond the point of disrespectful; the sexual transgression was the end. It was obvious then that he didn't respect me or love me, that he didn't really even like me."

In fact, she was giving this man more credit than he deserved. It wasn't just that he didn't respect, love, or like her; she did not exist for him as a person with feelings of her own worthy of the slightest consideration. She was just another novelty, something on his checklist. Her body and a syringe full of heroin were identical in his eyes, both objects to be used for his pleasure or edification however and whenever he saw fit. She meant nothing to him, and she finally realized that this was not because she was worth nothing, but because he could feel nothing. When his naked coldness was revealed to her, her illusions shattered, and the thrill was gone. She never again allowed herself to be treated this way by a man. Just as a brush with the law can scare a person straight, a brush with a pathological narcissist amid the right conjunction of disasters can scare a person sane.

What drew this tender, thoughtful, and highly intelligent young woman to such a man? The fervor of her physical description, even decades afterward, and the blind, self-obliterating nature of her surrender to him were the keys; they pointed to her past.

Maggie's sometime boyfriend was a malign caricature of her father, to whom he bore a striking resemblance both physically and mentally. "He looked a little bit like my dad, who also had a beautiful body at that age," she confirmed. Maggie's father had been a minor-league baseball player and a spectacular physical specimen, as well as a daredevil in his youth, and he too had a tyrannical streak. Maggie's mother, whom he'd swept off her feet when she was a teenager, married him at nineteen, the same age her daughter was when she fell for her athletic philosophy major. Both men called the shots with everyone in their lives. Maggie's self-effacing mother spent her life under her husband's thumb, doing his bidding. The entire family catered to his whims and feared his wrath, but he also had a generous, principled side, which his young stand-in conspicuously lacked. Seeing her parents' relationship and being bullied by her father as her mother also was predisposed Maggie to submerge her own needs and to be attracted to a man who would dominate her and who would confirm her conviction of her own inadequacy.

Why didn't living with her father and seeing the toll it took on her make Maggie run from a man who so resembled him? Her experience of her father was not consistently awful enough to prevent her from being drawn to someone like him—at least when she was young and insecure. Her identification with her mother and their close relationship also played a role in her choice. The unconscious urge to repeat problematic relationships from the past is both potent and insidious; our history is always alive within us and affects us our entire lives. The sexual and emotional magnetism that the man she chose exerted over her seduced her and overrode any rational objections she might have had.

Her father, like his look-alike, belittled the women in his

life and did what he wanted when he wanted—although, luckily, drug use was not among his vices. Maggie only began to
appreciate her own worth and to seek and then to find a man
who would cherish her when she stopped tolerating the kind of
treatment that her mother continued to endure.

Maggie's lover certainly had a personality that predisposed him
to addictions and to extreme experiences, even if he was only
experimenting with heroin at the time she knew him. But was
she herself what is popularly called a "love addict"? There is no
consensus among professionals about whether a predilection to
pursue futile love affairs is a true addiction, a physiologically
based craving like drugs or alcohol, or only a metaphorical equivalent.

   Love addiction is not included in the *Diagnostic and Statis-
tical Manual of Mental Disorders, Fifth Edition*, the latest catalog
of psychiatrically diagnosable conditions (or in any of the four
earlier editions), and, in my opinion, does not belong there.
There are many more "love addicts"—usually defined as such
by the sufferers themselves or by Web sites purporting to cure
them—than alcohol or drug addicts; although exceptions do
exist, it is hard to find someone of either sex who has not had
such an experience. These people do not ingest psychoactive
substances or have to "detox" by enduring physiological withdrawal, and most of them do not seek or require treatment;
addiction is different from compulsion,* a clinically more ac-
curate description of the experiences of obsessive lovers. Even

---

* Compulsive disorder, which is a subtype of obsessive-compulsive disorder
  (now known popularly as OCD), is characterized by physical and mental
  activities that feel involuntary and aversive to the afflicted person, including
  intrusive thoughts and uncontrollable-seeming behavior (such as stalking,
  among driven unhappy lovers). Symptoms can range in severity from

though who and how they love make them miserable, they often function well in other areas of their lives. The condition also tends to be self-limiting; those who suffer its pangs usually recover or improve over time, as Maggie did. Those who remain obsessive lovers into middle age and beyond typically have more serious underlying psychological issues that they are attempting to resolve.

Love addiction is often confused with "sex addiction," a different and more ominous type of pathology also omitted from the *DSM* because of a lack of consensus among professionals about its physiological substrate. Though it may not be a literal addiction, it is a serious and disorganizing affliction. So-called sex addicts use sex for comfort, stimulation, or escape. They seek sexual experiences indiscriminately with multiple partners (or via pornography), while love addicts are "hooked" on one person, and may not even be sexually involved with that person. One seeks a sensation, the other a relationship.

Behavior like Maggie's, so typical in adolescence, need not become an entrenched or inescapable pattern of loving that marks a person for life; more solid self-esteem, judgment, and knowledge of the world eventually protect most people from infinite recurrences. She went "cold turkey" by repudiating her unloving lover completely when she saw who he really was and never pined for him (even though she still found him attractive) or reproduced the same kind of slavish relationship with anyone remotely like him for the rest of her life—hardly the behavior of either a codependent personality or a recalcitrant love addict.

In her senior year of college, soon after she ended this hu-

---

distressing to disabling. In contrast, addictions always involve physical—not just psychic—dependency.

miliating affair, Maggie met the man she would marry two years later; it would have been difficult to find someone more different from her former heartthrob. "He was the first man to value me as a person, and by then, I was open to seeing it and feeling it," she told me. "He was mature himself and considered me his equal. To be appreciated by him was a relief and a delight."

THE OTHER MAN

David Shapiro was bewitched. He met Anna, a vivacious, voluptuous freshman, at the beginning of his sophomore year, and he had to have her. It seemed like this would be an easy conquest, as most things in college had been for him, both intellectually and socially. The friend who introduced them assured him that she was available and that her boyfriend, who attended another college and visited her only sporadically, would be "no problem." And so it seemed; in addition to being clever and alluring, she was completely willing to gratify David's every desire, and in no time, they were spending hours and hours in bed, on the floor, up in a bell tower, in delirious lust. He was new at love, with only one previous girlfriend—he had ended their yearlong relationship even though he cared about her because she had wanted to move in with him almost immediately and he knew he wasn't ready—but Anna's appetite was only matched by her enthusiasm and expertise, and she made no such demands. This was his first taste of what seemed like thrilling sensuality, the unbridled expression of desire, which was especially intoxicating for someone who had grown up in an atmosphere of extreme sexual repression. "I wasn't really looking for another girlfriend or a serious relationship," he said. "I wanted amusement, at least at the beginning. She was jolly and lively, extremely sexy and sexualized, and I'd never had oral sex before." The only stumbling block to bliss was the boyfriend, who proved more of an impediment than the go-between had asserted (in the manner of college sophomores, the go-between had his own designs on David's former girlfriend).

Anna threw herself headlong into their affair but barred the bedroom door on weekends, which she reserved for her steady. "He'd park himself in her room," David recalled, still annoyed about his exclusion. Even though he wanted a no-strings fling after his too-much-too-soon prior relationship, he wasn't pleased when he realized how many additional contenders for Anna's favors were hovering around. Anna admitted that she had had several "erotic friendships"; in fact, as he discovered, she specialized in them.

David was used to succeeding, but this was one of the few times in his life that he was confronted with an obstacle he couldn't overcome. He kept hoping he would prevail over his various rivals, of which the boyfriend proved to be only the most prominent, and win her for himself, but instead he found himself perennially condemned to be her other man. Since he had read his Freud, he figured that it had to be significant that she had the same name as his mother—as did his previous girlfriend. He knew something was afoot, although the knowledge did him little good.

Four months later, it was over. Anna #3 wrote him a letter telling him she felt too guilty about cheating on her boyfriend to continue their trysts. David spent the rest of his college career frantically trying to get back into her good graces, abetted by her continuing to flirt with him and kiss him passionately every so often in a perfect demonstration of maddeningly intermittent reinforcement. She toyed with him, but she never came back to him; he never displaced the boyfriend or rejoined the ranks of the auxiliary lovers. The more she rejected him, the more he hungered for her. To his shame and discomfiture, he found himself falling in love with her. What started out as a seemingly liberating interlude was turning into torment.

It is striking that David, a gallant and sensitive man, spoke graphically of his exploits with Anna in the same raunchy tone ("She was masturbating me before her boyfriend arrived, but I couldn't come. I wanted to fuck her . . .") that the demure Maggie had used when describing her lover's body and (lack of) sexual prowess. He, like she, was still trying to exorcise the specter of a disturbingly compelling and humiliating attachment, even though it had ended decades earlier, by objectifying and demeaning the object of his desire. This was his way of finally expressing the anger he had to conceal from himself when he was pursuing her. If he had let himself know how furious he was, it would have been more difficult to conceal it from Anna, and she might leave him for good. Turning rage inward to protect a problematic relationship is one reason obsessive lovers are so often depressed.*

David "mooned over" Anna long after his tenure as her lover was terminated, and his "four months of exquisite torture" morphed into two years of ordinary misery, much of it self-inflicted. They remained on friendly terms—despite the covert mutual hostility of their mutually teasing behavior, there were genuine warm feelings between them—and continued to see each other in various classes and activities. They also continued to tantalize each other ("She stayed away but not too far," he said) while carrying on brief affairs with others, with Anna's boyfriend never entirely out of the picture.

---

* Since Freud's revelatory paper "Mourning and Melancholia" in 1917 (*Standard Edition*, vol. 14), it has been a basic tenet of psychoanalytic therapy that depression (the contemporary term for melancholia) is anger turned against the self.

From the beginning, David had established himself as Anna's sexual and emotional confidant, a role he never relinquished despite his ambivalence about performing it. She told him about her problems as well as her exploits with her boyfriend and her other lovers, and he listened, disturbed and transfixed, to all the details. All her once and future conquests, her plans for seductions, and her anxieties were on display. She told him that her boyfriend, to her chagrin, never got her birthday cards "because he didn't believe in empty gestures like that"—after which David, aiming to be all that she could desire, bought her an expensive birthday present. He invited her to the prom, even though she wouldn't accept in case her boyfriend decided to ask her; he even met her parents.

Confession was intrinsic to the erotic charge between them. He became a perennial witness to, if no longer a direct participant in, "the traffic jam in her bedroom," forever hoping to parlay her trust into winning her away from his chief rival or, if that proved impossible, at least rekindling their affair. "Hearing about her having sex was the best I could do, and she didn't tell just anybody. I tried to get her back by being there all the time," he said. His rapt attention, he thought, was a way to make himself uniquely special to her, to stand out in a crowded field. In addition to inserting himself into her elaborate sexual adventures, it also gave him access to her inner world. "It was really an opportunity for her to boast and for me to lacerate myself," he commented in retrospect—a tumultuous combination of exhibitionism and voyeurism, with tenderness thrown in.

One night, her provocation was almost too much to bear. "She got really drunk at a party and asked me to take her home. I did—she trusted me. When we got to her room, she let me come in at last. She sat on my lap and then took off her clothes in front of me and got into bed. I lifted the sheet and kissed her stomach, and away I went; I was such a good boy. I felt both aroused and excluded; I was not in the inner ring, but I had a box seat. This was abject behavior. I was her love slave." The role of the ethical romantic hero had its gratifications and its drawbacks.

I wondered why David never even considered asking Anna to leave her boyfriend while they shared her or made any overt move to win her back later on. "I never said, 'You've got to choose between us,'" he admitted. "I never said, 'I love you. I want you to be mine only.' Passivity and timidity silenced me. It was impossible at that point in my life to believe that I could ever do such a thing." Instead, like Maggie, who sought to win her beloved's attention by the self-improvement strategy of trying to be "a little bit sexier or smarter," David relied on being a good listener and a mensch rather than the more dangerous direct approach. "It was clear that she wouldn't do it, and that would have been the end," he said. Losing her entirely was a risk he dared not take. "You're so tied to this person that you'll tolerate anything. Half a loaf, even a crust, is better than no bread at all."

Obsessed lovers fear, with good reason, that they will be abandoned if they say or do anything that can be construed as a demand; if a relationship is already foundering, making waves is the last thing you want to do. Pessimism about one's own power and desirability is intrinsic to the experience of a one-way love affair.

As much as he railed against them, David needed his rivals because he needed to be chosen over them. The excruciating position that a lover like him finds himself in with a partner who rejects him or ignores him or prefers another actually fulfills an unconscious need.* He not only tolerates the pain built into the situation but seems relentlessly to seek it. "I felt triumphant when she wanted me," he said. Being the man Anna wants, even for the moment, overrides everything. It confirms his desirability, lays fear and doubt to rest. It is the antidote to having been traumatically rejected as a child by the parent who is the center of your universe, which is worth any humiliation to achieve. What is obvious to any onlooker is opaque to the needy one: this was a competition he was never going to win.

David had been the center of his mother's universe when he was a boy, almost her auxiliary husband—but everything changed when he grew up. His mother felt betrayed and considered every potential girlfriend a hated rival. He never fully regained his special position with her, and it took years for him to understand and work through the reasons for his exile.

As a young man on the cusp of maturity, who had once been the protected darling of a volatile and enthralling mother, David was still unsure of his masculinity and his ability to assert himself. All questions vanished when he held Anna in his arms. All rivals were vanquished, and she was his alone. Such is the compelling, if tragically evanescent, nature of sexual passion;† it gives us the illusion that we have what we need or what we needed in the past. It is validation by proxy.

Anna's ever-changing bevy of suitors provided David with

---

* Freud wrote a prescient paper about men who choose unavailable women: S. Freud, "Contributions to the Psychology of Love: A Special Type of Choice of Objects Made by Men," in *Standard Edition*, vol. 11 (1910), 163–176.

† I believe that overt or covert sexual passion is a sine qua non in obsessive love. However, sexual passion is what psychoanalysts call "overdetermined"; it has a multitude of meanings and complex origins.

multiple chances to prove to himself that he was powerful and desirable. The price he paid, however, was that they also provided multiple opportunities to have his self-esteem deflated and his hopes dashed. The harder objects of desire are to snare, the more gratifying it is to win their dubious affection, and the harder it is to give up the prospect, even if you secretly know it is transient at best.

David didn't realize that Anna needed what he called "a solar system of men" revolving around her in order to shore up her own self-esteem, which had been seriously battered by a charming alcoholic father who severely disappointed her. They revolved around her while she revolved around the withholding and controlling boyfriend who was her father's latter-day representative. Equality with a man was impossible for her; she had to be controlled or in control.

The urgent need to be the special one that consumed both David and Anna had roots in their pasts; just as Anna was acting out an old scenario with her father, David was enacting a parallel scenario with his mother. Those who compulsively seek the role of the special one with an unavailable lover are usually trying to undo a childhood experience of a fall from grace, of being rejected by a parent who once seemed to favor them and then inexplicably turned away and chose someone else—typically a spouse or another sibling (or, in Anna's case, alcohol). This is a terrible blow to self-worth, because children tend to blame themselves and have very limited understanding of the motivation of the adults they depend on.

What classical Freudians call the Oedipus complex—a child's desire to have sex with the opposite sex parent by besting (or even wishing to destroy) the same-sex rival parent—is but the tip of the iceberg. Underneath the fantasy of romance with a parent is a longing for merger, for protection, for a secure sense of being prized, and for assurance that you will always be able to get what you need from someone who can in fact only inconsistently provide it. The fantasy of an Oedipal victory that drives so many wretched love affairs is frequently an attempt to undo an original Oedipal defeat, a rivalry for an exclusive love that you have already lost to another; we attempt to rewrite history when the truth seems unbearable. Trying to make an unsatisfying past come out differently is a very popular human project, even if it is doomed; sexual conquest is one of the most popular ways to create an illusion of success in this endeavor. The only real way to transform things that have already happened is to learn from them.

The nadir of David's doomed romance occurred in his senior year. "As soon as I came back to school at the beginning of the semester, I went to her room and sat there waiting for hours for her to come back, looking like I had nothing better to do. I figured her boyfriend would be coming later on, but I needed desperately to see her. I couldn't bear to be cast out; it would have meant that I was worthless as a man in her eyes." This time, however, the familiar situation did not feel at all exciting; it only felt humiliating. By the time she finally appeared, he had lost all hope of even a Pyrrhic victory. "Sitting there like that was a symbol of my exclusion and degradation—I wanted so badly what I couldn't have." He felt worthless in his own eyes.

Waiting Godot-like for a lover who could never be his had the same effect on David that the heroin/anal sex–request combo had had on Maggie: it opened his eyes. He could no longer deny the hopelessness of his passion, the impossibility of possessing someone who wasn't there physically, psychically, or sexually. As the chances of succeeding faded, the self-abnegation of his role in her life became more than he could bear. His desperate desire did not wane immediately, but he began to face reality. "Time helped me realize that I could never, ever, really have her—nobody could; she seemed in charge, but she turned out very much not to be."

Only after graduation, when they moved to different cities to pursue their adult lives and he no longer saw her regularly, did David fully understand his ensorcellment and extricate himself from it. Gradually, his ardor cooled along with his jealousy, and they were able to maintain affection for each other.

Their destinies radically diverged. Anna had a disastrous first marriage with a man who not only had another lover simultaneously but fathered a child with her. Soon after college, David met and married his (monogamous) soul mate. Their relationship was as enduring, as satisfying, and as mutually admiring as Maggie's with her husband.

As naive college students, Maggie and David felt compelled to pursue unattainable—and unworthy—mates unable to love, or at very least unable to love them, who shared character traits with their parents, including ones that drove their children crazy. Maggie sought someone with a beautiful body, a strong will, and a selfish streak. David was looking for a passionate but insecure woman with a need to dominate and hidden contempt for men. They both wanted to make relationships similar to the ones that had once disappointed them come out differently.

Both lovers idealized their objects while underestimating themselves and overlooking serious obvious character flaws (lack of basic consideration in Maggie's case, inability to be faithful in David's) that were insurmountable obstacles to lasting intimacy and satisfaction. The intensity of their sexual desire for the wrong people had unconscious roots in their histories, but at the time, it was so overwhelming that they lost all perspective. What looks like sex and feels like sex can have nonsexual origins. These deeper, earlier longings are often obscured by ignorance of oneself and the urgency of the body's demands, particularly in late adolescence. They were both exceedingly fortunate to grow up and out of obsessive love.

Graduation ends many a frustrating relationship by imposing a natural separation that often brings people to their senses and exposes them to a larger world of choices. With luck and with effort, reformed obsessive lovers can discover that being involved with someone who loves them back is a lot more gratifying—and actually more passionate—than the most ardent one-sided affair.

THE FOUNTAIN OF YOUTH

There is one thing that no man of fifty-five, no matter how fit or attractive, has any control over: he is no longer young, and there is absolutely nothing he can do about it. This is a fact that José Sanchez could not bear and spent five tumultuous years denying, almost destroying himself and everything that mattered to him as he wildly pursued a hopeless love affair with a woman half his age. He is the kind of man—strikingly handsome, rich, and successful—who, if surfaces were all-important, you would think could have any woman he wanted, except for the one on whom he felt his destiny depended.

José has cheekbones to die for, the physique of the athlete he still is, and the allure of the soap opera star he was in his twenties, when his smoldering, dark, Latino good looks got him frequently cast as alluring villains. He parlayed his early acting success into an international real estate fortune; we met long ago when I was looking for an apartment, and we stayed in touch. He has been married for years to a cabaret performer, and they have a picture-perfect family on whom he dotes—and yet, he was wretched and miserable amid all the trappings of an enviable life.

José was looking for someone in whom to confide his secret, and I found myself regaled with the details of a crazed passion for his twenty-five-year-old former receptionist that would have seemed absurd if he hadn't been so desperate and wasn't taking such appalling risks to satisfy; in most cases of impossible love that I was familiar with, the lovers mostly only damaged themselves. Being a middle-aged husband and father who is carrying on like an adolescent ups the ante for disaster.

He talked about her in a way that only the obsessed do. It was always a pressured monologue, and it was always the same. He had to relate every detail, interpreting and seeking meaning in her every utterance or action, like a fundamentalist minutely analyzing a biblical text. I feared that his misadventure would be exposed and would jeopardize not only his marriage but his children's welfare, and I told him so, but it made no impression; he was, and wanted to remain, entirely heedless of consequences.

José was single-minded to a degree I had never encountered before. It was as though the reflective part of his brain was switched off, and he had no interest in switching it back on. Simultaneously ecstatic and tormented, he did acknowledge in rare moments of sobriety that his aspiration to spend the rest of his life with her might be unrealistic, but he could not stop chasing his dream girl, because it was only when he was with her that he felt fully vital for the very first time. She was the answer to his malaise, the meaning of his life.

He seemed to be living in an alternate universe.

At the beginning of his courtship, José laid the world at his young lover's feet, whisking her off to romantic hideaways all over the Pacific Rim when he had business there, taking her to the best restaurants and introducing her to all the opulence, glamour, and sophistication at his disposal. He was forever thinking of their last encounter and planning the next one. He had never felt this way before, he assured me, sexually or emotionally. I got the impression that she was dazzled as well as genuinely taken with him, although she felt guilty that he was married, and she was uncomfortable with the idea of being somebody's mistress. His sense of their future together was much more definite than hers.

José always talked as if he had just seen or communicated with his beloved, but he was really reporting his stream-of-consciousness thoughts about her, even when they hadn't had any contact for months. She was omnipresent in his consciousness, the only real thing in his life, with the occasional exception of his son and his daughter. When he described their actual interactions, I got only the most superficial impression of what she was actually like and a great deal of information about how he felt when he was with her—a sure sign of self-absorption masked as love.

One indication of how distorted by his own desire his perceptions of her were is that he saw qualities in her that she did not actually possess. He extolled her simplicity, her spontaneity, her beat-up motorbike, all of which made her seem pristine and unpretentious, a welcome contrast to his world-weariness, his driven work ethic, and the materialism that surrounded him. It became clear to me, if not to him, that in fact she had no real direction in her life or much motivation to find one. He was overly impressed when she enrolled in film school, which demonstrated her artistic ability, and he was thrilled at the prospect of "helping her in her career" but had no reaction when she dropped out after one semester, after which she went back to her hometown in Washington State and worked in a convenience store trying to figure out what to do next. He saw talent and spiritual purity where there was mostly naïveté, confusion, and the desire to find someone to take care of her, as her father, with his girlfriends as young as she, never did. Like Maggie, who interpreted the risky behavior of the man she desired as daring individuality, José never seemed to reconsider who his lover really was even as she continued to demonstrate that she was not who he wanted her to be. She was a projective screen for his Pygmalion fantasies and his lost youth. When I remarked that the disparity between their ages and perspectives might not be easy to breach, he answered, "What do those things matter when you're soul mates?"

Later on, however, the thrill diminished for her, and she started pulling away as guilt and wariness took over. I could sense that she felt oppressed and disturbed by the intensity of his attentions; objects of obsessive preoccupation rarely enjoy being on the receiving end for any extended length of time. He became increasingly desperate and foolhardy as she did so. One weekend when he had business in Northern California, he drove eight hours each way to deliver a bouquet of rare orchids and left it on her doorstep. I wondered how his wife could fail to notice how distracted, irritable, and otherwise engaged he was, emotions he took few pains to conceal.

José seemed like a man possessed, outside of time even as he was excruciatingly aware of its passage. To my astonishment, I discovered that he and his chosen one had not been lovers for two years when I first learned of her existence, although he talked as if their affair was not only still ongoing but was becoming ever more intense and absorbing—which was true, but entirely in his head; with the exception of an occasional brief text message in response to a barrage from him, he rarely heard from her. He mentioned almost as an afterthought that she had already moved on to another boyfriend as old as he but who was not married. This did not seem to faze him or indeed to register as an impediment. He himself described his behavior as "stalking" her—showering her with gifts and letters, begging her to speak to him and at least to let him see her. She equivocated but gave him very little access. At some point, he actually proposed to her, which obliged her to point out that he was not in fact free to marry her even if she had been willing. His obsession increased as the possibility of satisfaction slipped away.

Eventually, José could no longer deny that the relationship had become unilateral. His frantic efforts to win her had failed. The gap between them was unbreachable, and she would never be his. The pressure had become too much to bear, and he had to do something, so he unconsciously arranged to be found out. Since he believed he had no control over his behavior, he needed someone else to stop him and to break the spell. He "carelessly" left an incriminating array of text messages on his cell phone in a place where his wife was sure to find it— all the while cursing his fate and insisting that he had no idea how he could have been so incautious. His wife's shock and horror at his betrayal were excruciating to hear about, and the fallout did not dissipate quickly. Before he felt both thrilled and awful, and afterward he felt only awful, but he regretted nothing.

Has José learned anything, or will he try to find another antiaging elixir? It remains to be seen whether he will face reality and try to understand himself or simply repeat the pattern and seek another much younger woman to give him the illusion of agelessness, another second chance to do his life over and—for a little longer—turn back the hands of time.

·   ·   ·

What made José act with such reckless, thoughtless abandon? His history explains why he was overwhelmed by his fantasy of a perfect love: he was seeking an antidote to a life that he believed had been forced upon him by his sense of duty and responsibility, one that he had gone along with rather than actively decided to pursue. He impetuously and heedlessly married his high school sweetheart right after graduation, and they had a child immediately. He then took up the role of devoted husband and father without making conscious choices about either obligation. Over the next three decades, he became increasingly claustrophobic, sinking into deep unhappiness with his lot that no success could compensate for or distract him from.

José was convinced that having married and become a father at so young an age had caused him to miss out on what mattered most—a sense of freedom. His feeling of being trapped in convention became unendurable, and his craving for passion and adventure only increased as the prospect of a too quiet old age loomed. He saw his passion as defying fate, asserting his will, rebelling, and starting over, but it really was an external solution to an internal problem.

Why did he not get divorced and find someone adventurous his own age, particularly now that his children were grown? Ironically, his sense of duty kept him locked in place. Only a force beyond his control, a love he felt he could not and should not resist, could permit him to escape and to assuage his guilt at the same time.

His new love represented the road not taken, the life he desired rather than one that seemed just to have happened to him, and he was willing to pay the price. He picked a much younger, impressionable woman because he wanted to control the outcome this time; here was someone he thought he could mold into his ideal, a tabula rasa to be inscribed to order, in contrast to the mature woman he found himself married to.

The affair was José's attempt to reboot his life rather than come to terms with it. Sex with a partner half his age gave him the illusion of becoming young again himself, a remedy for the malaise and built-in doubts of middle age. When he embraced his beloved, he felt, as so many middle-aged men (and women) do, "I'm still desirable; I can still experience and elicit passion. I am free to choose somebody thrilling." Having her would change everything, erasing his disappointments forever.

José became obsessed with recovering his youth through a lover because he had failed to grieve for his lost opportunities. He could not see that nobody forced him to stay in his conventional life, that doing so had been his choice. Recognizing the benefits as well as the limitations that choice entailed could have been a source of authentic pride and self-acceptance, both of which are prerequisites for real love, but recognizing them would involve rigorous self-examination.

Instead, he took a desperate, doomed chance on illusory happiness based on denial—refusing to accept that five decades were forever behind him, that it is not possible to build a mate entirely to your own specifications, that past actions cannot be undone, that another person cannot enliven you or give purpose and meaning to your life, and that there is no such thing as youth by association.

José would never have described his preoccupation with his muse as an addiction—she was simply the great and only love of his life in his eyes—but his behavior had all the earmarks of one, at least metaphorically: self-neglect, compromised judgment, single-minded pursuit of his desire regardless of the consequences to himself or others, insatiable craving only momentarily assuaged by scoring a sexual encounter. Even though he used no drugs, it was almost as though he were narcotizing himself by thinking about her, insulating himself from the disappointments of his life. Sex with her, or the memory of it, was his fix, a fleeting, ecstatic distraction from the dread that he had wasted his youth and now was trapped forever.

Contemporary brain research confirms that obsessive love like José's does indeed share many characteristics with physical addictions and also with gambling, a habit that can be as compulsive and destructive as alcohol or cocaine, though no substance is involved. This commonality explains the primitive urgency and the sense of being in the grip of forces beyond rational control that the obsessed experience; every compulsive lover I spoke to felt this way.

Functional MRI (magnetic resonance imaging), a recently developed noninvasive brain-mapping technology for observing activation patterns that underlie mental states, has led to a proliferation of research about "the brain on love" that has captured the popular imagination. Anthropologist Helen Fisher, whose studies of the neurophysiological foundations of love are among the best known, used fMRIs to explore the brains of newly enamored and recently rejected lovers.* She discovered that romantic passion and drug addiction have similar effects; both stimulate regions in and directly above the brain stem, including the hypothalamus, which synthesizes and secretes neurochemicals from which sensations of pleasure, arousal, focused attention, and high-risk behavior arise. The spurned

---

* Helen Fisher, Arthur Aron, and Lucy Brown, "Romantic Love: A Mammalian Brain System for Mate Choice," *Philosophical Transactions of the Royal Society B* 361 (2006): 2173–2186; Helen Fisher, *Why We Love: The Nature and Chemistry of Romantic Love* (New York: St. Martin's, 2004).

lovers' brains registered an inclination to pursue risky invest-
ment strategies and to make efforts to manage anger, but also
to ruminate and to engage in obsessive-compulsive behavior;
like José, they couldn't stop thinking about the one they had
lost.

fMRI research on the cerebral correlates of passion and
obsession, while intriguing, has been criticized by some researchers as lacking reliability and validity on the grounds that
it may be tracking only superficial changes and that sample sizes
tend to be small or of limited generalizability.[*]

One fact that the new brain research has demonstrated is
the centrality of the neurotransmitter dopamine in the experience of obsessive passion. Stanford neuroendocrinologist and
primatologist Robert Sapolsky described the role of dopamine
in his provocative TED Talk "The Uniqueness of Humans"
and in numerous publications.[†] Dopamine, released by the
hypothalamus, enables goal-directed (including very long-
term goal-directed) behavior, the anticipation of pleasure,
and responses to uncertain rewards. The system is activated
when something good happens unexpectedly, and you want it
to recur. Ventures that only pay off randomly or occasionally
become more deeply compelling than any others; we work the
hardest for tantalizing potential, though unlikely, gratifications, like winning the lottery or getting the attention of a
lover who responds only every once in a while. In conditions of

---

[*] E. Hatfield and R. L. Rapson, "The Neuropsychology of Passionate Love
and Sexual Desire," in *Psychology of Relationships*, eds. E. Cuyler and
M. Ackhart (Hauppauge, NY: Nova Science, 2009), 1–26.

[†] TED, "The Uniqueness of Humans," by Robert Sapolsky, September
2009, www.ted.com/talks/robert_sapolsky_the_uniqueness_of_humans;
Robert Sapolsky, *Monkeyluv: And Other Essays on Our Lives as Animals*
(New York: Scribner, 2005).

unpredictable reinforcement like these, dopamine levels explode. Driven by this chemical surge, what Sapolsky calls "the astonishing human capacity to hold on" can keep people playing infinitesimal odds for astonishingly long periods. This cycle, whose primary evolutionary function is to produce stick-to-itiveness and the ability to tolerate delayed gratification, can also end up encouraging playing the slot machines, investing in thirty-year mortgages, believing in the afterlife, and waiting around for women like David's beloved Anna to find time for you. As Sapolsky astutely observes, "'Maybe' is reinforcing like nothing else on earth."

Long before the discovery of dopamine, Bluma Zeigarnik, a Soviet Gestalt psychologist,* was researching a phenomenon that sheds light from another angle on the motivation of obsessive lovers' pursuit of their impossible dreams. Her discovery, first reported in 1927 and known as "the Zeigarnik Effect,"† demonstrated that people remember uncompleted or interrupted tasks (and, in the case of people who love those who don't love them back, uncomplete-able tasks) better than completed ones; in her original experiments, unfinished problems are 90 percent more likely to be recalled than finished ones. The mind has a compelling need for closure, a desire to end uncertainty and to resolve unfinished business—which

---

* Gestalt psychology (which is unrelated to Gestalt therapy) is a twentieth-century German school of experimental psychology that studies how people integrate and organize perceptual and cognitive information into meaningful wholes. The antithesis of behaviorism, which reduces behavior into discrete stimuli and responses, the Gestalt approach can be summarized as "the whole is different from the sum of its parts."

† B. Zeigarnik, "On Finished and Unfinished Tasks," in *A Source Book of Gestalt Psychology*, ed. W. D. Ellis (New York: Harcourt, 1938), 300–314.

helps explain the lasting impact of the "business" of hopeless love affairs, which can never be resolved, at least not with the other person.

In subsequent studies of the phenomenon, researchers found that highly motivated subjects who were asked to solve mathematical puzzles continued to work on their assignments even after being told the experiment was over. When they felt "tension," a physical component of anxiety, while executing these tasks, their memory for the details improved. Tension also led to intrusive thoughts about what they had left undone; the anxiety that tortures the obsessed increases their preoccupation. People take the lack of closure seriously. It is a constant irritant, like a stone in one's shoe, or in the case of unhappy lovers, in one's heart.

Is there any value in compulsive remembering? Reconsidering failures may be useful in finding solutions to similar problems in the future.* To my mind, the best possible use of this dogged cognitive persistence is to apply it to figuring out why one continues to pursue relationships that lead only to grief.

All this research reveals nothing but the neurophysiological substrate of these overwhelming emotions—the where and the what, but not the why: What in our histories and our personalities makes us susceptible to searching for love in all the wrong places? Why are some people more prone to miserable love affairs than others? Why do we pick the people we fall for and then continue to pursue them when there is not a chance in the world that they will reciprocate? How do we ever stop? These are questions for psychologists and philosophers, not

---

* C. M. Seifert and A. L. Patalano, "Memory for Incomplete Tasks: A Re-Examination of the Zeigarnik Effect," in *Proceedings of the Thirteenth Annual Conference of the Cognitive Science Society* (Chicago, 1991), 114–119.

physiologists. Obsessive love, as torturous as it is, is in most cases not a disease or a mental illness but part of the human condition.

Freud's renegade student Theodor Reik made the troubling and perceptive observation that people are most likely to fall intensely in love when they are anxious and their self-esteem is lowest,* which explains the timing of José's infatuation; he had reached an age when he was frantically looking for a way to rewrite his life and retrieve his battered self-image. Feeling inadequate, unhappy, and empty inside are virtually prerequisites for falling and staying desperately in love; at least temporarily, the ecstasy of desire seems to cure everything that ails you.

There is a connection between aversive states of mind— loneliness, shame, even grief and horror—and a propensity to feel overwhelming passion; this is one reason romances blossom in times of war or natural disasters, as well as during the private disasters of our everyday lives.

---

* "[T]he suddenness and vehemence of the beginning [of] passion mark the great effort made to escape an intense psychical distress . . . sometimes boredom or loneliness, a distaste or even dislike for oneself. . . ." Theodor Reik, *A Psychologist Looks at Love* (New York: Farrar and Rinehart, 1944), 43.

Pierre Janet, an early French psychologist and predecessor of Freud, said something uncannily similar: "If a man is depressed he will fall in love, or receive the germ of some kind of passion, on the first and most trivial occasion. . . . The least thing is then enough: the sight of some face, a gesture, a word, which previously would have left him altogether indifferent, strikes us, and becomes the starting point of a long amorous malady. Or more than this, an object which had made no impression on us, at the moment when our mind was healthier and not capable of inoculation, may have left in us some insignificant memory which reappears in a moment of morbid receptivity." Frederick W. J. Myers, "Professor Pierre Janet's 'Automatisme Psychologique,'" in *Proceedings of the Society for Psychical Research*, vol. 6 (London: National Press Agency), 196–97.

Psychopharmacologist Donatella Marazziti* noted that both passionate lovers and people with obsessive-compulsive disorder are deficient in the brain-soothing neurotransmitter serotonin. Low levels of this chemical occur in anxiety states, as well as in depression and aggression, and especially in states of intense jealousy. This finding led her to declare that "love is a type of insanity"—a judgment that may not be true for every kind of love but makes sense to anyone who has fallen into an obsessive abyss.

More potent than reinforcement, dopamine, and serotonin is the ineradicable specter of the past and the urge to reproduce it. Freud wrote about this unconscious force in a paper called "Remembering, Repeating and Working Through,"† in which he named it "the repetition compulsion."

The repetition compulsion is the universal tendency to keep making the same mistakes and re-creating problematic relationships ad infinitum. Freud, a notorious pessimist, understood this self-defeating behavior as a response to traumas that people cannot extricate themselves from, which condemns them to relive their worst moments forever.

Modern psychoanalysts appreciate the tragic magnetic pull of trauma, but they understand this urge not just as a need to reiterate painful experiences but as an attempt to master them retrospectively. People become stuck in self-defeating habits of relating either because they fail to understand the causes or because they are trying to change the effects. Like a dream, reenacting‡ is an unconscious communication to the self about

---

* D. Marazziti, "The Neurobiology of Love," *Current Psychiatry Reviews* 1 (2005): 331–335.

† S. Freud, "Remembering, Repeating and Working Through," in *Standard Edition*, vol. 12 (1914).

‡ What is now referred to as "reenacting" used to be called "acting out," a

unfinished business. By actively seeking what they originally passively endured, victims of trauma are searching for a sense of control. Finding new relationships that mimic the old ones is a way to work through suffering, not just to reproduce it blindly. Recognizing the affinity between a current problematic relationship and the traumatic original can be a revelation, and the first step to creating a new outcome.

BY LOVE POSSESSED

> *This man, this nobody, this lowlife—this man is loved,*
> *and rules a woman's soul.*
> —BIANOR, FROM *THE GREEK ANTHOLOGY*,
>   AD FIRST CENTURY

When David and Maggie were in college, lonely lovers had no trouble making themselves miserable waiting for their elusive objects of desire to come to them. They sat by the phone, hung around the person's dorm, or "casually" showed up at events, fabricated excuses to meet, inquired about their beloved's ac-tivities or whereabouts from unsuspecting third parties, and got updates from sympathetic friends who stood helplessly by. When I was their age and became inextricably entangled with a maddeningly inconsistent boyfriend, I recall feeling a burn-ing need to borrow records from his collection, to attend a concert he might be at, or to solicit his help with an inexplicable math problem at 1:00 A.M. Desperate lovers become shameless.

The Internet has changed the means, if not the motivation, for such behavior. It is now possible to act like a person possessed 24-7 and to comfort yourself with the simulacrum of unlimited,

---

pejorative term that referred exclusively to the negative consequences of behavior that actually has multiple functions, some of them beneficial.

secret access to the minutiae of another's life without his or her knowledge or consent, infinitely prolonging the agony and effectively guaranteeing that you will never have the distance to understand why you are frantically pursuing an intimacy that can never be anything but two-dimensional.

Forty-year-old advertising executive Monica Grey has subjected herself to eight years of very, very partial reinforcement—and an enormous amount of anguish and self-hatred—in cyberpursuit of a man for whom she feels both unquenchable passion and withering contempt.

By her own admission, Monica is an Internet stalker; she calls it "going down the rabbit hole" like Alice in Wonderland, because her compulsion distorts her sense of reality and disables her will. She goes online not to menace a celebrity or settle scores with an enemy or to reconnect with old acquaintances or flirt with new ones. Mesmerized by his Instagram feed, she tethers herself to her computer, immersing herself in the fantasy of sharing in what looks to her like the normal family life of her sometime lover, something she never knew as a child and hungers for desperately. She has trapped herself in the cycle of illusory connection—she cannot bear disconnection—and long-term torture, because even as she spies on him, she is constantly reminded that she is only an outsider looking into his life, not a real participant. "When I see his whole life played out online, I call it 'digital cutting,'" she said, with chilling accuracy. The instant gratification is always followed by long-term mortification. She hates herself for loving him.

The man whom Monica "follows" is divorced, but he and his ex-wife and their two children still live together in the same house, although his relationship with Monica is no secret. For years, he and Monica have been on-again, off-again lovers. She runs to him whenever he feels like seeing her, which is rarely;

most of their affair has been conducted unilaterally by her on her laptop. "I'm a welcome light distraction for him," she said bitterly, "an occasional fun, flirty dinner."

Even if theirs was a more typical relationship, they are ill-suited for each other and have little in common. With justification, her friends accused her of "dating down"; they were appalled to see her in thrall to a man whom she dismissed as "a part-time construction worker and fan of mixed martial arts." He was barely responsive and showed no concern for her welfare, failing to call her even when she was seriously ill. He was not even a good lover. "He was terrible in bed. It was the worst sex I ever had. He never satisfied me or tried to" was her withering assessment of his erotic talents. Still, she insisted, "I've never been more attracted to anyone in my life." Gratification and desire are not necessarily related.

Monica was astute enough to realize that his unappealing qualities were part of his attraction. "This guy won't run—he'll never find anyone else who would put up with him," she declared, demeaning them both. This was security of a kind; she could have him, more or less, forever.

Last year, Monica finally allowed her friends to persuade her to go into therapy. That interrupted her computer mania temporarily and jump-started the process of self-examination, but twelve months of "abstinence" left her feeling so bereft that she called him and arranged a meeting. "I reached out to him in a weak moment," she confessed. "I felt such a high when he responded. I had to go wherever it took me; I had to lessen the pain I felt at being without him." Of course, seeing him did nothing of the sort. We spoke a few days afterward, when the high from her adventure was already beginning to fade.

A seemingly logical rationalization had allowed her to act on what she must have suspected was a terrible idea—that seeing him in person would be a test of her resolve. "I had built up an image of the power he had over me, and I wanted to see if he still had it. It was a constant battle to control following him online. I felt like an addict waiting for my next fix, when maybe I didn't even need the fix anymore." That her urge to see him still seemed entirely beyond her control should have been a warning signal, but she ignored it. "I'm always just one step away from a relapse; it takes a huge amount of effort to fight this," she said. "If I look now, I'll go through a whole year of stuff nonstop. Why haven't I learned that I could end it? There should be something like AA sponsors to keep people like me 'sober.'"

In fact, Monica had all the support she needed in her sympathetic and very patient friends, but this time, she didn't call any of them for help in controlling herself. No external support in the world can restrain someone hell-bent on surrender. "I didn't tell my friends; they would be concerned after all the times they've picked me off the floor," she said. They might even be frustrated and furious with her, but she didn't let herself think about that. The obsessed tend to think of themselves as victims rather than as perpetrators of their own unhappiness and rarely consider the toll of their folly on those who truly love them and want to help them. This unconcern for the feelings of anybody else but the object of desire is an indication of the self-absorption that otherwise sensitive and caring people fall into when they give themselves over to obsessive love.

When they met at the trendy restaurant she picked, he behaved as he always did. "I noticed that he didn't look that great when he walked in," she said, both relieved and disappointed. Over his resistance, she tried to bring up how she felt, but as usual, he wasn't interested. "He said, 'I never meant to hurt you.

You've got to understand my situation'—it was all about him. We sat in the bar kissing a long time, and then I put him in a cab. He held my hand. At least, for the first time, I didn't ask him to come home with me."

Soon afterward, as always, the high dissipated, and the cycle of self-hatred, desire, and contempt began all over again.

Talking to this tormented woman was a sobering, painful immersion in the world of someone so deeply possessed by a timeless fantasy that she cannot see how much she is actually living in her own shocking past. At the root of Monica's compulsion is a history of extraordinary trauma and terror. "My mother left my father for another man, and he never forgave her but became insanely jealous and murderously vindictive. My father stalked my mother, constantly threatening to kill her, and those threats were real. I'm much closer to him than my mother, whom I never believed ever loved me, so I heard all about it. When he was supposed to pick up my brother and me for visitation, she left us alone on the street corner, because we were terrified that he would stab her or shoot her to death or hit her over the head with a baseball bat if their paths crossed. It was a constant battle between them; I've never had a nuclear family." Her lover's family situation, as peculiar and dysfunctional as the arrangement is, is not a waking nightmare for his children, and he and his ex-wife do not expose them to constant threats of horrific violence. Monica is seeking to acquire, or co-opt, a saner version of what she knew.

With the unerring instinct of the unconscious, Monica found the one man ideally suited to meet her need to redo her past. Every time she turns on her computer and sees her lover's two children smiling and waving with their parents at an amusement park, she dismantles the horror of her own childhood and becomes one of them. The horrors she endured still possess her because she has not fully experienced or grieved for—what Freud once called "abreacted"*—them. She still feels buffeted by her parents' madness, which was so gripping that they exposed their children to its fallout.

At the deepest level, Monica wants her beloved and his ex-wife to be her family; she wants to be their child, not his lover—the child of amicably divorced parents who are still providing a secure home for their children and a semblance of family life, parents who do not force their children to participate in their murderous mutual rituals of hatred. It is a perfect fit with her unmet needs. Desires can have different goals from what they appear to have, and what takes the form of sexual desire may have an entirely different underlying motive.

Another indicator that Monica is stuck in her past is her constant refrain that she has no sense of control over her life (she is prone to say variations on "I don't know why I choose the men I do—they choose me," "I'll accept any kind of treatment," and "Men always leave me when I was just beginning to feel comfortable"), which was tragically true in her relationship with her father, who sacrificed her welfare to his vendetta against her mother even though she loved him. She sees marriage as a chamber of horrors; it is no wonder that she is attracted only to unmarriageable men. Like José, she feels no

---

* "Abreaction" is a term from the early years of psychoanalysis (*Studies on Hysteria* was written by Freud and Josef Breuer in 1895), when Freud was experimenting with hypnosis to treat hysterical symptoms and noticed that reliving the full emotional force of traumatic experiences was therapeutic for his patients. Later on, he adopted interpretation as a preferable—and less explosive—technique, with insight as the goal. In contemporary approaches to treating trauma, including attachment theory and the various relationship-oriented approaches to psychodynamic therapy, abreaction has been resurrected in new guises and has lost none of its curative power.

sense of agency and, like him, believes she has no choice but to give in to her feelings, no matter how destructive she knows them to be. In order to live in the real world as an adult with some control over her own life, she has to realize that it is she who chooses the men who choose her.

A poignant image from one of Monica's dreams indicates some of the themes that may liberate her if she pursues them seriously. "I find myself in my lover's mother's beautiful kitchen, but there is no place for me to sit." She believes that she can never have what other people have—and, secretly, that she does not deserve to have the comforting joys of domestic life that this woman's kitchen epitomizes, where healthy appetites of all sorts are satisfied. Being nurtured feels forever off limits for her, and care is not something she deserves by right. This is a deduction from her childhood experience; children often hold themselves responsible for the way their parents treat them.

When she is not invading her lover's life online, Monica reads all the self-help Web sites the Internet has to offer and tries to follow their recommendations, but to no avail. "I wrote down ten things he said that should stop me from seeing him. I remind myself how selfish he is, that he has no empathy. I still cry when I think about his coldness. But when he was silent for two weeks after I last saw him, he seemed to regain the power that he used to have over me." Despite all this effort, she still thinks of him constantly. Advice, even sensible advice, changes nothing unless the recipient is receptive.

There are some indications, however, that Monica is taking the first steps toward disengaging with him online, without which nothing can fundamentally change. She has now texted him to request that he stop "liking" her posts. "I think it is finally becoming clearer to me how much pain I'm in when

I watch his life from afar," she said. "It is taking a long time to accept that I can never be part of his life. If I'm honest, I have to admit that the real reason I contacted him was that I hoped his situation had changed and that he might be ready to have me in his life. That will never, ever happen." Saying the truth can lead to believing it.

Is freedom within Monica's reach? I believe that there is hope for her, with resolve, support, and continued commitment to therapy. She already knows the outlines of the unspeakable terror that she is trying to undo, but she has to recognize that she will be trapped as long as she continues to hope that it can be magically altered by having the man she covets—a universal theme in obsession. In her case, reenactment and self-soothing by Internet stalking are symptoms of a serious post-traumatic stress disorder and must be identified as such to be treated effectively. She needs a profound, emotionally alive understanding of what she endured and how it affected her. Reexperiencing the terror in the nurturing holding environment* of a therapeutic relationship—the "kitchen" with a place for her—and a caring therapist, as both guide and witness, salves the deepest wounds.

These four obsessive affairs, so different on the surface, serve similar functions. Their hidden themes are identity, desirability, and redoing history. Each of these driven people was trying to re-create past experiences or relationships in new guises. For

---

* According to the pediatrician and psychoanalyst Donald Winnicott (1896–1971), a founding member of the British Object Relations school in modern psychoanalysis, the "holding environment" of the therapeutic relationship offers the patient the same comfort and sustenance as a mother's loving arms give her child. D. W. Winnicott, *The Child, the Family and the Outside World* (New York: Perseus, 1987).

the duration of their doomed romances, all four were under the spell of the repetition compulsion, pulled inexorably back into their unmetabolized longings and losses. Maggie found her father again in her philosophy major, David tried to regain his mother's exclusive love through Anna, José strove to revive his younger self, and Monica was revising the devastating experience of being her estranged parents' child.

It is much easier to say what doesn't work to control this emotional imprisonment than what does. Like chronic dieting, the cheerleading advice and behavior tips on online self-help sites, such as making lists of the beloved's hateful behaviors or obnoxious qualities or imagining him or her covered in vomit—are of limited long-term value. The only way out of pain is through it.

Obsessive love is built on a tissue of illusions: that by having sex with someone you can possess that person's soul; that you can transmute past defeats into present triumphs without understanding or mourning; that you can make the unloving love you by constancy, uncomplaining availability, and molding yourself into what you think that person wants. The only remedy is to recognize, acknowledge, and grieve that you have attached your hopes and handed over your destiny to someone who does not deserve them and who can never satisfy your desire.

Is there an effective way out of the self-inflicted madness of hopeless attachments? W. Somerset Maugham, in *Of Human Bondage*, his autobiographically inspired novel about a humiliating love affair, hints at the path to freedom. It is usually long and slow, with many setbacks and small advances, insights that slowly eat away at the desperate desire for what you cannot have, which begins to look less appealing than what you can. Paradoxically, it is inaction, or what looks like inaction, but is actually intense self-examination and loving self-restraint, that opens your eyes to possibilities for real mutual surrender and fulfillment. As Maugham asserted, "Self-control might be as passionate and as active as the surrender to passion."

3

VENGEANCE IS MINE

The Dark Side of Rejected Love

THE WAGES OF SIN

She opened the hood, unscrewed the radiator cap, and methodically stuffed the bits of frozen tilapia she had painstakingly cut into little pieces as far down into the radiator shaft as she could reach. Then she closed it, confident that when water circulated through the heating system, an ineradicable stench of rotten fish would fill the car belonging to her sixty-year-old husband's twenty-six-year-old lover (who was also their joint employee), insulting its owner's femininity in the grossest terms and forcing her to ponder her foul deed. This would certainly make the employee rue the day that she e-mailed her paramour a photograph of herself naked in front of his own family Christmas tree, an act of heedless bravado documenting the yearlong affair that his wife had discovered only days earlier.

Not only would the culprit now have an inescapable reminder of her guilt, but she would never, ever be able to sell the car.

The proverb says that revenge is a dish best eaten cold, when one can savor it more. But in this case, even though the instrument of revenge was frozen, the passionate hatred with which it was wielded was red hot. It is telling that the Internet lists many variations on how to stink up a car to get back at someone, suggesting the popularity of this activity, as well as of the actions that provoke it.

I heard the story from a close friend of the perpetrator. This confidante had talked the betrayed woman out of her original plan, which was to send an illustrated, incriminating letter to the young woman's mother. The employer and her now-former employee had been on such intimate terms that she knew the mother and had even been her houseguest in Mexico. Her friend had argued persuasively that the tilapia strategy was preferable, because only the guilty party and no innocent bystander would suffer the consequences. It was, the two friends agreed, a fitting penalty for a serious crime of the heart that would otherwise have gone unpunished.

There was plenty to punish, as it turned out; the incriminating photograph was just the tip of the iceberg. As soon as her eyes were opened, the wife discovered that, even as she and her employee were regularly going out to lunch together and having heart-to-heart talks, the lovers had been conducting an extensive erotic e-mail correspondence, that they had trysted regularly at out-of-town business gigs, and—the final blow—that the young woman who had been like a daughter to her had recently miscarried his child.

Why did she feel compelled to dramatically punish her husband's paramour (she had already dealt with him by starting divorce proceedings), and why did she only damage her rival's property rather than try to mentally torment, hurt, or even kill the paramour herself, as women scorned often do in tragedies and in the tabloids? I understood instinctively why she chose to punish the woman in this intimate way rather than her husband; unrealistically, most women (and many men) expect more loyalty from friends—even when they work for us—than from lovers or spouses, and therefore, betrayal by a friend seems more unforgivable. Since love is a passion, we are not shocked when it blows off course. Given the nature of the betrayal she was punishing, this woman believed that simply trashing the car would not have sufficiently expressed her outrage. In addition, although the wife was vindictive, she was not violent, except perhaps in her fantasies. She wanted the guilty woman to remember, so killing her was out of the question as well as against the law and the sixth commandment. Tilapia filled the bill.

The underlying purpose of her vengeful act was to restore her own self-esteem and sense of control, to undo an overwhelming feeling of powerlessness. "I didn't want her to get away without suffering as she had made me suffer," she told her friend. "I felt so much better knowing that in the hot Miami sun that fish would stink, and the smell of it wouldn't go away." Thanks to this ploy, she believed that the pervasive olfactory evidence of guilt would prevent the paramour from driving away scot-free. And it worked—at least on the surface. "She was the happiest woman," her friend told me. "She was liberated."

But was she? Neither the car saboteur nor her friend questioned whether it really was possible to guarantee that the paramour would suffer as she herself had suffered or even suffer at all. The car saboteur felt compelled to force her rival to feel *something*, even if it was not the regret she wanted her rival to feel. However, there is no guarantee that revenge will have the desired effect, a fact often ignored in the frenzy of enacting it.

By doing the most insulting thing she could imagine, the wife wanted to humiliate her rival as she herself had been humiliated. However, having a car's resale value destroyed, even if it makes the owner feel as rotten as her car now smelled, is far less devastating than having a marriage destroyed in a double betrayal of trust. Whether the intended victim actually was horribly insulted or was simply furious or dismissed the sabotage as the behavior of a crazy person acting out jealous rage, the perpetrator would never know. In fact, nobody can neutralize a grave injury that has already occurred by inflicting one in return. The past can never be undone, even though its meaning and impact can evolve over time, and the anguish can diminish.

Authentic liberation from the pain of betrayal involves more than turning the tables. It is hard emotional work and requires a much bigger commitment of time and mental energy than even the most cunning act of vengeance. Delivering retribution is a Pyrrhic victory unless the betrayed person then turns inward and processes the impact of what has befallen her. In this case, the wife would have to confront her own blindness and misplaced trust and understand their origins in her own history. Only serious self-examination could then enable her to rebuild her life on less shaky ground. She would have to mourn for her losses—by confronting the fault lines in her marriage and her husband's character, acknowledging that she had been helpless to prevent another woman from taking his love, and working through her hatred for the two of them for betraying her and for herself for being oblivious. Revenge may be a dish best eaten cold, but the best revenge of all is living wisely and well—learning from the past and applying those lessons in the future.

Is there such a thing as healthy revenge? The auto vandal genuinely felt better afterward. Her spiteful glee at getting even lessened her losses—of her marriage, her trust, her former friend and employee, her emotional foundation—at least temporarily. As long as she had no illusions that it was a lasting solution to the task of recovering her self-respect, it served a purpose. Had she gone on to defame her rival on the Internet, kill her cat, try to ruin her life, or become obsessed with her, she would have continued to be victimized by the betrayal and allowed the affair to warp her permanently. But if the tilapia gave her momentary solace in extremis and if in addition she had no illusions that employing it circumvented the grieving process ahead, it was money and effort well spent, even if technically illegal.

I heard from her friend that the erstwhile employee vanished and that the wife got a healthy divorce settlement. But I had to ask one final question: why did she specifically use tilapia to do the job? "It was cheap, and she probably had it on hand in her freezer," the friend replied. "I certainly wouldn't choose Copper River salmon as *my* revenge fish."

The woman who advised the betrayed wife against sending an incriminating letter to her husband's lover's mother spoke with the authority of personal experience. "I told her not to do it, because when you send something like that into the world, it comes back; it really does," she told me. "I know, because it happened to me. I lived it." She took this stand because she wanted to spare someone she identified with from her own fate—a fate she believed was retribution for an act of vengeance she herself had meticulously plotted and carried out a decade earlier (she was forty years old at the time) after discovering that her boyfriend and her own closest female friend had betrayed her.

Hers was a subtler, secret, and darker revenge than car

vandalism. Instead of ice, she used fire—photographs, artifacts, and names written on slips of paper incinerated with a curse in a black magic ritual.

"I lived with Don for years," she said. "Right before we broke up, he started an affair with my friend Sandy. He denied it, but I knew it was true from seeing them together." Here too, e-mail confirmed an illicit relationship between two people who had been trusted and whose characters had never been suspected. Here too, the woman friend's behavior hurt more, especially since she had been one of a group of people who had long shared a summer house with the couple. "I felt so betrayed by her—I couldn't believe that a girlfriend would do that to another woman, because my girlfriends were my family," she explained.

When she found the incriminating e-mail exchange, she let all their mutual acquaintances and housemates know what had happened. She wanted to defame their characters, and she succeeded. "I made it my business to tell everyone we knew in common about them," she said. However, there were unanticipated consequences to her revelation. "People were shocked—but in telling them all, I created a division among our friends." It was satisfying to expose the transgression, even though she lost some friends and sowed dissent that resulted in the disbanding of the close-knit group. "I felt better. I was vindicated," the avenger said. "It felt good to show them that they couldn't just get away with doing this and not have to pay for it." She was willing to pay the price in lost friendships herself in order to assure that their actions had consequences.

But sweet though it was, broadcasting the affair was not enough to sate her urge to get back at the couple. She wanted to cause more insidious and permanent damage than simply public censure; she wanted to destroy their chances for happiness. She picked a night with a full moon to carry out a rite intended to curse them. "I needed a sense of cleansing, so I took sage and a candle and things of theirs—including a photo of Sandy I found at our upstate place, and a piece of paper with Don's name written on it—and I burned them together to deny them their love. I wanted their love to fall apart. If I couldn't have love, I didn't want them to have love; it was the only control I had over an uncontrollable situation. I felt helpless to change what happened, to do anything about it. To me, this was a way of getting power back when I had lost it. It gave me the strength to go on." Like the woman she later advised, she too had been desperate to recover a sense of agency after betrayal, and revenge was the only way she felt she could do it, even though she was frightened of the forces she might be unleashing. "I was also a bit scared, since I felt I was dealing with something I didn't really understand in my own little black magic ritual," she admitted.

As it turned out, she came to believe that her own long-term losses undid any short-term gains she had achieved from performing her satanic ceremony, despite the comfort she derived at the time. "A friend told me that wishing other people ill comes back twofold on you, and it did," she said. "It ended up backfiring. Don has been in a good relationship with someone else for eight years, and I've yet to have a good relationship myself."

What in fact caused her enforced solitude? Was it retribution from the universe for summoning the powers of darkness as she herself believed? Or did that explanation come from her own guilty conscience, as I believe? In either case, she was convinced that she herself had been the one who was punished by her mental cruelty and condemned to a life without love.

MURDER ON THEIR MINDS

Heav'n has no Rage, like Love to Hatred turn'd,
Nor Hell a Fury, like a Woman scorn'd.
—WILLIAM CONGREVE, 1697

Humiliation inflames many victims of betrayal, and some it unhinges. Most get over it or perform nonlethal acts of revenge that get it out of their systems. Then they lick their wounds and go on with their lives. But the truly vulnerable of both sexes become obsessed with vengeance and hell-bent on evening the score. The compulsion to undo a sense of personal annihilation by annihilating the perpetrator (or the perpetrator's paramour) underlies every crime of passion.

The sorceress Medea, heroine of Euripides's tragedy, is the archetypal passionate-lover-turned-avenger that Congreve had in mind. Her retribution against Jason, her unfaithful husband, was horrifyingly complete. Medea's advice and magic arts allowed Jason to obtain the coveted Golden Fleece and had saved his life on numerous occasions. He pledged eternal love to her, married her, and had two sons with her but then deserted her for a more politically useful bride. Medea, deranged with jealous rage, wreaked a memorable and torturous vengeance on him. First she sent his new love a wedding present of a dress that burned her alive when she put it on, and then she murdered her own children and served them to their father. So intent was Medea to punish Jason by obliterating everything he loved—and leaving him alive to suffer the anguish of these losses—that she destroyed even the most beloved parts of herself. Her overpowering love became relentless hatred.*

The two most noteworthy modern-day Medeas were considerably less noble than the original, and the men in their lives behaved no better than Jason. The cases of Amy Fisher (whom the tabloids christened "the Long Island Lolita") and Jean Harris (the spurned mistress of the cardiologist known as "the Scarsdale Diet Doctor")—Fisher attempted murder, and Harris actually committed it—still resonate in the imagination. Their stories were told in screaming headlines and trashy made-for-TV movies† (and, in the second case, also serious books‡) rather than in immortal poetry, but the same tumultuous emotions compelled them, and the same personality traits underlay their violent behavior. Their trials saturated the media; the Harris case was front-page news for a year, and the Fisher case never seemed to go away. Both became household

---

* It is intriguing that authors who have written about the pair have shown considerably more sympathy for Medea than for Jason. In Euripides's play, Medea never pays for her crimes and is conveyed in a dragon-drawn golden chariot sent by her grandfather, the sun god Helios, to Athens, where she remarries and has more children. Jason fares far worse. In Apollonius of Rhodes's third-century BC epic *Argonautica*, Jason is punished for breaking his vow to Medea by dying, miserable and alone, when his rotted ship, *The Argo*, falls on him while he sleeps, crushing him under its stern. Dante has him suffer an even more wretched fate: as a treacherous seducer, Jason inhabits the Eighth Circle of Hell in *The Inferno*, where he is compelled to march about endlessly while being whipped by devils. Breaking vows was taken very, very seriously in the classical world and the Middle Ages.

† All three networks made movies about the Fisher case, a first in television history. *Newsweek* rated them with garbage cans for trash content. The Harris case inspired only two made-for-TV movies, which were at least superficially more tasteful.

‡ Critic Diana Trilling's *Mrs. Harris* and journalist Shana Alexander's *Very Much a Lady*.

words, and there was an unquenchable public appetite for details of both affairs.

The sordid saga of Amy Fisher, the adolescent girl gone murderously amuck, galvanized national attention. At age seventeen, she shot Mary Jo Buttafuoco, her thirty-five-year-old lover Joey Buttafuoco's wife, in the head and nearly killed her. Incensed that Joey had not left Mary Jo, she was determined to eliminate her rival and almost succeeded. She served a seven-year sentence for a plea-bargained first-degree aggravated assault charge and never expressed a moment's remorse. After her release, she capitalized on her notoriety by becoming a porn star.

The ambiance of the Harris affair was more elegant, but the circumstances were no less sordid. Harris, the proper and accomplished fifty-six-year-old headmistress of a girls' school, murdered sixty-seven-year-old Dr. Herman Tarnower, her philandering lover of fourteen years. He had long been flagrantly and unapologetically unfaithful to her, but this was the first time he had chosen a woman thirty years his junior. Harris ostensibly went to Tarnower's house to commit suicide but instead shot him four times at point-blank range when she saw the lingerie of her much-younger replacement in his bedroom. Despite her protestations of innocence and of abiding love for her victim, Harris was convicted of second-degree murder; hoping to be exonerated, she had refused to plea-bargain. Her fifteen-year sentence was commuted after she served twelve years. The case was the subject of two books, and Harris herself wrote two others. Although she made significant efforts to redeem her life—while in prison, she started a center for inmates' children and a foundation that provided scholarships for them—she felt like the victim herself until her death at eighty-nine and never faced the hatred that underlay her love. She could never admit that she had bound herself to an unworthy man—even after she killed him.

AN EYE FOR AN EYE

The motives and psychodynamics of Amy Fisher and Jean Harris are similar to those of their mythic predecessor: none of the three could endure her own helplessness or tolerate that her rejection and shame should go unpunished. How and why does love get converted to hate and the compulsion to destroy, and why are some people more susceptible to this transformation than others?

Intimate betrayal causes what Freud called "narcissistic injury"—a grievous wound to a person's sense of self-esteem and potency in the world. For those with certain fault lines in their personalities caused by early trauma, narcissistic injury easily morphs into what Heinz Kohut* later labeled "narcissistic rage," a far more poisonous emotion that frequently culminates in violence.† At the extreme, bloodlust overrides everything else, and the rejected lover is consumed by it; he or she comes to embody it. The only means of undoing the shame and impotence that engulf the self is to destroy those who caused it.

Nobody is exempt from experiencing narcissistic injury in childhood, because nobody is the exclusive object of a parent's love, and no parent is always perfectly attuned or needs to be.

---

* Kohut (1913–1981) was the founder of self psychology, a modern psychoanalytic approach focusing on the development and maintenance of a person's sense of self. With his emphasis on the centrality of the therapist's empathy in the analytic process, he has been a major influence on my thinking and my therapeutic stance. Kohut's most significant works are *The Analysis of the Self: A Systematic Approach to the Psychoanalytic Treatment of Narcissistic Personality Disorders* (New York: International Universities Press, 1971), *The Restoration of Self* (New York: International Universities Press, 1977), and *How Does Analysis Cure?*, edited by Arnold Goldberg with Paul E. Stepansky (Chicago: University of Chicago Press, 1984).

† Heinz Kohut contrasts narcissistic rage with "mature aggression," the more nuanced, less automatic, and not massively destructive response of a more integrated personality to damage inflicted by others.

But children whose parents cannot empathize with them and whose needs are regularly ignored can develop a type of character pathology in which intense aggression is easily aroused and difficult to modulate. Such people—the psychiatric diagnostic terms for their condition are "pathological narcissism" or "narcissistic personality disorder"—are cold and self-involved even when they love, and they also suffer from inner emptiness and an inability to regulate their emotions. They lack the resources to withstand the inevitable traumas of life. These are the people who become compulsively vengeful. The shocking behaviors of these avengers fascinate the more restrained among us even as they horrify us; they act out what we hardly dare to imagine.

Most people do not become criminals when they are betrayed; religious scruples—they take seriously God's biblical pronouncement that "Vengeance is Mine," even when sorely tempted to make it theirs—a sense of personal morality, self-awareness, or good counsel restrain them. Those who are lucky or wise have other internal resources that survive even betrayal.

HIS MOTHER'S SON

Cedric Walker is a forty-six-year-old massage therapist—barrel-chested and powerful, with extravagant dreadlocks, a softly lilting voice, and a laid-back manner. A childhood injury left him with a pronounced limp, for which he compensates with his upper-body strength. He takes his vocation seriously and becomes so absorbed when he is working that he hardly speaks. He is the last person you would imagine capable of seriously contemplating violence against anybody, and it seems inconceivable that he could ever harbor thoughts of hurting a woman under any circumstances, let alone of devising the perfect torture for an unfaithful wife. But he comes from a West

Indian culture where violence is considered the natural and proper punishment for adultery—particularly when it takes place in the marital bed—and where there is no dearth of enforcers standing ready to either murder the culprits or curse them should you be unwilling to do either job yourself; in his country, he assured me, the law looks the other way. This was the environment in which he had to struggle against the siren call to vengeance.

Cedric was forty-four and his wife was thirty-seven, and they had been married five years when she betrayed him. At the time, he had a job at a resort that took him away from his hometown for three weeks out of every month. Supporting his wife was a masculine point of honor for him. "She was living in the house we owned, so I was paying the mortgage—I didn't let her do it," he told me. "I said, 'Keep your money.'" One night, Cedric got a call from his best friend at four o'clock in the morning, informing him that a flashy black SUV was parked in his garage. This had aroused his friend's suspicions since he knew that Cedric didn't own a car. The friend also knew that the car belonged to a locally famous musician and deduced that the musician was in bed with Cedric's wife. "He asked me, 'Do you want me to take care of it?'" Cedric said, "I told him, 'Just take a photo of the car and the license plate, and I'll deal with him when I get back'"—a conversation that in this context would be universally understood as an offer by the friend to commit vengeance by proxy and a statement by the cuckold that he intended to do the deed himself. I asked him how you find somebody to "take care of it" if no friend is there to volunteer and you yourself are unable or unwilling to carry it out. "You know people," he said with intentionally vague certainty. He explained what he himself might be able to do. "A relative of mine is an undercover cop. If I killed somebody, he would do what he has to do to make it work—to overlook certain situations. People have affairs, but if you bring it home, vengeance comes in."

But Cedric neither used the services of his friend or his other resources nor acted on his own behalf. "All I had to say to my friend was 'It's okay,' and it would have been done, but that's not who I am," he told me. Why, then, did he ask for photographs? "I wanted them for the divorce hearing. If I have proof, she can't get alimony from me." It was one thing to pay her expenses if she were honorable, but quite another if she was not.

Honor killing may have been his first impulse when he got the news, but his plans evolved into something more effective than murder, something that felt entirely justified as well as morally acceptable. "I'm not a killer," he said. "I don't think killing somebody solves anything—if she dies, it's over." Expressing the same sentiments as the car saboteur and her friend, he said, "You want to wound, make her pay attention." I wondered why he thought only his wife should pay. "That man couldn't do anything to her if she didn't allow it—she's the guilty one," he said, and I had to agree.

Since black magic was a readily available and undetectable option, had he considered using it against her? He had clearly entertained the idea. "I know about it because I grew up in a place with that," he said. "My grandfather was a voodoo priest, and I know a woman who had someone send a demon to make a woman rival's husband crazy." But he dismissed it on moral grounds, even though he didn't doubt its horrifying efficacy. "My father would have nothing to do with it; if you dabble your hands in it, there's no coming back." Black magic was a real option in Cedric's world, and rejecting it took a level of self-control

that was far from universal in his culture. In doing so, he emulated his father, whom he revered for his good sense and good
example.

Then Cedric told me what he had planned to do to his wife
while she was still unaware that she had been found out. It was
a punishment that was dark, but very much of this world rather
than the diabolical one. "I thought about lacing a condom with
hot pepper and having sex with her, so she would feel extreme
pain and evil like I was feeling." To inflict genital torture that
paralleled the mental torture she had inflicted on him seemed
only just. That his rival was able-bodied added to his humiliation and stoked his hate and outrage. "She knew I was crippled
when she married me. If she didn't want to be married to me
anymore, she could have said so, but she didn't. She betrayed me
and was still taking my money," he explained. From the satisfaction with which he described his sadistic plan, it was clear that
he had seriously considered acting on it.

However, his work as a healer came to his rescue, and he
decided not to act on his plan. "I'm a massage therapist," he
explained. "How could I touch someone's body to heal them
if I harbored violence in my mind? You are a vessel. You can't
hold anger for a female, because that anger is going to trigger
when you're touching a female, and she would feel it. You've got
to keep your vessel clean. Otherwise, spite will come around
back to you and destroy you. Massage is my true love. She
chose me, I didn't choose her, and I'm happy that she did." As
if in explanation for his steadfast tenderness toward women,
despite how one had treated him, he added proudly, "My mother
raised a good son."

How did Cedric acquire his enlightened self-control? "Ego
strength" is the term from classical Freudian theory that

describes the capacity of a person to call on emotional restraint in a crisis—in this case, to override hate and the desire to wreak vengeance. It is the antidote to narcissistic rage. This ability to resist acting out and to maintain one's identity under duress is not based on fear of punishment—going to hell or going to jail—but on the self-esteem engendered by empathic parents who prize their child and instill discipline lovingly. Even if parents fail to provide it, a person can acquire ego strength later in life though self-awareness.*

Empathic love and the inspiring example of both his parents protected Cedric and kept him from acting out his rage on his unfaithful wife. He identified with his father and turned his back on black magic because his father had done so, but in this crisis, brought about by a woman betraying him, the forces of restraint that most helped him were the two women—one real and the other symbolic—whom he loved and who loved him. One was his revered mother; the other was his vocation, which he envisioned as a beloved woman who could never betray him, to whom he had pledged inviolable fidelity. These two feminine ideals consoled him and inspired him to act honorably. Their presence within him neutralized the harm his wife had done him and allowed him to overcome his hunger for vengeance. Together they provided inner sustenance deeper than the hurt he suffered; they bolstered him when he needed them most. He had so deep a reservoir to draw on that nothing could destroy his sense of self. The thoughtful, passionate self-restraint that these two abiding loves engendered salved his wounds and stayed his hand.

---

* The set of skills that underlie ego strength and other cognitive organizational and planning abilities has been located by contemporary neurophysiologists in the prefrontal cortex and is now widely known as "executive function."

The empathic love and inspiring example of good parents and a person's own efforts as a mature adult to overcome the lust for vengeance that betrayal excites offer more lasting solace than tilapia, guns, or curses can ever provide.

4

BETRAYAL

KEEPING FAITH WITH THE UNFAITHFUL

At five minutes to five on Thursday, April 22, 1993—she remembers all the particulars—Deirdre Black came home from work and opened the front door of her apartment. At the entrance, she found her charming, garrulous husband, Ben, standing with his bags packed. Without ceremony or explanation ("I need some space" was all he said), he walked out the door she had just walked in, never to return. She was thirty-six. They had been married for five years. Over the next several years, she emerged from this devastation with her self-esteem, her ability to love, and even her dark sense of humor intact. The unusual vow that she made to herself soon after it happened saved her.

Deirdre was a friendly acquaintance of mine, an intense, capable, flawlessly turned-out, green-eyed Irishwoman whom I used to run into regularly at our neighborhood espresso bar. She was also a profoundly pious Catholic, the only one I've ever known at all well; since I am a liberal and an agnostic Reform Jew, our worldviews clashed in many fundamental ways (we both knew, and did not discuss, that many of the social policies she was seriously against I was seriously for), but we always appreciated each other. When I saw her there in line again after a six-month hiatus, I was alarmed by the change in her appearance--she seemed wan—and, concerned that she might have been ill, I asked her how she was. That was how I learned, to my horror, what had befallen her. I knew Ben slightly, as well—she was a brooder, but he always seemed to be in a good mood—and never imagined he could treat anybody with such casual cruelty.

Little did I know when we bumped into each other that she had only recently regained her ability to speak and eat and was still mostly just going through the motions of living. It emerged as we talked that for two months after Ben's exit, she had been so grief stricken and shocked that she became virtually mute, perhaps for fear of what she would know once she heard herself say it aloud. Voicing sentiments like "I hate him," "I hate myself," or "I wish we both were dead," which many people in her situation would share and some would consider a relief to express, would have violated her stringent sense of how a devout Catholic ought to feel and concretize thoughts that she struggled to suppress.

During that time, her weight dropped to eighty-five pounds because she could barely eat from despair and self-punishment— her family and friends virtually force-fed her—and her immune system was so compromised that she contracted a grave illness and had to endure a long course of intravenous antibiotics. She felt doomed, disoriented, and utterly alone. "The planes of the universe had shifted, and there was nothing I could do," she said. "The entire situation was impossible in every way, too painful, unendurable." She contemplated suicide but fought the urge. "I had to rule that out countless times," she admitted. "I dragged myself bodily through every single hour. I wasn't thinking about anything but whether I could live until the next day." She believed that it would have been an intolerable sign of weakness to commit a mortal sin when she was already so horribly sinned against; if she added bad behavior to bad fortune, she would have no honor left. At that point, the only thing left for her to cling to was self-control. Despite everything, she prided herself on not having missed a day of work the entire time. She had never even been late. "People depended on me," she explained. Dependability is an aspect of fidelity, and fidelity was to become her raison d'être.

Deirdre then told me something that I never imagined anyone would think, let alone enshrine as a prime directive and credo. It has confounded me and resonated over the two decades that have passed since her ordeal, during which we have become intimates: as she lay prostrate trying to find a reason to go on living, she made a split-second but irrevocable decision "to remain faithful to Ben, no matter what, for all eternity." It was a private vow, not even spoken aloud, but as fervent as any nun's.

I was moved by her seriousness of purpose, but the therapist in me was horrified; surely, it was seriously masochistic to swear fealty to someone who acted toward you with such depraved indifference. Why bind yourself to your tormentor, forsaking all possible others who might in fact treat you well and make up for your loss? Since she was such an exacting person, was she punishing herself, scrutinizing and blaming herself for character flaws that could have made him leave? Did she think

she had inadvertently alienated him or not loved him unself-
ishly enough? In my own life, I had certainly continued to care
for people who did not deserve my devotion, but I never did it
as a point of honor, let alone an act of faith. I couldn't decide
whether this was a self-created prison or a unique route to liberation.

Initially, it was not easy for even a trained empathizer like
me to follow Deirdre's logic or to grasp something so alien and
counterintuitive. I wanted to comprehend everything that was
packed into that startling statement. I kept trying to pin her
down. What did her love consist of? How can you love someone
and not respect him? How can you love someone not worthy of
your respect and still respect yourself? None of these were issues for her, because she saw her oath of fidelity as strictly between herself and God; Ben had become irrelevant, although
paradoxically he was the ongoing object of her devotion. Her
vow was a declaration about her own nature and how she intended to conduct herself—the only things she felt were still
entirely under her control.

Deirdre's notion of fidelity is nothing like mine; no fan of
the "hate the sin, love the sinner" mentality, I believe a person
has to deserve love. But since Ben was out of her life for good,
mutuality did not matter to her. In fact, Deirdre and I had very
different feelings about mutuality even in ongoing intimate relationships, where I considered it a sine qua non and she did
not. She expected nothing from Ben in return and knew that
she would never honor him, trust him, or see him again. "My
decision had nothing to do with Ben," she explained in one of
our many talks over the years. "Once he was gone, it was only
about my relation to God. Marriage is never just between two
people; it's a sacrament, a promise you make." God, she passionately believed, had joined them, so no mere woman like

herself should put them asunder. Would her promise still be valid even if he tried to kill her? I wondered. "That would be different," she said without pausing. "I wouldn't have to stick around for that—that's crazy. You don't keep walking over broken glass." Would it hold if their marriage were annulled? "No annulment has happened yet, so I don't know what I would do," she responded, but I had a feeling that fidelity to Ben had become so central and habitual for her that she would maintain it even then; she had made preserving the sanctity of their marriage single-handedly the defining characteristic of her identity.

Ben's vanishing was, paradoxically, an aid to her self-restoration. It meant Deirdre never again had to deal with him outside her own mind, so she could think and feel whatever she wanted about him in complete freedom with no real-world consequences. Since the worldview she asserted was absolute and unilateral, nothing Ben could ever do to her could destroy it. She was placing herself and her value as a human being beyond his influence forever. "Thankfully, I've never had the expectation that all relationships have to be equal to be worth preserving," she explained. For her, fidelity is not a transaction with another person; it is a sacred duty. There doesn't have to be any quid pro quo. "I'm a very faithful person," she said simply. "It's not a commodity, it's not wampum." It is her essence.

Keeping faith as Deirdre conceived it was her new vocation, defined and implemented in her own way. Her stance would require neither celibacy nor sexual fidelity to Ben in the future, either of which would have been self-punitive under the circumstances. She could continue to believe in the sacredness of marriage, while leaving open the possibility of remarriage. And, contrary to Catholic doctrine, forgiving Ben was out of the question. "That's God's job," she declared. She disputes that a wronged person has a duty to grant absolution—one of the things I find refreshing and independent-minded about her. Deirdre was not trying to make herself a candidate for sainthood; she was asserting a principle to sustain her "when it would have been easier to die."

Anyone who endures so soul-destroying an experience feels impotent and isolated. "You go through it alone," as Deirdre said—like death. But she was fortunate to get a crucial piece of help from an irreproachable source early on.

A conversation with her father at once playful and serious galvanized her will. "One day, he asked me, 'Is there something I can do?' and I said, 'Yeah, I'd like it if you punched him in the nose.' I wanted him to knock off and smash Ben's little Leprechaun nose. He was quiet, and then he said, 'Well, you really don't want me to do that—you'd like a shortcut to figuring this out, and there isn't one.'

"I wanted my father to punch him because I knew if he did it, Ben's nose would break—if a nose that small could actually break—and my father's hand wouldn't. I couldn't pull it off myself—I'd end up with a broken hand, which would not be the outcome I had in mind."

Deirdre wanted to outsource her desire for violent retribution to a surrogate (as well as ultimately to God the Father) so the wish would not possess her, and it worked. "I was so distracted with delight at the picture in my mind of him actually punching Ben! Seemingly ridiculous things can sometimes give you the strength to go on."

She allowed herself to enjoy a fantasy of revenge—which every betrayed person entertains and must negotiate. In this, she was unwittingly following the advice of Theodor Reik, one of Freud's early followers, on how to maintain mental health despite the assaults of the world: "A thought-murder a day keeps the doctor away."*

But she also appreciated her father's realism. Preoccupation with wreaking vengeance, he knew, keeps a victim a victim. It is an attempt to turn the tables in order to avoid feelings of sorrow and helplessness, but since the past cannot be undone, it never works. His logic made sense to me; for years, I had told myself and my patients, "The only way out of pain is through it."

There was a darker, unconscious side to the way Deirdre swore eternal devotion to the man who had abandoned her. She described the process with a startling image. "I felt like it took me a week to pull that trigger, but it actually happened very quickly." The gunshot metaphor she used to describe her instantaneous decision could as easily characterize a murder or a suicide. But rather than killing Ben or herself, she managed instead to destroy the harm he did her. She was pulling the trig-

---

* This delicious and profound observation is from Theodor Reik's autobiography in which this gifted therapist and writer on masochism and the criminal mind (he was one of the first psychologist/psychoanalysts without medical training and a forerunner of the current relational orientation in psychoanalysis) relates how he grasps a patient's reality through intuition, empathy, and self-exploration. Running from the Nazis, being rejected by the medical establishment in the United States, and his own temperament undoubtedly contributed to his understanding of the consolations of sadistic fantasy. Here is his interpretation of one of his own dreams:

"It seems that I go out of my way to retaliate with fantasies against a person who has tried to humiliate me. Such fantasies have, it seems to me, psychotherapeutic value as well. When not accompanied by guilt-feelings, fantasies of such a violent kind protect me, I suppose, from becoming neurotic. If it is permitted to joke in such serious matters, I would say they are to be recommended as useful counter-advice against a boy-scout mentality. A thought-murder a day keeps the doctor away." *Listening with the Third Ear: The Inner Experiences of a Psychoanalyst* (New York: Macmillan, 1983), 43.

ger on her own pain, eradicating it. This was an act of healthy violence—"sublimated," in the language of psychoanalysis—which was one of the reasons it succeeded.

I began to understand how Deirdre's pledge both reinforced and transformed her self-image, but did she do anything different as a result? On the surface, it seemed as if nothing dramatic had changed. Then it dawned on me that the very ordinariness of the actions she started to take—beginning to eat and speak again, never missing work, seeing a therapist, and consulting her confessor—indicated that something fundamental had shifted and that she was coming back to life (she called it "un-freezing").

The things she didn't do were as significant as the ones she did and required at least as much self-discipline: she did not stalk Ben or pine for him, nourish fantasies of reconciliation, attempt to insinuate herself back into his life, try to ruin his reputation, scrutinize him on Facebook when that favorite tool of the obsessed became available, or even seriously wish him ill.

Slowly and subtly—almost mystically—she began to rein-terpret the purpose of her life. She concluded that it consisted in being of service to those she loved, in ways small and large—from running errands to keeping vigil during their illnesses. These were things she was already doing. But taking a solemn oath and sticking to it casts everything in a different light and infuses the ordinary with significance. It can change a person more radically than any drug or many years of therapy.

Ben did not make it easy for Deirdre to keep faith with him. Her patience was sorely tried by his refusal to behave with even common decency toward her, which continued long after his precipitous exit. For ten years, he refused to divorce her, effec-tively preventing her from marrying again in her childbearing years. He never cooperated with annulment proceedings and still has not. He never apologized or (according to her lawyer) seemed to suffer pangs of guilt or remorse and later went on to remarry and have a family without ever looking back. "What he did is despicable. He almost destroyed me and thinks he hasn't done anything," she said. Nonetheless, she would not allow him to destroy her integrity or her ability to care, even for him. He broke her heart but not her soul.

Deirdre's vow was the lodestar that guided her back into the world and kept her there during that first problematic decade. Afterward, she no longer had to exert any effort. Practicing fidelity daily made life worth living again. It restored her pride and her joy and helped her regain her health. Her tie to Ben lessened naturally when she found a man more worthy of her devotion—even though she did not publicly announce their marriage for several years to protect herself in case he, too, might fail her.

Those who suffer in love are routinely counseled by well-meaning therapists, friends, and self-help authors to run in the opposite direction from "the toxic person" and never look back—advice that is hard to follow, though usually sage. Deirdre did the opposite; she made use of her toxic person to save her own life and to reset the planes of her universe. It wouldn't work for everybody, but it certainly worked for her.

THE AFFIRMATIVE NO

What are the tasks that anyone who has been betrayed must accomplish? Grieving for one's losses—for bad choices, for lost time and destroyed hope and misplaced devotion, for the shame and self-laceration (conscious or unconscious) that all these things evoke—this is fruitful sorrow. Learning to live with doomed longing for an unrequited beloved (one who is unwilling or unable to reciprocate devotion) until it diminishes as life goes on. Recovering the ability to trust oneself and other people instead of retreating into terminal self-doubt and paranoia. Neutralizing the inevitable rage and hatred directed against oneself and the other. Restoring self-respect and a sense of control over one's own destiny.

What was done to you and how it was done, who you are, and how you think determine how you cope with a betrayal of this magnitude. A former patient of mine, and I myself, responded to circumstances not unlike Deirdre's in ways that were qualitatively different from hers, yet there were underlying commonalities, and all three of us ultimately achieved similar ends.

Barbara, a lovely young woman, announced in a session that she was suddenly, thrillingly in love. She was in the midst of a whirlwind courtship with an exciting man who couldn't wait to marry her, even though they had only just met. I was suspicious and counseled waiting until they knew each other better—which made her furious with me—but instead, they moved up the wedding. They started looking for an apartment immediately after returning from a lavish honeymoon; the down payment was her parents' wedding gift. Several months later, after missing many appointments and being evasive and defensive when she did show up because she was beginning to have doubts about him, she came to a session aghast. She had gone to her bank to withdraw a small sum and gotten a notice that her account was overdrawn. Her new husband, it turned out, had looked over her shoulder the last time she used the ATM, copied her PIN number, and then emptied her account of the $100,000 her parents had given them. Then he disappeared.

Barbara was grief stricken, horrified, and humiliated— reactions that were not made easier by reminding her of her father, who had been discovered to have a second simultaneous family across the country when she was a teenager. A year of intensive self-examination in therapy put her back on her feet, during which time she got a job as a boutique manager and learned to curb her impulsiveness and improve her taste in men.

Two astonishing things then happened in quick succession: her former husband called her asking to reconcile (he told her he had reformed), and she got a call from the FBI. It turned out that she was the third woman that he had stolen from in similar circumstances. The agent even knew about the phone call she'd received and asked if she would agree to a meeting so that her ex could be apprehended. I wholeheartedly encouraged her to do so; this was the most gratifying, sane revenge I could imagine—getting even by doing justice.

The stratagem worked. She later testified at his trial, where she met three more women whom he was in the process of fleecing, bringing the grand total of victims to six. Barbara was instrumental in sending this psychopath to the federal penitentiary. Even though the money was lost, she felt enormous pride and a sense of restored power that she had prevented him from harming anyone else. Then, after a long and careful courtship, she married a stable, hardworking man who genuinely cared for her.

I suffered a shocking betrayal in my twenties (not, alas, the first). Like Deirdre, I made a vow, but one with a very different focus from hers. The man I had lived with for five years and planned to marry announced as unceremoniously as Ben had that he was leaving me. He added, for no reason other than to give me pain, that he had had an affair with a close mutual friend the previous year. I subsequently learned from someone else that she was only one of many lovers. I had never imagined, never suspected, and felt shattered; how could I have not known who he really was? His deviousness, assisted by my unconscious need not to know, contributed to my blindness. His behavior, past and present, cut off all possibility, at least in the short term, of my retrieving anything of value from our time together; fidelity to a promiscuous and sadistic liar in any way, shape, or form was out of the question for me; indifference was hard enough to achieve.

Working on my doctoral dissertation kept me occupied initially, but what ultimately got me through was my single-minded determination, voiced aloud to myself and recorded in my diary, to discover the causes of my blindness and never to repeat them. Fearlessly pursuing insight was my badge of honor, my route back to self-respect. I started with the fact that in my own history, as in Barbara's, lay a philandering father and a mother who for years made herself oblivious and then martyred herself by staying with him anyway even after the truth came out. Understanding and grieving—and a wise analyst—painstakingly changed my life and the choices I made.

There are many ways to become mistress (or master) of one's fate after a betrayal, but they all have things in common: conscious effort and a fighting spirit, embodied in what I call "the Affirmative No." The Affirmative No incorporates self-enhancing outrage, independence, and courage. It is a stance through which a traumatized person actively proclaims her will by rejecting the role of victim. This is not an act of negation or rebellion; it is an act of self-assertion, subjectively defined. Deirdre's vow exemplified this. It reestablished a sense of self that had been battered almost to death. Her thoughts and actions announced to Ben and everyone else, "I refuse to allow you to obliterate the things I hold most dear; they cannot be taken from me. This is the essence of my life, and here I stand." Her antidote to passive suffering was swearing fidelity, just as Barbara's was furthering justice and mine was pursuing self-knowledge. Unable to change our predicaments, we actively changed their meaning and our relationship to them, and in the process, we discovered that we could exert power when we thought we had none.

Will is misunderstood by many contemporary therapists as a purely behavioral tool involving techniques like assertiveness training and one-size-fits-all affirmations—superficial caricatures of a process that can activate the deepest healing capacities of the self. Will is underrated as a therapeutic agent, an instrument of transformation and self-determination—sometimes the only tool a person can call upon in extremis. There is nothing natural or spontaneous about it. To make a blessing out of a curse is a genuine triumph of will, and transforming shame into pride a rare form of alchemy.

FAITH REWARDED

Betrayal forced Deirdre, as it does every betrayed person, to contend with the demons of her nature. Her vow and the actions that sprang from it converted her self-hatred and negative grandiosity (the clinical term for the common assumption people make that they themselves are the cause of everything bad that befalls them) to unassailable pride in the way she conducted her life. When she realized nothing could stop her from behaving with love toward others, she was finally able to behave with love toward herself again.

Two decades later—we last discussed their relationship on what would have been their twenty-fifth anniversary—Deirdre has remained true to herself and to Ben, after her fashion, but the nature of her love for him has changed: she has finally stopped missing him. "I don't have room for him anymore with all the other people I love," she declared. "That frequency is no longer one I tune in to."

Keeping faith is no longer something she has to work at; through long practice, it has become her natural state of mind, and she employs it in all areas of her life. "Now," she says, "it feels very peaceful, very easy, and calm." The self-doubts and humiliation that bedeviled her have faded away along with the ever-decreasing potency of Ben's betrayal in her mind.

Along the way, she has miraculously managed to preserve a revised version of her first husband, stripped of his vices. This adorable Ben visits her regularly. "He's in my dreams," she confessed with a tender smile. "Sometimes it's night after night for two weeks, sometimes once every three months. I'm always glad to see him; I always care about him. Of course, it's tricky to figure out what I'm supposed to do about my second husband." Here, at long last, is a moral dilemma she can contemplate with pleasure.

Deirdre, Barbara, and I accomplished the essential thing a person must do to transcend betrayal and to help prevent its recurrence: we each transferred the locus of our self-respect from the one who abandoned us to ourselves so that no one could wrest it from us ever again.

Defining your own truth and then living according to it—whether you do it by making a vow, testifying in court, or committing yourself to unflinching introspection—changes your sense of self and sets you free; it makes you fearless—or at least more courageous—with every significant person in your life. When you're not so insecure, there are things—offhand cruelties, insensitivities large and small—you don't tolerate, things you don't have to deny. You no longer hold yourself responsible for everything or believe that it's up to you to make every relationship work. You expect and demand to be treated by the one you love as you treat him. Once you are the one who defines the meaning of your life, nobody can gainsay it. This act of self-assertive defiance immunizes you—at least to a certain extent—from ever allowing someone else to control your destiny ever again. Then you can love and be loved in return.

5

UNREQUITED LOVE
My Golden One

MY YOUNG SELF SPEAKS

If you do not love me I shall not be loved.

—SAMUEL BECKETT

When I was nineteen years old, I fell passionately in love with a man who meant far more to me than I did to him. I surrendered my will to him and only felt fully alive when I was in his arms. I needed him too desperately to accept that he didn't love me.

Unrequited love affairs are hardly unusual (especially at that age), but the aftermath of this one was: I buried the most telling details of our relationship for nearly fifty years, barely alluding to him in therapy and mentioning him to my husband only in passing. For all those decades, I hardly gave a conscious thought to the one who had briefly been the center of my universe—who had *been* my universe and who had left me bereft. The only trace of him was in dreams—opaque ones.

I only recovered the full truth about what really happened between us when I reread the diary I kept at the time. The black morocco cover fell apart as soon as I opened it, and I had to hold the whole thing together with rubber bands. What I read there—every emotion, every conversation, every encounter painstakingly recorded in my own handwriting—did not seem like memories, but living presences in my body and my psyche, fresh, raw, and unmetabolized.

My young self was speaking directly to me from that tattered volume. I saw how, in order not to lose him, I had tried to stifle any emotions that might have displeased him when I was with him and to censor unacceptable feelings even when I was alone. I had erased all this from consciousness because the experience was too painful in itself and evoked pain from earlier in my life.

As I read on, I realized with a jolt that I also held in my hands the key to an anxiety dream that had recurred for decades. I knew it referred to the period in my life when I had known him—in sleep I returned to the city in which we had been lovers—but I'd never been able to grasp the meaning of these nocturnal visits until I opened the diary once more.

Those gold-edged pages also revealed an aspect of my character that I had conveniently forgotten because it didn't fit with my self-image. Despite my efforts to suppress my rage at him for how he'd treated me, I had actually expressed it in two acts of revenge against him—the first one witty and self-possessed, the second far darker. It was the only time in my life that I acted this way. Unrequited love always has a sinister side that no lover wants to admit to.

In the process of recovering the excruciating details of my

doomed affair, I also retrieved its full, fervent, thrilling intensity and the joys that were intermingled with the anguish. Despite my abject behavior, I even saw precursors of boldness and insight in myself.

The impetus for turning to my diary and uncovering the secrets from this pivotal chapter of my life—secrets that had never surfaced in twenty-five years of intensive analysis—was an eerily parallel experience I had at age sixty-five: my most intimate friend left me alone when I was seriously ill. Her abandonment led me back to his, and it caused me to reencounter myself as a young woman frantically, hopelessly in love. To this young woman I owe the insights into the nature of passionate unrequited love—and how to escape its clutches—that I might otherwise never have discovered.

MY GOLDEN ONE

I thought of Michael as "golden" from the moment I saw him. We were both avid folk dancers, and he first appeared at a dance early in my sophomore year in college. He was like nobody else I had ever known. Tall and lithe, he moved like a sprite, with musicality and joie de vivre. Brightness seemed intrinsic to him, and I was sorely in need of brightness in a city infamous for its freezing wind and bleak winters, at a university whose unofficial motto was "Where fun goes to die." Michael had a roguish smile, a profusion of blond curls, sly amber-colored eyes, and an aura of gleaming ease and aplomb; at twenty-four, he seemed to dance through life. His wit and his wildness intrigued me. When I found out that he wore a black leather jacket as he drove his sleek motorcycle, played the oboe, and was more than willing to help me with my incomprehensible math homework, my monochromatic world burst into color because he was in it.

The only problem was that he was a doctoral student from

another university on a science fellowship of uncertain duration. At first, I panicked that I would lose him just as I had found him, but I rejoiced when his tenure was extended first three and then six months. I was longing to fall in love, and I didn't want to miss even a temporary opportunity to do it.

I flung myself into passion because of my dark emotional state at the time. This was the nadir of my life. I was almost unimaginably lonely before I met Michael, beyond even the usual late-adolescent angst. In addition to my disappointment with the university, my beloved roommate had taken a year's leave of absence, and nobody had replaced her as my confidante. I was living alone in a tiny dormitory room that seemed like it was on the edge of an abyss; one weekend when I was sick I didn't speak to a soul. My last high school romance had been so excruciating—my boyfriend was both unstable and unfaithful—that I hadn't sought another in two years.

The most unsettling thing of all was that my family, which had seemed a bastion of stability, was disintegrating. At the age of sixteen, I had been the one to discover concrete proof of my adored father's infidelity—I found two women in our house alone with him one night. Even worse, my mother never left him. I felt there was nowhere I belonged, nobody I could rely on. Utterly unmoored and in dire need of a haven, I turned to Michael to provide it. He was my remedy for emptiness, my bulwark against hopelessness, and it worked—at least when I was with him and he smiled at me. In that cold desert where it always seemed to be winter, it was easy to mistake charm for warmth and desire for love.

Our romance began promisingly enough. In addition to his endlessly patient help with my homework, we played in the snow and rode his motorcycle to the zoo, to coffeehouses, and to concerts—I didn't care that it was freezing—and talked into the night. We had so many interests in common, and he had such a lively mind and clever tongue that I didn't realize he revealed hardly anything significant about himself other than that he was afraid of the dark.

Michael seemed to be welcoming me into his world. He showed me the lab where he did his research, and he cooked for me, the first time a man had ever done so. We kissed for the first time while we were baking a cake. I found his combination of domesticity and sensuality both comforting and alluring. At the time, I never consciously made the connection between our frequent after-hours trips to Michael's lab and having accompanied my father, who was also a wry, self-contained scientist—a doctor—on his nightly hospital rounds, but the subliminal link between the two was compelling.

Much too soon, though, unpredictability crept into this routine, and Michael's elusiveness began to trouble me. Every moment of our time together was on his schedule; he rarely made a date in advance and failed to show up at events at which we'd planned to meet. He spent hours with me one day and then disappeared for a week without any explanation or acknowledgment. I never considered calling him myself, much less objecting, because I felt so lucky to have him at all, so overjoyed to be alone no longer.

Ominous premonitions appeared in my diary. I wrote, "I feel myself rushing into something I'm not at all sure is there or can be there, and my recklessness terrifies me. I have no idea how to control it or to keep any kind of balance." I noted anxiously what was happening to me, but the good parts felt far too good for me to heed my own internal warnings. All the symptoms of unrequited love were there—one-sided preoccupation with the beloved's every move, legitimate anxiety about reciprocity, a willingness to tolerate bad treatment just to be near him.

I spent undue amounts of time and effort trying to interpret his motives—a favorite pastime of the besotted. When he didn't call or show up, I became preoccupied with figuring out what I could possibly have done to alienate him. The problem had to be me, not him; otherwise, I was helpless to do anything about it.

"Is there someone else, here or elsewhere? Is he still interested in me?" I asked myself early on. When I went to his apartment the first time, I noted that my dorm was one of the "frequently called numbers" listed by the phone; I was overjoyed.

Soon, however, I had all the proof I needed that my fears were justified. One moonlit night, a month after we started spending time together, we walked to the frozen lake. Michael stopped suddenly, turned to me, and said with a serious edge in his voice I'd never heard before, "Jeanne, how vulnerable are you? The more time I spend with you, the clearer it becomes that I want to share my bed with you—but I may take that very pleasant situation more lightly than you. I'm not sure how much I can give. You may be more involved than I am." Then he put his arms around me and said in a far more insinuating tone, "But I do think we should be lovers."

When I read what he said to me, I wanted to rush back in time and yell "Don't do it!" to my younger self.

At the time, I was so aghast that I didn't say a word in response, although I wrote it all down verbatim afterward.

This is where my memory began to fail. Until I reread my diary, my version of this monologue had been heavily edited. I recollected the unadorned declaration of desire—it felt frank and adult, cool rather than cold, at the time—but I had erased the caveats that accompanied it. I was too frightened by what they implied: I could not stand to know my effort was doomed from the start, that no matter what I did, he would never be mine.

Michael's declaration of intent, which seemed like openness and candor, was actually his way to manage his guilt preemptively. It put me off balance from that moment on, intensifying my insecurity, confirming all my dread. Despite this, I plunged ahead. I stayed overnight with him, barely chaste, a week later. It was the first time I spent an entire night with a man. "A glad night," I reported in my diary, "but something says that I will never have his love, never at the level I want." All the warning signs were there—I enumerated them in my diary, railed against them, and proceeded to ignore them. Acting consciously and wisely on what you know to be true, overriding inner compulsion on your own behalf, requires far more self-possession than I had at that point in my life.

Michael's behavior toward me really was confusing. There were times when I clearly interested him—I made him laugh, and I was a worthy sparring partner—and times when he withdrew from me or rejected me, sometimes in close succession. Since I idealized him, I assumed he knew what he was doing, when in fact I see now that he had to have been as buffeted about by his emotions as I was by my own.

I longed for consistency, merger, and ardor, while he wanted occasional interludes of diversion, amusement, and pleasure. What drew me to him was obvious to me—he sparkled so— but why on earth he selected someone like me, so utterly unsuited to his wishes for minimal involvement, I still cannot understand. I can only assume that my attentiveness and emotional intensity appealed to him as much as they caused him to flee.

Even after he made his position perfectly clear, I continued to cherish the fantasy that I would find a way to get through to him. Like Sleeping Beauty or Snow White in reverse, I would awaken his ability to love me; I believed that I held the magic key to his heart. The seductive grandiosity of this conviction was unshakable. When you are in the throes of this kind of desire, "never" is an unutterable word, because it is the death of hope; obsessive lovers strive to keep hope alive at all costs, even when it is clearly a lost cause.

One thing I tolerated silently but found disquieting was that Michael told me about his attraction to other women the first time I stayed overnight with him, and he continued to do so, often when we were in bed together. I wasn't yet savvy enough to realize that recoiling from this wasn't prudishness on my part, that his behavior was at the very least offensive and off-putting, an indication of faithlessness, in thought and deed. There were echoes of my father's conduct in it as well that I must have willed myself to overlook but could clearly see when I read the diary.

Although my elusive beloved often behaved coldly toward me, he never struck me as an inherently cruel man. He seemed motivated by self-protection rather than perverse pleasure in causing pain. However, as a teacher of mine when I was in analytic training years later said, "You don't need a sadist to have a sadomasochistic relationship."

My Golden One vanished once again after our first night together. I couldn't conceal my tension when I saw him later on. "There's been a lack of humor lately," he chided me. It is a reflection of my emotional state that I took this not as a failure of empathy on his part but as a legitimate criticism of me.

Michael wanted to keep things between us in a major key at all times. Light banter was his preferred form of expression, and it had to become mine if I wanted to avoid estranging him. Cultivating irony, what he approvingly called "our wit and repartee," became my main task. I felt as though I were playing a role in a surreal comedy of manners in which I had been cast against type. Only he had the script, and I had to improvise my lines.

My subservience—being on call and amusing on demand—took a toll on me because it was so unnatural. I wasn't a passive or compliant person even then; in fact, I was the opposite—strong willed, opinionated, outspoken and direct to a fault. That I suppressed my real personality so dramatically reflected my urgent mission to keep the relationship afloat.

Michael eventually explained the reason for his increasing aloofness; there was "a conflict about another relationship" with a former girlfriend in another city. He did not elaborate, and I asked no questions, such as why this conflict had not kept him from me in the first place or why, since full disclosure seemed so important to him, he had not told me up front. I also didn't let myself consider what it said about his character that he was being unfaithful to her, as well. Having a shadowy rival made me even more insecure than before.

Why did I remain silent? Contemporary psychoanalytic attachment theory and trauma studies provide clues.* It has long been known that creatures in danger can defend themselves by fighting, fleeing, or freezing. Freezing is a radical self-protective state caused by shock, the psychic equivalent of playing dead in the face of an existential threat. In my case, the threat was not being devoured by a predator but being aban-

---

* Philip Bromberg's powerful paper "One Need Not Be a House to Be Haunted" in his book *Awakening the Dreamer: Clinical Journeys* (Mahwah, NJ: Analytic Press, 2006), 153–73, presents a compelling clinical example of dissociation.

doned by someone I needed and dared not risk displeasing, who also left me feeling helpless and alienated (the technical term is "dissociated") from my authentic self. I performed a desperate act of emotional survival by putting my intolerable feelings away in cold storage.

My performance must have improved subsequently, because he became my lover two weeks later. For a moment, I was happy.

He had shown up at a dance and taken me home with him. "Never have I felt so abandoned, so possessed," my diary says. "I spent much of the night watching him sleep beside me, hardly believing I was with him."

This magical interlude was immediately sullied by doubts. I urgently wanted reassurance that I meant something to him beyond our second "glad night" but never dared to ask. Why, I wondered, did he turn away from me when he slept? Why did he never call me just to talk? Why did I know nothing about his past? I never pressed these questions in the interest of not rocking a very leaky boat.

I could not understand how a man could be passionate and sensually connected but then wake up in the morning eager to separate and go about his business, the openness fleeting and confined to the darkness. I didn't have enough experience to know that this wasn't the case with every man.

I waited by the phone—these were the days before cell phones and texting, but I'm sure the state of mind hasn't changed materially since then—afraid to do anything or go anywhere in case he called. Every once in a while he did, and we would share another unbridled night, the illusion of connection revived once more. "When I am with him I feel, 'Love is embodied in you,'" I wrote. I would endure anything for this.

Right before spring break, when we had spent a rare day together as though we were a normal couple, he told me he was flying to Philadelphia to see an old friend. For romantic atmosphere and to combat his fear of the dark, he lit candles in the bedroom at dusk. He was unusually tender and expressive, emerging smiling from the shower to lay his damp golden head on my breast, only blowing out the flames at daybreak.

When we woke voluptuously at noon, he told me, obliquely, the real reason he was going—"to see the dog" that his not-so-former girlfriend had inherited from him. He would not be coming back for several weeks.

I was crushed rather than outraged. What did I do with my anger at him for tantalizing me and then treating me so callously? I had a dream of being fondled by a man with green-and-blue hair whom I was trying to kick. While I couldn't express it in waking life, my rage seeped into my dreams.

Every once in a while, I wrote something in my diary that was not about Michael. I had deep conversations with other people, sang and played my guitar, wrote poetry, and learned ancient Greek. I also forged a close friendship with a man whom I did not desire, who would remain an integral part of my adult life for many years. My most encouraging observation, because it became the foundation for my future vocation, was "How I love to see words balance and sing. Writing does more for my ego than making love." An obsession with a problematic lover, as intense and disabling as it seems and as much as it colonizes one's consciousness, often coexists with normal life.

I assumed Michael had left me for good, and I felt desolate, but after he returned from Philadelphia, he came to see me again. "I'm not ready for intense monogamy," he told me. "I can't split my personality, and I don't want to lie." I asked whether he had told his old girlfriend about me. He had not; telling the truth in matters of the heart seemed reserved for my ears only.

Then I asked something I never should have asked. "But what about our last night together—wasn't that good?"

"Good," he said, "but not good enough." He added, as if to soften the blow, "It's not as fatal as you seem to think. I'm simply asking for my freedom."

Even after such an insult, I never considered leaving him.

As our remaining time together grew short, I kept trying to reach him. I said it grieved me to part from anything that mattered to me, yet I welcomed the grief because it meant I had felt deeply and needed to express it. "I even had trouble leaving the Parthenon," I told him—another object that was golden in the sunlight—"because it was so beautiful and I knew I'd never see it again." He made a joke out of this, grinning, bowing, and pretending to shake hands with an imaginary building. Grieving was not in his repertoire.

Finally, I said the naked truth. "I just want you to hold me. I want your physical presence, because soon there will be nothing."

"I'm sorry," he said, "but I'm going home alone to sleep and think, and I'll call you later." When I went home alone, I felt inconsolable.

He surprised me once more when he eventually called, days later, to ask if I wanted to see his tabla (an Indian drum; the vogue for Indian music was in full swing); it was in his hometown several hours away, in his bedroom in the house where he had grown up. He was going there on the motorcycle to plant some trees for his mother. I took along a paper to work on while he dug the holes.

It was a little frame house on a street of nearly identical houses with neat but barren yards separated by chain-link fences. The interior was dark. There were heavy curtains on the windows and Catholic devotional art on the walls (he had never mentioned that he was Catholic) as if from another era, another world. His mother was due home from work in a couple of hours, and we were staying for lunch. He was greeted by a big shaggy dog who was overjoyed to see him.

He took me upstairs to his tiny bedroom, unchanged since his high school years. I admired the tabla—he put Ravi Shankar on his old record player—and I was fascinated to see photographs of him as a crew-cut teenager, looking anything but cool. Everything there was a window into a past he had never mentioned—that he had been a runner, played various wind instruments in the school orchestra, won various academic honors, read Stendhal's *On Love*. Then we spent a ravenous hour in the bed where he had slept in the years before he turned into the striking, graceful, seemingly insouciant man I knew. The combination of physical and emotional intimacy before parting was the consolation I had longed for.

But then, to regain a sense of control and put some distance between us, he mentioned a girl he wanted to seduce when he returned to graduate school, and he warned me not to interrupt him while he was working in the yard; clearly, he had done enough relating for one day.

His mother arrived, a plainly dressed woman who seemed much older than my own mother, although they were contemporaries. He kissed her forehead with real tenderness. It was clear that she adored him and that the feeling was mutual. Then she proceeded, over a lunch of Spam and watermelon, to regale me with stories about her Mikey—how he charmed everyone, what a wonderful son he was, how he took care of her. It was almost an infomercial for my benefit. For the rest of the afternoon, I lay writing in the grass in the backyard and watching him happily working. I felt no need to interrupt.

That night when we returned to the university, he took me

dancing. Afterward, we had what I had hungered for more than anything, a serious conversation about our pasts. Unprompted, he spoke at length and with feeling, telling me that he was six months old when his father had died, that his mother had been left destitute. She had "a bleak life as a clerk" and had devoted herself to raising him, sacrificing everything for him, never re-marrying. They lived just above the poverty line, and—this was the only moment that bitterness over an old humiliation crept into his voice—his clothes came from a low-end mail-order catalog. No wonder he became such a good cook and a stylish dresser, and no wonder he couldn't bear to get too in-volved or to say good-bye; he'd endured but never fully pro-cessed more than one devastating loss—his father's death, his mother's depression, his straitened childhood. He had reason to be afraid of the dark side of life.

This was the only time Michael ever opened himself to me unsparingly. Although I didn't know it, the whole day was his unspoken farewell.

His actual leaving town a week later was, to borrow Michael's way of putting things, "rather different" from our last, moving idyll together. On the day before his departure, I hadn't heard a word from him and did not move from my room to make sure I didn't miss his call—but every hour passed in silence. Was he really not going to come and say good-bye? I typed ten pages about my feelings in the third person to get some perspective and stayed up all night waiting for him.

The phone finally rang at 10:00 A.M. the next day. He was coming over, stopping by on his way out of town, on his motor-cycle. He had arranged that our last moments together would be in public, at the front door of my dorm. I put myself together and greeted him without complaint. He seemed remote. I tried to set his image in my mind.

Then he told me where he had been, even though I hadn't asked. He had spent the night "consoling" a woman who was "broken up" about his leaving, one of the legion he had told me he was attracted to. "She was just released from a mental hospital," he added by way of explanation, "and she's even crazier than you." With that, he put his arms around me, kissed me, and said, "We won't lose touch." As he rode away, I stood riveted to the spot in shock.

"How long before I can read this and look back without the pain stifling me?" I wrote afterward. It was to take another forty-eight years.

My dear friend, the man who had stood helplessly by while the awful endgame unfolded, fed me and took me downtown to the symphony that night for a performance of the Bach Double Violin Concerto. During the slow movement, one of the most tender and passionately entwining pieces of music every written, the sonic equivalent of fulfilled love, all my pent-up shame and rage and grief and longing overwhelmed me, and I sat there sobbing in my seat. It was the only time I have ever openly wept at a concert and the only time until now that I wept over him.

THE GOLDEN CONDOM: REVENGE, SWEET AND BITTER

I had no faith at all that Michael meant what he said about staying in touch; I thought it was a getaway line, not a promise. Once again, I was wrong. Soon I got a letter from him, printed in red ink. He referred to things we had said and done but omitted any mention of, let alone any apology for, his brutal exit. I was intensely agitated to receive it but responded in an arch style as close to his as I could manage. My hunger to maintain a connection with him, no matter how meager and unsatisfying, had not changed.

He proved more faithful as a correspondent than he had been as a lover. Every few weeks, I received a couple of pages precisely printed in red ink. Every time, I strained to find the right tone in which to craft a reply.

This odd, taxing correspondence had been going on for several months when I received a letter from him that was not quite as chatty or nonchalant as the others. It was a request for advice. He wrote to ask me, since he knew I knew about such things, how he might go about sexually satisfying the girl he had mentioned to me the day I met his mother. She was timid and naive, and he wasn't sure how to put her at ease. Could I make any recommendations based on experiences we had had together?

Nothing he had ever said or done held a candle to this. Did he really consider me a female Playboy Advisor? Then, an idea burst upon me fully formed of how to reply to what I came to call "The Sex Tips Letter": I would send him, anonymously, a golden condom, which I would create for the occasion. This would be my way to say "Fuck you" to him for behaving as though we weren't lovers but rather partners in the seduction of an innocent girl like the sophisticated, ice-cold, coconspirators Vicomte de Valmont and the Marquise de Merteuil in the scandalous French novel *Les Liaisons Dangereuses*. I meant it as an insult in kind, my attempt to humiliate and ridicule him for making such a sordid, selfish request of me. My implicit message was "Maybe wearing this will impress her and turn her on, since you can't seem to do it on your own." The gilding, a reference to his coloring and his narcissism, made it even more preposterous. I was so outraged that I didn't care how he felt about it, or me, and I expected no answer. I intended it as an exorcism of his hold over me.

There were some logistical problems to work out before I could implement my plan. How would I acquire the raw materials? In the first place, in that era of the Pill, I had never even seen a condom, much less purchased one. An older friend of mine came to the rescue and provided several specimens, since it might take some practice to perfect the gilding technique. She also offered to be present when I produced the glittering item I envisioned. I bought a can of gold spray paint at a local art supply store.

Then there was the problem of finding a suitable venue in which to fabricate the object. I had just moved out of the dorm and into an apartment with a light fixture in my bedroom ceiling. Heeding the warning on the can to "use only in a well-ventilated space," I raised the window sash and covered the floor and the nearest wall with newspaper. Then I opened the foil packet, unrolled the unfamiliar contents, attached the open end with paper clips and string to the chandelier, and began spraying. Having never done anything remotely resembling this before, I had no idea what to expect—certainly not what actually happened: the chemicals in the paint made the latex expand at least thrice its normal size and length. Here was a condom to reckon with, one as big as his ego. After my co-conspirator and I laughed heartily at what I had wrought, I let my eloquent creation dry for the rest of the day, folded it up, and sent it off to him in an envelope marked "Fragile," with no return address.

In record time, I got a call from him, the only one since he had left town. There was a hint of chagrin as well as eagerness in his voice; now that I had called his bluff, he was dying to talk to me. He saw at once that I must have been the source. He seemed abashed, but mostly he thought it was hilarious; I had exceeded even his high standards for wit and repartee. So thoroughly delighted was he that he told me he was coming back to the city at Christmas and wanted to see me. Concealing my astonishment, I replied, truthfully, that I wasn't going to be in town when he planned to be there; for once, I had no intention of changing my own schedule to suit his. Then he said words I never imagined I would hear him say, the sweetest words in the world, an unimagined triumph: "I'll wait for you."

I had unwittingly discovered—when I was done trying—the way to his heart, at least temporarily. I had evened the score with my cheeky art project. He felt compelled to pursue me because, at long last, I had rejected him. I should have enjoyed my moment of glory, written him off, and moved on, but I wanted him even more since I had gotten him to admire my gumption.

Right around the time that "The Sex Tips Letter" from Michael arrived, Jonathan, another dancer—also a tall motorcyclist-scientist who played the oboe—took me out on a real date. I had no idea how I was going to negotiate the surfeit of suitors, with Michael waiting for me to return after Christmas and Jonathan in residence. Fate, however, intervened to prevent me from enjoying my triumph as planned. Another of Michael's red letters arrived. It was brief, sober, and terrible. He had not only succeeded in seducing the young woman in question even without the benefit of advice from me but had also gotten her pregnant. He wouldn't be coming to town for Christmas because he had to take her to Mexico for an illegal abortion, the only kind available at the time.

The news made me sick. His selfishness and his careless-
ness did more harm to this poor woman than anything he had
ever done to me. I got away with nothing damaged but my
self-esteem; she risked dying.

He called me, unexpectedly, late one night in early Janu-
ary. I could feel the urgency in his voice; the veneer of non-
chalance was gone. "You know you're the first person I turn to
when I want to talk," he said by way of explanation. I had never
imagined anything of the sort, yet here he was, seeking me out
when he was in trouble. This was the fulfillment of the fantasy
of everybody who has ever loved an unresponsive person.

"So why didn't you talk to me when you were here?" I asked,
emboldened.

"There wasn't much to say," he said—and then told me for
the next hour, in wretched detail, everything that had happened in Mexico. Fortunately, the young woman had lived.

He was frantic, desperate, and on the verge of tears; I
had never seen him like that. As reprehensible as I found his
conduct, the specter of so self-contained a man revealing his distress to me—and only me—was both unnerving and gratifying. Despite everything, I also pitied him.

After we hung up, I wrote in my diary, "The thought crossed
my mind when we were talking how ordinary it all was, and he
was. Why had I tormented myself so over him?" "Ordinary"
was the last adjective I would ever have imagined using to describe him until that moment. My Golden One was nothing
but base metal.

I couldn't tolerate this insight very long, however, and very
quickly I converted him in my thoughts back to "extraordinary."
He still filled my need to win the love of an unattainable man,
a need I could not yet relinquish. To face the truth about him

would mean I had lavished myself on someone entirely unworthy of my devotion.

I told Jonathan nothing about this conversation. "Somehow when I am alone," I confessed to my diary, "all of Jonathan's tenderness melts away before the bright glances of Michael's elfin eyes." When you are in thrall to an obsessive love, a reciprocated one seems less alluring. You prize what you cannot have more than what you can.

Michael told me he was coming back in July, and we arranged to meet. Unbeknownst even to myself, I was planning my second act of vengeance against him. The first had been for insulting me by asking for sex tips; the second would be bending him to my will to punish him for crimes of the heart against me. I wanted him to stay with me and be my lover once more, but this time, I vowed, unconsciously, that I would be in charge.

Fastidious reporter though I was, it is striking that I did not record how I arranged an assignation with him without my current boyfriend's knowledge. My deviousness disturbed me too much to admit even to my diary.

Seeing him again and dancing with him again seemed to undo a year's worth of frustration, anguish, and humiliation at his hands. We went back to my apartment, where we spent hours making dinner, talking, listening to music, and embracing by candlelight, all tension cast aside. "He moves like a blond cat," I wrote later in my diary. "I wouldn't have wanted to miss this." We finally fell asleep fully clothed on my bed. To seduce him when we awoke in the morning seemed the easiest, most natural thing in the world. I encountered no resistance.

The sensual romp that I orchestrated was in fact a coldly calculated (if disavowed) act of retribution on my part. Ever since the day I met my hated, beloved tormentor, he had exerted control over me—control made worse by my complicity. Turning the tables on him, forcing him to do what I wanted when I wanted it, was meant to be my payback.

I felt neither powerful nor gratified afterward, however. Instead, I sat bolt upright in bed, pale and shaking in agitation, engulfed by a wave of guilt, shame, and sorrow. It was a full-fledged anxiety attack that seemed to come from nowhere.

At the moment, I thought I was punishing myself for being untrue to Jonathan, but that was the least of it; I was overwhelmed by Michael. He was floating away even as he lay beside me, just as he always had. Controlling the superficial conditions of our encounter had not changed how he felt about me or wiped away the harm I had already allowed him to do to me. He was still the same fundamentally unreachable man, and my love was as unrequited as ever. My attempt at payback had failed.

My unwonted emotional outburst did get a reaction from him. It was exactly what I should have expected. He neither asked me what the matter was nor made any attempt to comfort me. "It's not the end of the world," he said from a thousand miles away. "The sun's still shining." He had no desire to engage when it wasn't easy anymore. He left soon afterward, with a cursory kiss on my forehead. I never saw or heard from him again.

After I closed the door behind him and crawled into bed to put myself back together, I wrote, "I saw one glistening hair of his on my pillow, and for a moment remembered only his loveliness." I remember it still.

Not until four months had passed with no word from him was I forced to accept that this really was the end. It was then that this man, who had prompted me to behave in ways I never did before or have since, inspired another uncharacteristic action. For someone who yearns to preserve everything that is meaningful, it was a radical departure. "I just read all Michael's letters and tore them up," my diary announces. "I had planned to save one pleasant one, but I decided that it too had to go. Into the garbage with the whole relationship. I console myself that all of them lie in pieces in my wastebasket and can give me no grief anymore." A symbolic act of demolition was the only way left to exert any kind of control. This was the last time—until now—I would ever write his name.

I shredded the physical evidence of the most damaging attachment of my life, but even that couldn't eradicate the psychological residue, so I tried to bury my unmanageable emotions. I told my diary that it was time "to wrap these feelings in cellophane and thrust them into a dark place in my mind." This, too, proved ineffective. While I did not utter or write his name again for almost half a century, Michael simply moved into my dreams, where, under deep cover, he continued to give me grief for decades more. You can suppress your unbearable feelings about a tortured love and throw the evidence away, but you cannot destroy them. The only way to diminish their power, to stop being haunted by them, is to face them, figure out their meaning, and understand their impact.

I stayed with Jonathan for two years and ended our relationship when I graduated. It took another decade, and a devoted male analyst, before I was able to find the man who has cherished me for thirty-five years of marriage, and whom I cherish.

THE GOLDEN FANTASY AND RELENTLESS HOPE

My Golden One stayed hidden in the recesses of my mind for almost five decades. I discovered him again serendipitously

only after my woman friend betrayed me. When I saw that the
two experiences evoked similar feelings, I realized I needed to
exhume him, because I clearly had unfinished business with
him. I had reached the point in my life when I finally felt able
to withstand the whole truth about what had happened between
us. I asked the questions I had always avoided while I still imagined that he could somehow be mine: What function did this
alluring but dangerously cold man serve for me? What kept me
coming back? What experiences in my past was I trying to repair (or undo) by being his lover? Why did I doggedly continue
to hope despite overwhelming evidence that getting his love
was hopeless? There had to be more going on that was as deeply
buried as Michael.

My explorations were aided by two psychoanalytic articles
that I discovered as I was searching the literature for insights
into unrequited love. They described my behavior with such uncanny accuracy that it seemed as if the authors, too, had read
my diary—or perhaps lived through it themselves.

The title of psychoanalyst Sydney Smith's study "The
Golden Fantasy"* resonated immediately. According to Smith,
the goal of this fantasy is to find someone who meets all one's
needs "in a relationship hallowed by perfection," like an ideal
mother in the "golden age" of infancy. Anyone who seeks such

---

* Sydney Smith, "The Golden Fantasy: A Regressive Reaction to Separation
Anxiety," *International Journal of Psycho-Analysis* 58, no. 3 (1977): 311–324.
My relationship with Michael did not exactly replicate the fantasy Smith
describes, but it had many of the same dynamics. Dr. Smith was for many
years clinical director of the Menninger Foundation, a major American
psychoanalytic training and treatment center then located in Topeka,
Kansas. This paper is a classic in the field because it identifies a particular
type of problematic relationship in a compelling, poetic way. Since I had
independently used the same term to describe my own beloved, it had special
significance for me.

an experience as an adult harbors an "emotionally charged memory" of early traumatic maternal loss that never healed. Perpetuating this impossible dream prevents mourning by denying that the original abandonment happened and cannot now be undone.

The Golden Fantasy is usually a shameful secret and one that is extremely hard to relinquish because you feel helpless without such an all-giving person, as though you were still a young child without resources of your own. You cling to the possibility of recovering the perfect bond because to renounce it "is to give up everything, to lose the primary source of comfort, even one's sense of meaning . . . without [which] the world becomes a place without hope"—an eternal winter of the psyche.

A craving to be loved and a fear of being rejected pervade the emotional lives of those in thrall to the Golden Fantasy. They feel particularly desperate when they are alone, even as adults, and believe that separation from the indispensable person is unbearable, so they go to inordinate lengths to preserve such relationships at any cost. One of Smith's patients said, "Without [him] reality seems so drab, so lifeless, and offers me nothing to keep me going"—virtually a quote about Michael from my diary.

All this resonated for me, but one fundamental fact didn't fit: Smith traced the origins of this fantasy back to an early traumatic loss of a mother's care. The loss had to be severe, such as serious failures of empathy or wholesale abandonment, and the person who suffered it had to be painfully aware that it happened, which was not the case for me. If anything, my mother was too present in my life—a vital, opinionated, often demanding woman—and I had idealized her. I had always assumed that my choices of unavailable men to love (Michael was not the only one) derived from the way my father disappointed me in my adolescence by his flagrant infidelities.

One of Smith's examples enlarged my thinking. He described a woman who decided to marry the man who was courting her when he fed her from his fork on a dinner date. "She found this act of caring so gratifying, so compelling in its promise of a regressive* fulfillment in the relationship, that her indecision was ended." I realized that Michael's feeding me satisfied a deep hunger in me for more than food. His cooking—coupled with his homework help, inviting me to his lab, the way he smiled at me†—were so compelling because they signified to me that he was a mother/father amalgam to lean on when I had just irrevocably lost both my parents as sources of security. No wonder I held on to him for dear life.

Prompted by Smith's article, I began to recall times when my mother had indeed abandoned me. There had been grave early lapses in her ability to provide a reliable "holding environment"—pediatrician/psychoanalyst D. W. Winnicott's name for the stable primordial world and a symbolic extension of the mother's loving arms—that every child needs. The most terrible of these were two suicide attempts when I was five and eight years old. At other times, this otherwise vibrant and devoted woman was so desperately anxious that she could become hysterical or furious, or turn coldly away when I was frightened. I rarely woke her when I had nightmares as a child, preferring my father's calm, reassuring competence.

My father had replaced my mother. He was much better at

---

* Regressive experiences harken back to an earlier stage of life.
† Heinz Kohut, founder of self psychology, called "the gleam in the mother's eye" the essential act of delight and appreciation a mother gives an infant.

being "the mother of physical comfort"* than she, for all her other gifts. No crisis or emotional reaction of mine ever threw him; I felt safe in his hands.

The golden age of my father's total devotion did not last, either. Death and depression stalked him. The diagnosis of a faulty heart valve that could have led to an early death, a three-month hospital stay for another dangerous illness, and massive disappointment in his marriage and his own life left serious psychic scars and led to his compulsive womanizing by the time I entered my teens. His own woes interfered with, and ultimately curtailed, his emotional availability. Although both my parents loved me, neither one consistently provided a sense of fundamental emotional safety.

I had turned to my father when my mother failed to comfort me, but when he too failed me, there was nowhere else to turn. Then I met Michael.

I finally understood that I had been seeking a new edition of my maternal father, but why hadn't I picked a consistent one? What made me recruit Michael and then refuse to fire him when he fell down so disastrously on the job? Martha Stark's revelatory study of obsessive love, "Transformation of Relentless Hope,"† provided the answers. It explained why, against all odds, I felt compelled to seek blood from this particular stone, and why so many others do the same.

"Relentless hope" is Stark's poignant phrase for the state of

---

* Psychoanalyst Leo Stone's term for the early role a mother plays in her child's development. Leo Stone, *The Psychoanalytic Situation* (New York: International Universities Press, 1977).

† Martha Stark, "Transformation of Relentless Hope: A Relational Approach to Sadomasochism," lifespanlearn.org/documents/STARKtranform .pdf, April 2006. Dr. Stark, a psychiatrist and psychoanalyst in the contemporary relational tradition, teaches at Harvard Medical School.

mind that drives a person to pursue a relationship that feels simultaneously unsatisfying and indispensable. The mission of the relentlessly hopeful lover is to convert a disappointing parent-substitute into one who meets his or her fundamental needs. It is fueled by a passionately held conviction that it is possible—indeed, necessary—to persuade another person to change. Relentless hope differs from "normal" hope because it is actually the denial of hopelessness, the refusal to acknowledge and to mourn for the irreplaceable, traumatic loss of a parent's love in childhood, which feels unbearable to contemplate. Trying to reproduce the Golden Fantasy leads inevitably to relentless hope, the driven perversion of optimism.

The typical scenario is to choose someone who shares essential characteristics with the lost parent and to labor ceaselessly to transform him—whether by turning oneself into the kind of person he would respond to, by getting him to act or feel differently, or by some combination of the two. The underlying fantasy is that the object* is unwilling, not incapable: That it "could give [if it wanted to] . . . and would give [if you] get it right." "If only I could get the words right, so I can get a loving or comprehending response," I had written in my diary, as if the fault for failing to get it were mine. Every time I had got ten a glimpse of how limited my power actually was, I had cautioned myself in my diary to "expect nothing, be prepared for indifference, for his saying he is incapable—but that would be the end of hope."

I found Stark's formulation eye-opening because it demonstrated that the unrequited lover does not simply suffer passively but actively attempts to control the object of her affection.

---

* "Object" is the psychoanalytic term for a person in whom one is emotionally invested.

Suffering is not the goal; it is an unfortunate but necessary by-product of urgent efforts to force one's will on an unwilling other—a far more active role than is usually ascribed to so-called masochists. The gratification one seeks is to wield the power to get essential needs met, not just to endure bad treatment as a perverse source of pleasure. This felt closer to the truth than any other explanation of the behavior of obsessive lovers that I had ever seen, and points the way to changing it through understanding.

The way I acted with Michael had every characteristic of the maddening, desperate, and ambivalent ties that Stark depicts. As she says, "Choosing a good object is not a viable option. A good object does not satisfy. Rather, the need . . . is to re-encounter the old bad object—and then to compel [it] to become good." Why do you endlessly pursue modern-day equivalents of the "old bad object"? Because it was the only one you had to rely on as a child, and is the only model you have now. Without it there is nothing. By attempting to undo a trauma, you guarantee its endless repetition. Only recognition, grieving, and insight rob it of its power.

The author offers as a grimly funny example a woman with a recalcitrant alcoholic father who chooses to love not a teetotaler but another recalcitrant alcoholic. She then tries to reform him, even though "a panel of 10,000 'objective' judges would probably have been able to predict" that it would never happen. You override even the best advice if taking it leads to conclusions you cannot bear to know.

The problematic beloved frustrates you not only by withholding himself but also by intermittently giving himself; this fosters the illusion that he could be consistently available if only the conditions were right. As Stark says, "[He] initially tantalize[s] by offering the seductive promise of . . . relatedness, but . . . later devastate[s] by rescinding that enticement."

The beloved's ambivalence is a prerequisite for his being chosen. We have uncanny radar for people who meet our unconscious needs; it is part of the universal human compulsion to relive and remake the past through intimate relationships in the present.

Although the enticement keeps you coming back, it also makes you hate the perpetrator and yourself. Stark describes the rage that this behavior provokes as the compulsion to punish the disappointing object whenever the impossibility of converting it becomes undeniable. The golden condom and the disastrous seduction were my attempts to punish my object when I could no longer deny the impossibility of changing him into what I needed him to be. No masochist—all relentless lovers are masochists—likes to be reminded that she is also a sadist, but this fact must be confronted if she ever hopes to break the cycle.

The costs of holding on to the illusion of control are obvious, but the relentless lover has reasons for clinging to it. Pursuing an unrequited love is an attempt to achieve "belated mastery" by making the past come out differently. According to Stark, relentless hope wards off unbearable helplessness and despair. If you believe that accepting the truth cannot be endured, you have no other choice. Questioning that foregone conclusion— and identifying what you are doing to maintain a fantasy—is an important step toward eventually refuting it.

How does anyone ever break out of this all-engulfing, self-destructive, tragic pursuit of relationships that offer, as I lamented in my diary, "at least thrice the pain as pleasure"? It starts with making the choice to look at reality—both past and present—rather than to look away from it; you must force yourself to acknowledge that changing another person is both your secret desire and a doomed enterprise.

This decision is an act of will, which is under your control, unlike the original traumatizing parent or the current unloving lover. Exercising will builds esteem from within through action on one's own behalf; it disproves the premise that only another person can provide it. The result, long in coming and always worth the effort, is the experience of authentic agency in your own life, a sense of self that cannot be destroyed because it is not dependent on anybody else. You are putting your destiny in your own hands.

This can lead to requited love with someone who can give wholeheartedly. Grieving over relentless hope allows real hope to be born.

THE INTERPRETATION OF DREAMS

I don't remember when the dreams started, but I know that they troubled and perplexed me for at least thirty years. They made regular appearances, at least bimonthly, for all that time. They were so much a part of my nocturnal life that I named the series after the city in which they inevitably took place—the city where I went to college and where my relationship with Michael unfolded. Each one had the same theme, expressed the same emotional content, and provoked the same reaction in me on awakening, which was to be greatly relieved to discover that it was "only" a dream.

Simultaneously baffling and riveting in their intensity and their verisimilitude, these anxiety dreams—they were not true nightmares because I woke up troubled rather than terrified—eluded my most strenuous efforts to unravel them, frustrating all the skill at dream interpretation I had honed over decades. As many people intuitively understand, any dream that recurs with such regularity is trying to tell you something that you urgently need to know (and resist comprehending), but this particular one staunchly refused to reveal its meaning to me, try as I might to coax it forth.

With minor variations, the scenario was always identical: I find myself in an unrecognizable version of the neighborhood of the university, lost, alone, and disoriented. I have to get to a class I've somehow neglected to take, but I have no idea where to go or even what the subject is. There is nobody I can turn to for assistance even though there are other people around. As I desperately and unsuccessfully try to get my bearings, I realize why I'm there: I must get another Ph.D. in a field that is unknown to me and that is taught nowhere else, but I don't know why I have to do this. Worst of all, winter is coming. I have to endure it all alone, all over again, in order to complete my research, interrupting my current life to finish this arduous project. How am I going to endure the cold, figure out where I'm supposed to go, or even meet my basic needs for food and shelter? I seem to have no resources—no purse, no phone, no credit card, not even a pencil and paper—and there is no haven for me, no comfort or solace. Sometimes I protest aloud to no one in particular that I already have a doctorate in my field, that I've had it for years, so why do I need to go to such lengths to obtain another one? I always wake up as I'm trying frantically to find my way to the bountiful supermarket that was one of my favorite places when I actually lived there.

The imagery and the emotional tone of these dreams depict the mental state of a person beset by what D. W. Winnicott labeled "the unthinkable anxieties," primitive experiences of being overwhelmed by unmanageable emotions that cannot be processed because they occur in infancy before the development of language and the organization of cognition. I was reexperiencing two of them specifically—"having no orientation" and "complete isolation because of there being no means of communication."* The infant (and the adult who feels like an infant) falls prey to them when what Winnicott called the holding environment is disrupted.

My Golden One never appeared in any of these dreams as himself, but when I reread my diary, it suddenly became clear to me that he was my third experience (after my mother and my father) of a disrupted holding environment. Michael was the frigid "place" in which I was stuck, trying unsuccessfully to find help and sustenance (directions and food) when I felt I had no inner resources. Figuring out our relationship was the essential course of study that I had avoided since 1967; I had to go back to the source of the problem and reexperience the emotional state in its full intensity in order to complete my "education" in the meaning of my obsession with him.

As soon as I figured out what our relationship meant to me—that he was my imperfect replacement for my imperfect maternal father—the dreams stopped as if by magic, never to recur.

Just as I began to write about him, the dream paid me one final visit. The setting was the same, but this time Rick, my husband, was with me. I said to him, "Let's get out of here. I don't have to endure this. I really don't have to prove anything now. I already have my Ph.D., and that's enough—and besides,

---

* Jan Abram, *The Language of Winnicott: A Dictionary of Winnicott's Use of Words* (London: Karnac Books, 1966), 171. The other unthinkable anxieties are Going to Pieces, Falling Forever, and Having No Relation to the Body.

I've written six books." I had only written five at the time; the one in which this essay appears is the sixth.

I knew then that I had finally graduated, and with the most advanced degree, from the School of Hard Knocks of Unrequited Love.

PART II

DIFFICULT LOVE

6

THE MAN WHO COULD NOT LOVE

LONG-DISTANCE CALL

I saw my patient Peter only twice in the ten years I was his therapist. He lived, literally as well as psychologically, in a distant state, so we had weekly phone sessions the rest of the time. He originally contacted me because he had read a book I wrote about life with problem siblings, and he thought I would understand what he had endured by growing up with his seriously disturbed older brother, James—a topic he had never discussed with anyone. James's rampages, as well as the way his parents ignored them, continued to have a chilling effect on all Peter's relationships, including the one he had with himself. At age forty, married and successful in business—he was an energy executive—his life was still both defined and confined by the traumatic atmosphere of his childhood home. James's noisily menacing behavior and the even more frightening silence of his parents' nonresponse and seeming obliviousness to it had tormented him daily throughout his first two decades. No matter what James did—cursing and screaming at everyone, throwing the television set, or trying to set the house afire—his parents ignored it and behaved as if nothing were happening. They made no attempt to stop James or to shield Peter from these terrifying outbursts.

Many parents are overwhelmed by having a troubled child, but Peter's parents had themselves had a repressive upbringing and a cultural background in which discussion was not a part of family life. Their paralyzing fear of their own rage prevented them from taking any action whatsoever. The situation and their reactions to it unnerved them so deeply that they shut down entirely and psychologically absented themselves from the scene. Every evening, after James wreaked havoc, they would go about the business of eating dinner and blandly discussing the news of the day, after which they retreated—his father to his office (he always locked the door behind him to create a physical as well as a mental barrier to the chaos outside) and his mother to the kitchen (cooking was the only way she knew how to nurture her family)—as if nothing were amiss, leaving Peter to fend for himself. I had heard similar stories countless times before from other patients, but this scenario seemed especially relentless and damaging to the sensitive boy—Peter was ten years younger than James—who was forced simultaneously to witness his brother's pathological lack of self-control and his parents' pathologically excessive self-control. There was no way for him to get attention, much less find a refuge from dread, rage, and sorrow. All emotion—his own or anybody else's—was unmanageable, even life threatening; from his perspective as a child, he lived in fear that James could become dangerously violent at any time. What benefits could Peter possibly get from other people? The daily diet of silence and violence to which he had been subjected had battered him to such an extent that he had learned early on to barricade himself emotionally; he concluded that love provided no solace and human bonds no sustenance.

From our first conversation, I had a sense that this was not going to be a typical therapeutic encounter. Peter asked to have sessions mostly by telephone (this was before the days of Skype) because he only rarely came to New York. I was reluctant, since I rely on and enjoy the personal contact and all the nuances and bodily cues that are subliminally communicated when my patient and I are in the same room, and I sensed that making a connection with him would be hard enough without additional obstacles, but I was willing to try. In this, Peter knew himself well; he turned out to be freer and more communicative on the phone than when we met in my office, and he probably would never have been able to endure the sustained emotional onslaught of in-person therapy. The very remoteness allowed him to feel more protected and more in charge of the process—critical things for someone so damaged by human interactions—so he could experience and express more than he would have in any other circumstances. Even so, his ability to relate to me fluctuated wildly within virtually every session, and it often vanished altogether.

Peter insisted on paying for six months' worth of sessions in advance—something no one had ever done before or has done since—because it was "more convenient." But I believed the real reason was that prepayment meant writing fewer checks and thus being reminded less frequently that he had to pay to have somebody to talk to. It also served to guarantee my attention;

since money was the only commodity he thought he had, he assumed it was mine, as well. Leasing me, I thought, was his way of preventing himself from becoming attached to me—and he (unlike his parents and himself as a child in relation to James) would then be less at the whim of my moods. It gave him the illusion of control.

THE SIBLING MASTER

Peter sought me out, he told me, because he always tried to find "masters" to study with in his areas of interest (martial arts was another one of these), and he had the financial resources to hire them. I was gratified by, but also wary of, this flattering description because of the expectations it set up and the grandiosity it implied; what if all I had to offer was just an ordinary relationship, something that had never given him anything but pain and fear?

In addition to our long-distance arrangement and our unusual financial agreement, Peter's attitude toward therapy was also new to me. He seemed to be looking for nuggets of wisdom, which he would go off to digest on his own, periodically returning for another helping. He planned to tape our sessions; he wanted news he could use and talking points to carry around in his pocket to help him initiate conversations with people he knew. Relating to and sharing his emotional life with another human being was not something he understood or actively sought; growing up in his family provided no model for needing or trusting or communicating with anyone. As a therapist, I used self-awareness, empathy, and my knowledge and experience to enter his inner world and accompany him back into his childhood, but this did not seem to be what Peter had in mind. Harry Stack Sullivan, founder of the interpersonal school of psychoanalysis (and quite a character himself from a seriously

disturbed background*), defined the analyst as "an expert in human relations," a job description I was not at all sure suited me.
I feared that I might end up feeling exploited and discarded and
that my would-be acolyte would be bitterly disillusioned. Being
a dispenser of life lessons seemed an unnatural assignment, the
opposite of the unique if strange intimacy that I was used to
sharing with my patients. How could we ever really connect?

I might not have had the kind of wisdom to impart that
Peter envisioned, but I certainly had empathy about his sibling
problem; treating "Normal Ones"—my term for the higher-
functioning brothers and sisters of the physically or mentally
impaired—had long been a therapeutic specialty of mine. I was
one myself; my own older brother, Steven (who was seven
years my senior), had never been as frightening or as destructive as James, but he had social and school trouble throughout
my childhood and always seemed to be angry. My parents,
though not as emotionally incapacitated as Peter's, also had
no idea how to help their son or to address the tumultuous
environment he created in our house. Steven and my mother
screamed at each other regularly, while my father mostly tuned
out; he gave up on his son early on and turned to me, his daughter, who then became his heir apparent. Of course, neither
Steven nor James was ever sent for therapy, which would have
exposed to the outside world their parents' private shame for
having a disturbed child; this type of refusal to confront or to
seek treatment for even serious pathology is all too common
in dysfunctional families. At least my mother had wanted to
take Steven, but she capitulated to her physician-husband's

---

* Sullivan, like Peter, was a gifted, abrasive loner, and his only friends
  growing up were the animals on his parents' farm—which was more company than Peter had. Sullivan also coined the term "participant observer"
  to describe the analyst's role.

resistance. I never realized how profoundly I was affected by the whole situation until I wrote about it in middle age.

I coped with the tension quite differently from the way Peter did. Emulating his parents, Peter battened down the hatches; he retreated into himself and imploded, becoming inwardly furious, never sharing his feelings with anyone. On the other hand, I felt compelled to connect and made it my business to be my parents' darling and confidante—as attentive and delightful to them as Steven was burdensome and unappealing. Relationships were my source of power and sustenance; self-sufficiency was Peter's.

I also understood from personal experience why Peter was mesmerized into passivity and had failed to confront his parents or his brother. I was fifty—considerably older than Peter—when I finally broke the spell of forced obliviousness and inaction that my family wove around everything to do with Steven; at a dinner with my mother and brother years after my father's death, I could endure Steven's sullen silence no longer and told him to think about leaving the restaurant if he was going to refuse to talk. He stayed and at least minimally participated, but I remember my mother's horrified expression, as though I had committed a shocking breach of etiquette. When Steven died at sixty-four, we had been estranged for years, despite my attempts to reconcile in his last years. All this had a powerful underground influence on every aspect of my life (including my choice of a profession), which, as I discovered in my research, happens to anyone who grows up in families like ours. You do not leave your troubled siblings at home when you move out; they follow you into every subsequent relationship. These were things Peter didn't have to explain to me, and it helped him feel understood for the first time.

I thought I'd heard every possible awful sibling story in my practice: the doctor whose epileptic brother smashed the windows of movie theaters on family outings and tried to commit suicide when she was left to babysit for him (her mother screamed and cried while her father looked the other way), the lawyer whose schizophrenic brother tried to set her afire (her parents' only response was to stop keeping matches in the house), the teacher whose autistic brother urinated in her mouth (her father begged her to try to understand and befriend him), and the editor whose borderline older brother punched him in the face and broke his teeth ("He didn't know his own strength," his mother explained). But I had never encountered anyone whose life had been constricted by the experience as severely as Peter's. The parents of my other patients all lived in a state of denial but were at least occasionally emotionally related to their higher-functioning children. In Peter's family, the tension was unrelenting, his parents' response entirely zombielike. They never complained or cried or showed any outward sign that they were living and forcing Peter to live in a madhouse without keepers. Relationships were nothing but torture.

Most of the Normal Ones I have known become helpers and caretakers in their personal and professional lives—a disproportionate number of members of the various "helping professions" (medicine, special education, rehabilitation, and assorted therapeutic specialties) learned at home—but Peter rejected the caretaking role with a vengeance; he only felt in control if he gave absolutely nothing to anybody. He worried that he might come across as arrogant and authoritarian to others, but he had no idea what to do about it.

We had our work cut out. Peter had concluded early on that the only way to survive with his sanity intact was to emulate his parents, which required him to remove himself from his own and other people's emotions as they had done. He had shut himself up in his own mind, letting no one in and sharing himself with no one. At work, he concentrated on expertly arranging sustainable energy deals; solitary sports and intensive study with his "masters" filled his leisure hours. But he admitted that he was terribly lonely for human contact, even though he fled from it. Intimacy of any kind was a language he could not decipher; he hired me as his translator.

One of my teachers at the psychoanalytic institute where I trained used to say, only half humorously, that "the most important prerequisite for a vocation as a psychotherapist is a depressed mother"; based on my history, I think that a suffering but inaccessible father and a damaged sibling should be added to the list of qualifications. In addition to empathy, you have to have a certain relentlessness and perseverance—and perhaps a touch of masochism—to reach someone like Peter.

The first time I saw him, I was unexpectedly charmed by his sincerity, his intelligent gray eyes, and his boyish manner. He was so short and slight that he almost disappeared on my couch. Despite his athleticism—he was an expert fencer—his shyness and awkwardness of manner combined with the monotone in which he spoke made him seem like an alien who had applied himself to the study of human ways with only partial success. He was such a peculiar combination of physical grace and mental regimentation that he seemed to be two people incompletely melded together.

It surprised me to learn how successful he was professionally, since he was no glad-hander and shunned all nonbusiness relationships. Efficiency and attention to detail got him through. I was also astonished when he told me that he had a wife—an attractive and thoughtful woman with whom he barely spoke; they had not had a real conversation for most of the fifteen years they had been together. She occasionally told him, and showed him by how miserable she looked in his presence, that she despaired of ever reaching him, even though she stayed with him for reasons I understood no better than her husband did. They did share interests; both loved travel, and she had a reclusive streak herself. Somehow she tolerated his silence and appreciated him. But she regularly became so frustrated with his callousness (one time he let her go to the emergency room alone when she injured herself) that once she seriously threatened to leave. He begged her to stay, promised to reform, bought her a sports car—and soon reverted to spending more time with his computer than with her. Her unhappiness made him feel bad. He knew that she needed more from him, yet he could only regret that he could not provide it, as if doing anything was beyond his control. Still, neither he nor his wife wanted to be alone.

One of the most telling things that Peter revealed to me was his relationship with their dog—a huge, beautiful, and affectionate creature of an unusual breed. He left its care and feeding entirely to his wife—I thought it was her substitute husband—and never even petted the animal for fear that it would require more attention and involvement than he was willing to give if it became attached to him. Any relationship whatsoever seemed to him a potential prison of unrelenting demands. Like his parents, he never imagined he could set any limits on anybody.

I asked him once what it was like to be in the room with his wife, his dog, or even the garbage in the kitchen, all of which he saw as demanding his attention simply by sharing his space. "I draw into myself," he said. "They're there, but they're like a chair—I'm totally disconnected from them, and they have no effect on me. I go off and find a distraction as soon as I can."

"But," I countered, "you wouldn't say that unless you had to defuse the effect they have on you; leaving mentally or physically allows you to get rid of their demands without having to interact with them." He had learned to wall himself off and to escape early on: a child's vision of independence that was actually a trap.

At first glance, Peter seemed almost Asperger's-esque, yet his palpable anguish and longing for a mutual human touch told another story. He tried desperately to have a simulacrum of a normal life, which he "put on from the outside" by giving lavish gifts to clients and parties for remote acquaintances. He told me with embarrassment that he practiced smiling in the shower before he went to work to temper his oddness, but it did not help. I had never met a lonelier person or one who was more cut off or frightened of the very contact that some part of him clearly missed.

This strange, remote, yet tormented man aroused a conflicting welter of feelings within me. I admired his intelligence, his perseverance, and his courage, and I could sense the anguish beneath his often forbidding façade. But relating to him took a toll on me. He aroused a depth of rage and despair that was hard to contain, the intensity of which caught me unawares every time, even though I tried to prepare myself for it. My countertransference—the technical term for the therapist's reactions to a patient based on her own unresolved issues in intimate relationships*—was particularly intense with him;

---

* Heinz Kohut, the founder of self psychology, said that "analysis is always conducted on the front lines," by which he meant that the deepest conflicts of both participants can be aroused at any time. There is a constant, unpredictable, unconscious dialogue. Hopefully, one's own treatment—in my case, twenty-five years total with two different analysts—alerts you to the most critical pitfalls so that you can resolve them before they over-

clearly, Peter represented every difficult man I had ever cared about and wanted to reach. At least at this point in my life, my frustration and my wish to retaliate by cutting him off or saying something hostile or withering when he rejected me—which I had rarely been able to do with my own personal inaccessible loves—were conscious, and though the impulses plagued me, I rarely acted them out with my patient.

He always started our phone sessions robotically, announcing with a fixed combination of frustration and conceit that nothing had changed and that he did not remember what we had talked about the week before and had not taken any of the actions (writing in a journal, for example) that I had suggested and that he had agreed to perform. With disturbing frequency, he would do something really outrageous and offensive; once when he seemed out of breath and background noises made him difficult to understand, it turned out that he was race-walking during our session so as not to "waste the time." On another occasion, I could hear him talking to someone in the background; he was consulting an auto mechanic about a problem with his car in the middle of our session. Discussing anything to do with our relationship or how he was treating me was irrelevant from his point of view, and he let me know in no uncertain terms that he considered any time spent on these topics a waste of money. In a flash, his voice would become so flat and his manner so cold and distant that it seemed as though he was not speaking to a living person. There was no way in. The

---

whelm the relationship. If it really feels unmanageable, you consult informally with friends and colleagues or, on rare occasions, pay a supervisor to advise you. I was all too painfully aware of what Peter provoked in me and why, which allowed me to repair the unavoidable rifts between us—the process through which I and many other analysts believe the most important work actually happens.

way he addressed me, as from a height, made me so angry and hopeless that I could hardly contain myself.

Yet often, later in the same session, he would warm up. Then we would have a human-to-human exchange, often full of self-awareness, about why he had just behaved so obnoxiously, which usually had to do with feeling needy or unimportant; even if I had done nothing specific to arouse those feelings, he believed that his very dependency on me put him at a disadvantage. So he kept me continuously off balance, both to thwart my having any power over him and to have me experience firsthand the emotional roller coaster that was his constant, though hidden, state of mind. I hated being periodically erased by him, although I was beginning to understand him—and I was also endlessly tantalized by the prospect of getting through to this most recalcitrant of men. I tried hard to be patient with both of us.

Why couldn't Peter leave his childhood experience behind or modify it? Why, I asked him, did the entire inner and outer world become the living room of his youth, with every person (and even the resident canine) he encountered playing the role of James or his parents? He could only say that the experience had been so awful he never got past it, that he feared that he might be irreparably warped by it, that he was too scared to change and didn't know how. Living "underground" was safe, and better safe than sorry. Nonetheless, he was clearly mindful of what he was missing: life itself. It is never easy to answer why one person with a traumatic background overcomes it and has remarkably normal relationships, while another shuts down as he did—but his flashes of insight, and even of passion, about his predicament and its meaning made me believe that his seemingly impenetrable façade was a defense, rather than the fundamental truth about him. After all the tumult of his childhood, I saw that maintaining a state of equilibrium and calm, free from emotional upheaval, was paramount. This project consumed him to such an extent that he didn't realize he had the capacity to tolerate a much wider emotional range, even when he felt it, either because expanding his inner horizons would force him to grieve over the waste of his life until then or because he was afraid of demands that would be made on him once others saw that he was open to emotion.

The odd but insightful interpersonalist Sullivan's concept of "selective inattention"—in which a person avoids being flooded with anxiety by turning his focus away from disturbing emotions, people, and experiences—helped me understand why Peter continued to be so utterly suspended in his past. The problem with this defensive "security operation" (another Sullivanian term) is that you have to pay attention in order to learn from experience, which can never occur as long as you are constantly running away.* I paid attention to him, and he knew it, which allowed him to begin, even if inconsistently, to pay attention to himself. I did not attack him as James did (even when I wanted to), but I also didn't allow him to behave like his parents. I was a different kind of parent, whom he recognized was trying to understand and to communicate and who did not abandon him, even when I was frustrated. Since I came from

---

* Even though I was never trained in Sullivan's approach to therapy, and his system and his style did not resonate for me, I was struck by how many of his concepts illuminated Peter's predicament. I think this is partly because he resembled Peter in his personality; Sullivan was so adept at treating seriously disturbed patients that his colleagues said when he spoke with schizophrenics, they no longer sounded schizophrenic. He gave me hope, because he believed that if you made real contact with a patient, you could help him, no matter how bizarre or alien he seemed. M. Blechner, "The Gay Harry Stack Sullivan: Interactions Between His Life, Clinical Work, and Theory," *Contemporary Psychoanalysis* 41, no. 4 (2005).

the world outside his family, I offered him a new pair of eyes. There were moments when I thought he was learning to look through them.

Many times, in between withdrawing and insulting me, he told me softly that he considered talking to me his last chance to join the world. This was very moving to me. He almost never missed an appointment, all the while announcing that he dreaded making every call, although he admitted that he felt better as we went along and also after the session ended. His recall of our conversations was spotty at best, however, and he needed me to prompt him. Eventually, I got over being annoyed at this implicit demand (perhaps he wanted to make sure I was really paying attention?) and told him what had transpired between us. Then he could resume our dialogue. I was learning to take him as he was.

Over time, I realized in more depth why he seemed so surpassingly disintegrated and peculiar. For Peter, caring for anybody was a danger to be avoided at all costs, because if he noticed or responded to another's needs, he would feel compelled to put his own needs aside entirely and do whatever that person demanded of him. Reciprocity and naturally maintaining boundaries were both inconceivable to him; where would he have seen either (or would it have registered if he did see) before we met? An impossible bind loomed before him: he was unable to live with people or without them—and this included me. His dreams revealed this to both of us with compelling immediacy.

THE FIRST RUNG

Dreams, I told Peter, tell the truth—particularly truths about ourselves that we would rather not know but need to know; they have fascinated me my entire life, and I taught dream interpretation for many years. Luckily, he grasped this principle intuitively and took his dreams seriously from the start; he knew they were his and his alone. Until our last couple of years together, he hardly remembered any, but then, when he was finally ready to attend to them, they started to reveal his emotional life with astonishing clarity. He saw that each was an eloquent and poignant metaphor for his existential predicament. Psychoanalyst and animal researcher John Mack, in his profound book *Nightmares and Human Conflict*, says that these terrifying dreams are "involuntary poetry," and Peter's certainly fit this description.

In the first dream he recounted to me, he was living in an underground bunker in a war zone and only dared to stick his head out periodically before retreating to save his life. The meaning of this siege mentality was obvious to both of us: his carapace of imperious indifference served the same function as a turtle's—to protect the vulnerable creature inside. It had formed so early and covered him so completely that he could not conceive of surviving without it. He feared that feeling anything, let alone caring about what others felt, would deplete his precious, limited resources. He carried his bunker on his back.

But Peter was not yet ready or able to give up his refuge—he had nothing reliable with which to replace it—and so this dream and his insights about it led exactly nowhere. At my wit's end, I tried another tack, more behavioral: I went on a campaign to get him to do little things at home, at work, and with me—like taking out the garbage (he kept himself magisterially aloof from all household chores), initiating the briefest personal conversation with his wife, going to the company coffee shop, e-mailing me any thoughts he had between sessions—but to no avail. Even when he did a little something—he actually took the dog for a walk once—it was always a one-off.

Whatever we accomplished during the hour he unwove like Penelope during the week by very active inattention and grimly determined inaction.

A combination of willfulness (his only means of self-assertion was to refuse to do what was asked of him) and terror of the unknown still kept Peter locked in place. He neutralized my every attempt to nudge him forward. I felt like I was the psychotherapist of Bartleby the Scrivener, the tragic hero of Melville's story who responded to every request by saying, "I prefer not to." He accused me of only doing it for the money, and I began to wonder if he wasn't correct.

But on rare occasions (but on more occasions than ever before) there would be flashes of another Peter. He would answer some inquiry of mine seriously and passionately with the impacted intensity of years of suppression. When James, his former tormentor, lay dying, Peter wrote him a poem declaring that he loved him, recalling this tragic man's aesthetic gifts and the good moments they had shared that had been unknown to me until he read it to me. The poem was found next to James's deathbed; Peter had gotten through to him at the end, something I had been unable to do with my own brother, and he knew I was glad for both of them. At the same time, Peter also threw his considerable expertise and energy into charity work. His efforts garnered millions of dollars in contributions that strangers admired and were touched by. Was he beginning to open himself to self-expression?

Then, just when I started to believe that we were actually making inroads and no longer had to start from scratch repeatedly, he did something so chillingly detached that I was unprepared for it even after long experience: I was hospitalized unexpectedly—and for an extended period of time—with a serious illness. I informed all my patients and received many touching responses. Peter reacted to my announcement without a word of concern, only an awkwardly worded question about whether his next regular session time would still be available, which of course was impossible under the circumstances. His utter lack of empathy shocked and hurt me, although on some level, I realized that he was denying my vulnerability and the anxiety that my unavailability and possible loss stirred up in him. I berated myself for grandiosely thinking—and not for the first time—that I alone could unlock his hidden heart. Had he regressed with a vengeance to his familiar aloofness because he was panicked by the fear of losing me—or was he simply showing his true colors? Had I barely made a dent with all my efforts? I berated myself for my blindness and egoism at having cherished the fantasy that in extremis I would be exempt from his withdrawal. However, when I confronted him with his behavior and told him how heartless it seemed—I did not hold back how hurt and angry I was—he sincerely apologized.

Shortly after this highly charged exchange, Peter surprised me by informing me that he had reinitiated a relationship with his aged mother (his father had died years before). He had been visiting her regularly. The more feeble and demented she became, the tenderer were his attentions; he actually talked to her with great patience. He was such a good son that the attendants of the nursing home constantly remarked on his devotion and told him that they wished others would emulate him. He even recalled, and discussed with joy, good times with her that he had never mentioned before, when they were alone together on summer weekdays without James. He could embrace her wholeheartedly because he knew there was a time limit on what could be expected of him—he would have a reserve left after she was gone—so he gave his considerable all. This inspired me to go on with him. When she finally died, Peter delivered a loving eulogy in which he revealed for the first time publicly what his family life had been like. ("The undercurrent of disruption and the threat of violence consumed so much of my mother's life that it would be a dishonor not to acknowledge it at the end of her life," he said. "May the unrelenting, enduring, and shocking suffering that our family had to privately endure be released on this day.") The mourners wept and embraced him.

In his next session after this apotheosis, however, he fell completely and totally silent as soon as I picked up the phone, and he stayed silent. Shaky starts for these encounters were typical of him, unused as he was to conversation in the world outside our calls, but now he said not a word for the entire forty-five minutes, which he had never done before. This would have been awkward in person, but on the telephone, it was unbearable. I felt imprisoned in the empty air space, and his withdrawal now felt like a refusal, not an inability, to make the effort. Had I convinced myself—I had certainly done it with other men—that he had more to give, that he had the capacity to feel more, than he really did? At this point, he was capable of knowing what he felt (frightened of intimacy? hopeless? furious and under my thumb?) and of expressing it; not doing so was willful. At the end of this interminable session, I gave him an ultimatum in my calmest voice: "If you don't make the effort to talk to me, I won't continue to work with you. Otherwise, we're wasting my time and your money. I'll give you one more chance in our session next week, and that's it." I was not at all sure that he would even bother to call.

I had no idea what he would do; was it really over between us—and in this lousy way? I was wary about how the next session would unfold and was prepared to make good on my word to end the charade; part of me even anticipated breaking up with a touch of sadistic pleasure. I had an urge to retaliate for all the disappointment and frustration he and every unrelated boyfriend in my past had caused me and I had not-so-patiently borne. I took a perverse fantasized pleasure at finally having the power to end a frustrating relationship—a power I had never thought I had in the past.

I braced myself for his next call. Something in my voice must have told him that I'd meant what I'd said, because he broke his silence at the very start by telling me a dream in anything but his usual monotone:

"I'm climbing a cliff, a vertical cliff. It's so real. I'm looking up to see where I can grab next. It's so windy up here that I could drift away. I can't go up or down safely—if I move at all, I'm going to fall to my death. I'm frightened, but I say okay, I'll try to let go."

He understood that this dream was a topographical representation of his existential dilemma, and he promised to think about it. I was hesitantly pleased that he took it seriously and had read the metaphor accurately. I decided to bide my time. Still, I worried, was this another fencer's feint to get me back in the match?

But Peter was true to his word and began the next session by recounting, in a voice full of feeling, an even more powerful dream:

"This time, instead of being up high, I was down low—I was at the bottom of a body of water. My feet were stuck on the bottom. I couldn't stay there any longer, but I couldn't get up to the surface. I realized I'm going to run out of breath here. I can't float—even gravity wasn't working in my favor. I'm going to die. Then I see that there's a wall on the side, like a ladder with grooves for my feet. I grab it, I hold on, I go up it, and I make it."

The threat of losing me and not being able to do anything about it had caused him to fall from the height of arrogance to the depth of despair, and from either place, there seemed to be no way out—until he saw the ladder and grabbed on at the last minute. He asked to continue for another six months, and I agreed, on the condition that he never again give me the silent treatment. My reactions were a complex mixture of professional gratification, genuine caring for him, and a touch of pleasure that I had "won." This I accepted as a normal human response; a saint couldn't do this work.

Then, just as we were ending, he added something poignant and revealing. "I'm afraid if I'm cured, I won't be able to see you anymore." This was the first time he had ever admitted that I mattered to him. I promised, holding back tears that luckily he could not see, that we could still be in touch even if he was no longer my patient.

Somehow I wasn't dismayed or offended at his initial backtracking the next week, when he suggested, as was his wont, that I must have felt happy not to lose the income. I expected it and saw through it and called him on it; I felt convinced that too much had changed for him to revert utterly. I said, "You know it's not true that I just see you as a revenue stream. You pay me for my time, but you can't pay me to care about you—that's freely given. What's the real reason for your discomfort?"

"If this works, it means that I've been wrong all my life," he said. "I thought of throwing you out to prove it hadn't been a waste."

Then, unprompted, in a quiet, intimate voice I had never heard before, he talked about what his last dream meant to him:

"There were iron bars cemented into that wall. It's strong. I realize you are that ladder—my path out of this. It goes far beyond the surface of the water. It goes all the way to heaven, for the rest of our lives—we've really got something, you and me. I'm so afraid to say it, but we've done something together that's wonderful. We've made both of us better. It's been mutually beneficial. We've gone through things that could have ended our relationship, but we've gotten through them. You're someone I can really count on. It's like a marriage; this is a third thing we've created. Why would I want to throw that away? It gives me a comfort that my parents couldn't give me. Holding on to the rungs of the ladder is like a child holding on to his parents' hands. But they never held my hands."

Through the lucky convergence of his needs and my own and a mutual willingness to continuously repair the unavoidable ruptures in our trust of each other, the man who could not love was finally ready to take a chance on the real thing.

In the last paper he wrote before his death, Heinz Kohut described how he offered a desperately suicidal patient two of his fingers to hold on to. Why did he violate a boundary that many analysts consider sacrosanct? He explained that he felt that an interpretation would not do; he had to give himself—and the patient didn't kill herself. Because of different interpretations of the appropriate physical boundaries between patients and therapists and the loaded symbolic nature of touch in a therapeutic relationship, psychoanalytic theorists of various persuasions have debated this act ever since. Did he go too far when simply telling her "I'm here" would have done the trick, or did he hold back too much by only giving her two fingers when he should have extended his whole hand?* Based on my experience with Peter, it's clear to me that he did exactly the right thing; he was giving her what she had needed as a baby, when two fingers of a loving, sustaining parent were all she could grasp. I was struck that even though I did not (and could not) literally give Peter my hand, he described our work together with the same image; he had finally learned to use me as a physical source of consolation and stability, a pathway out of terror.

I had no illusions that what lay ahead for us would be a straight route up to earth and air, let alone to the stars, but he had reached out and grasped my hand. We were on the first rung together, at long last.

---

* Howard Bacal and Lucyann Carlton, "Kohut's Last Words on Analytic Cure and How We Hear Them Now—A View from Specificity Theory," *International Journal of Psychoanalytic Self Psychology* 5 (2010): 132–143.

7

THE TANTALIZING MENTOR AND THE PASSIONATE PROTÉGÉ

THE SPECIAL RELATIONSHIP

He was a star—dazzling, handsome, and rich, at the top of his game, still an enfant terrible at age forty-four. He wrote his first bestseller, the first of his fifty books, at twenty-one. By twenty-nine, he had founded a controversial journal of opinion, of which he was editor in chief. By forty-one, he was hosting a hit interview show on television, and his name was a household word. He had a glittering wit, a glamorous life, and an eye for talent.

That eye alighted on a brash and brilliant teenager who sent an article to the magazine, unsolicited, at the age of fourteen. The article became a cover story, and its author, as if destined for the post, became the editor in chief's protégé.

Since the protégé was my boyfriend when he was officially appointed heir apparent and became my husband two years later,

I had a ringside seat at the progress, deterioration, and restoration of this tempestuous relationship over the next three decades. The bond between these two, which began with mutual admiration and idealization, came to encompass the entire gamut of emotions—with the exception of sexual attraction—between mentor and protégé:* awe, exhilaration, devotion, fear, envy, rage, shame, rivalry, disillusionment, sorrow, and gratitude.

Most protégés start out as teachers' pets, the kind of students whose report cards say "a pleasure to have in class" and whose teachers from grade school through graduate school remember them as fondly as they remember their teachers. To qualify for the position of a genuine protégé, however, a depth of intensity and intimacy that goes beyond the role of favorite student has to develop. The candidate must be seen as the bearer of a mentor's legacy and, in particularly charged cases, even identity—a professional, intellectual, and psychological heir.

These relationships are always more complicated than simple arrangements for the giving and receiving of good counsel and are more volatile than they appear. They are a precious, memorable, and extremely compelling variety of love, and as such are sown with pitfalls for both participants. Because both parties are amalgams of parent/child, lover, and friend, the potential for profound gratifications, and for devastating disappointments, is built in. As in all intimate connections, transferences and projections† in both directions, as well as unfulfilled

---

* I am not referring here to "mentoring" as the term is used in the corporate world. Important as these relationships are—and they often share some of the same qualities as classic mentor/protégé ties—they tend to be more circumscribed and not as potent or interwoven in the lives of both participants.
† Transference is an unconscious reexperiencing of intense emotional aspects of a childhood relationship, usually with a parent, in a current relationship.

and unfulfillable longings of all kinds, are undercurrents—the wish to relive one's youth, to have obstacles in your path whisked effortlessly away by someone else, to control the future, to have your life work perpetuated unchanged, to be admired or inspired without ambivalence. Though these bonds can morph into partnerships, friendships (or enemy-ships), rivalries, and even marriages, during the initial stage, they are by definition never relationships of equals; there is always an implicit power differential. Even if they last long enough for the couple to become near peers, echoes of the original hierarchy never entirely fade; they resonate for a lifetime.

Mentors can be of the same or the opposite sex and are typically fifteen to twenty years older than their protégés, which makes them slightly older than most lovers and younger than most parents. They are most commonly drawn from the ranks of teachers, supervisors, older colleagues, and bosses. Their principal function is to serve as experienced and trusted advisors, but they are often much more than that. The best of them have a combination of discernment, tact, generosity, and self-control. Like Plutarch, they believe that "the mind is not a vessel to be filled, but a fire to be kindled."

There are psychological prerequisites for each role. The mentor sees in the protégé a younger, malleable self, someone who can be formed in his or her own image; the protégé seeks a reliable, nonjudgmental intellectual or emotional guide, as

---

It occurs universally in psychotherapy—the therapist's transference to the patient is called "countertransference"—and in virtually every other significant relationship throughout life. Projection is the unconscious attribution to another of one's own, usually unacceptable, emotions or personality traits. The person onto whom projections are "beamed" is called the "projective screen." Mentors and their protégés project their own positive as well as negative characteristics onto each other and experience both positive and negative transferences toward one another.

well as the embodiment of the mature self he or she hopes to become. Both perceive—or think they perceive—an essential like-mindedness that sets their relationship apart. Each is a projective screen for the other. Not every good, or even great, teacher is mentor material, and not every good student aspires to be a protégé; there has to be a certain synergy, a personal fit, and a gift for a particular type of intimacy with someone who is not on one's own level, with all the demands and exposure that either role entails. Unconscious needs and ways of relating rooted in the past, as well as conscious affinity—at least for salient aspects of the other person—are essential.

Explicit or implicit sexual tensions between mentors and their protégés are one of the most treacherous maelstroms to navigate. While some of these relationships are blessedly exempt from boundary violations of this kind—as was my thirty-year tie with my first boss and role model, a vibrant, attractive man whom I adored with very little ambivalence and a complete sense of safety despite his well-deserved reputation as a ladies' man—many are not. These relationships inhabit a gray area where fantasies flourish and the urge to succumb is great on both sides. Few women I know, myself included, have not had to field unwanted advances from male mentors. When I taught graduate school in my thirties and my male students gazed at me with wide-eyed admiration or earnestly sought my advice, I gained a new appreciation for the temptations my own professors had endured, felt more sympathetic toward them, and judged them less severely.

Unacknowledged desire also has its perils, prompting the guilty or unwilling lover to reject the object of his or her longing, breeding shame, confusion, pain, and mutual anxiety. Breakups between mentors and protégés have an anguish all their own.

• • •

The first mentor, Mentor, wasn't so great at the job. Before leaving to fight in the Trojan War, Odysseus, king of Thebes and hero of Homer's *Odyssey,* asked this old friend to oversee the royal palace in Thebes and to educate and advise his young son, Telemachus. Mentor failed miserably at both assignments, leaving Telemachus to fend for himself during Odysseus's twenty-year absence and allowing the palace to be overrun by unwanted suitors who harassed Odysseus's wife, Penelope, and lived off his estates. Mentor only rose to the occasion and acted like a proper mentor when Athena, goddess of wisdom, assumed his form and spoke in his voice. Then he was able to instruct Telemachus properly and help the young man assert himself.

All modern mentors could use Athena's help in discharging their duties, but all too many seem instead to be possessed not by her but by Eros (god of desire), Ares (god of war), or some combination of the two.

THE PERENNIAL PROTÉGÉ

I have had a panoply of mentors all my life—ten major ones—beginning in grade school and continuing, in subtly altered form, into the present. I still seek and find them, and they find me, even though they are now often younger than I am, and the current manifestations have many of the same qualities as the memorable ones of my youth. While not all these special bonds ended well, the men and women I have emulated, including those who ultimately disappointed me, did me far more good than harm. They have fulfilled me more deeply, taught me more, and had a more enduring influence than many of my relationships with men I loved.

I have experienced many permutations of this unique and

compelling relationship. Most of my mentors delighted and inspired me or became my friends, but some disappointed me, dropped me, turned on me, or tried to seduce me. I identified with the best of them. They became part of me, and I incorporated their ways of thinking and acting into my adult self. I still see them and hear their voices when I need encouragement.

Being a protégé comes naturally to me; I learned the role at home. It has become so thoroughly integrated into my personality that it feels instinctive. I was the favorite of both my parents, their confidante and the fulfiller of their dreams (my father took me on his rounds at the hospital as a child and introduced me as "my assistant," and the original name my mother gave me on my birth certificate was one she thought I could use as a pen name); my brother, unfortunately for him, lacked the protégé gene and could not meet their emotional needs. The role of being the chosen one, the "master's" favorite (and often his voice, as well), has been a powerful archetype in my life. Subsequently, both men and women chose me for a position that can be simultaneously arduous, thrilling, and oppressive, even if filling it is your fondest desire. Having spent so much time as a child relating to adults and intuiting their psychological requirements made being my teachers' prize pupil easier than fitting in with most others my own age. When my husband watched part of a lesson with my swim coach (I was sixty and my latest mentor was fifty-five at the time), he noted with merriment how intent and connected with him I was. "Still the perfect student, aren't you?" he observed.

I wanted to learn what they had to teach me. I also cultivated the ability to concentrate my attention on them, to make them feel special, to reflect a gratifying image of themselves, and to become what they needed. This empathic enthusiasm was never contrived, because I really meant it; the same impulse led me to become a psychotherapist, a vocation I first felt in my preteen years. For a while, I even thought of becoming a professional translator, which required some of the same attunement to another's innermost thoughts.

The gift of being an ideal audience and helping others articulate what one has heard are prerequisites for being a successful protégé. These qualities made me a sought-after assistant—but also kept me from fully discovering and pursuing my own ideas independently as a writer until middle age. And since maintaining my special position was critical to my sense of self, I had intense anxiety about disappointing those I admired so much. What if I wasn't good enough for them? Even the perfect student isn't always perfect. Fears of fraudulence haunted every one of these relationships, even the best of them. Such fears are extremely common in protégés.

My first memorable protomentor was my fifth-grade teacher, a middle-aged woman with a prim appearance and an ardent sense of mission. She taught me to write and, with an eye to my future, gave me books on female "health heroes" like Marie Curie. Teachers like her intuit things about you—including abilities you actually turn out to have—before you know them yourself. "Possesses initiative," she commented on my report card. This made me proud, even though I had to look up the word in the dictionary. Years later, when my first article was published, she sent me a congratulatory note.

College gave me the opportunity to become the designated protégé of multiple mentors and would-be mentors. This way of relating was so ingrained that several professors whose areas of expertise were of only peripheral interest to me wanted me to be their assistant and to pursue a doctorate in their discipline. One who was on leave from another university encouraged me to follow him back there to work on his research, and another even cherished hopes that I would become a pioneering female rabbi, a profession for which I was utterly unsuited. I found these requests more awkward than flattering—how do you refuse the offer to be someone's acolyte without risking his displeasure? Will the person turn on you like a rejected suitor? At least none of them was vindictive, though none was pleased when I followed my own inclination to become a psychologist, rather than theirs.

One of the most painful relationships I ever had was with a mentor whom I sought out and truly revered, a renowned psychologist who was as much a humanist and moralist as he was a social scientist. A slovenly man in his late forties, he looked vaguely amphibian, with eyes that were both sad and merry, and the undergraduate course he taught, the first in the field I ever took, was entrancing. I wrote papers that he loved and went to see him frequently in his office, where we talked about his work and my future. When he left the university to teach elsewhere, he gave me my pick of any book of his I wanted as a parting gift. We had no further contact until five years after I graduated, when I was living in New York City and he called me entirely unexpectedly. He asked me to come to his hotel room to read and critique a paper he had just written about the psychology of King David; analysis of biblical figures was one of his specialties. He was in town to deliver it at a scholarly meeting and wanted me to make comments before he submitted it for publication. I was astonished and honored that he remembered me and sought me out. Flattered to be asked to comment on his work, as though I were a colleague when I was only a twenty-five-year-old graduate student, I went eagerly to meet him. I read the beginning of the typescript and made some observations, and then we caught up on my life and his. He asked me about my boyfriend and my plans. After an hour,

I rose to leave, promising that I'd read the paper closely and send him more comments. He walked to the door, but instead of opening it for me, he stood in front of it, barring my way. Then he said, in a voice I had never heard before, words I could never have imagined him uttering, which I remember exactly: "I want to kiss you the way you ought to be kissed." Instinctively, I recoiled in shame and horror and blurted out, "No!" I pushed past him and fled down four flights of stairs to avoid being on the same floor with him a minute longer. Nothing like this had ever happened to me before, and I was completely unnerved. Had I unwittingly encouraged him? Shouldn't I have suspected a more than scholarly interest when he invited me to his room? I didn't blame myself; I chalked it up to naïveté and the blindness of idolatry. He seemed pitiful, not a practiced seducer. And I never imagined I had stirred desires I did not feel in the slightest myself. I was deeply shocked, since he had a wife and many children and was at least twenty-five years my senior. I felt humiliated for both of us—for me that I had been clueless, for him that he had so disastrously misread my intent. I was appalled by his desperation and his naked loneliness, things I had never been privy to in all our previous conversations and did not want to be.

I never heard from him again, and for years, I avoided any professional gathering where I might see him, although a woman who had taken his course with me and knew nothing of this incident told me that she had run into him at a meeting a few years later, and he had asked after me. I still shudder when I recall the scene, though I also still remember with fond admiration many of the profound insights and witty observations he made when our relationship seemed an uncomplicated delight. Eventually, I found it almost unbearably sad.

Soon after this sordid denouement, I discovered yet another

mentor, this time a female psychologist, and our relationship had the opposite trajectory. A diminutive Italian with a ferocious intellect, she was my supervisor in psychological testing. There was a fifty-year disparity in our ages and what seemed like an unbridgeable gap between our levels of expertise with the Rorschach inkblot test, which every psychologist at the time had to learn to administer and score. She was a direct heir of Rorschach himself, having studied with his most famous student, and she had a major reputation in the field. When she asked me about my experience with the test during our first session, and I told her the truth (that I had studied it for one semester and administered it only once so far), she literally threw up her hands and said, "How can I teach you? You know nothing, absolutely nothing!" I slunk out of her office feeling wretched and reported this humiliating experience—which was especially terrible because it was so unusual for me to be rebuked by a teacher—to my analyst, who knew her. He assured me that she was just an anxious perfectionist and that I should not despair. Slowly she discovered that she could indeed teach me something; watching a patient come to life from her interpretation of his responses on this subtle and complex instrument was a thrilling demonstration of clinical reasoning. We became fast friends, she made me frittatas, we went to museums together, and she took to introducing me as her "last and best student." I knew and loved her until she died at ninety-six, at which time I found out that she was not only exacting but valorous: she had distributed an anti-Fascist newspaper in Mussolini's Italy during World War II and had been imprisoned for her efforts, which was particularly perilous since her family was Jewish. I subsequently taught the Rorschach test myself based on the profound understanding for its poetry and depth that she bequeathed to me.

Personality is more important than gender in determining

the fate of these relationships, which always have an unconscious component. Mentors of the same sex can behave quite differently. People tend to make the same assumptions about male and female mentors as they make about men and women in general. Having had both a warm, nurturing male analyst and a cool, intellectual female one, I have ample evidence that these stereotypes do not always apply.

The mentor who gave me the most practical help, whom I met in middle age after I wrote my first book, was like a fairy godmother, but one who eventually could not tolerate the change in the dynamics of the relationship when her "godchild" no longer accepted all her magic spells and the behavioral dictates that accompanied them. She was a decade older than I, a savvy, generous, and wickedly funny bestselling author. We soon discovered, to our mutual delight, that we had a great deal in common. I was overjoyed and honored to be taken up by her, and she taught me, with enthusiasm and skill, how to do publicity, which included expert advice on how to be interviewed as well as on makeup and wardrobe. She gloried in my success, and I felt boundless gratitude. We became intimate friends, sharing confidences, meeting regularly for lunch and going out with our husbands, even celebrating holidays together.

Then I wrote a second book. By this time, I was less of a novice and considerably less tractable. I reverted to my own natural style, and she felt no compunction about criticizing my hair (too short), my makeup (nonexistent), and my wardrobe (too unconventional for her taste), all of which she insisted would put me at a disadvantage. This time, I spoke my mind. "I took all your advice, and I can never thank you enough for all you've done for me," I said, "but I never felt completely myself. This time, I have to do it in my own style. People will just have to take me as I am." She didn't argue with me, but she was clearly

offended that I was rebelling against her authority and no longer took her opinions as gospel.

We never had an acrimonious falling-out, but her calls and
our lunch dates became less frequent. There were no more eve-
nings out or invitations to her country house. Soon we were no
longer in each other's lives, not speaking for months and then
years on end, our once-intimate bond becoming no more than
a cordial former friendship. I was grieved and baffled.

Why did she drop me? Here is what I think: she was playing the part of her own controlling mother vis-à-vis her younger,
rebellious self; I also represented the daughter she never had—
and she, a version of the opinionated mother I did have. When
mentors and protégés are the same sex, mother/daughter or
father/son dynamics are hard to avoid. Although her success
was far greater than mine, she probably envied my independence of mind and the fact that her own most important work
was behind her. I was no longer an awed beginner who needed
and hung on her advice, but a younger peer, and she could not
adapt. My admiration for her never diminished, but her ability
to change roles as I matured professionally was limited. I lost
her when I came into my own.

THE END OF THE AFFAIR

Finding a mentor is falling in love, even if the union you seek
is psychic rather than physical—there is the same longing, the
thrill of discovery, the preoccupation with the perfections of the
chosen one. The intensity of your desire to please and to drink
in everything your mentor has to offer can threaten his equilibrium, even if he responds to it. The intoxication of discovering
a remarkable role model prevents you from understanding at
the time that the person you esteem, despite his gifts, has the
flaws humans are prey to. You cannot imagine that his un-

acknowledged insecurities could make him even more anxious about the relationship than you are yourself, causing him to behave coldly or inexplicably and to put distance between the two of you just when you hoped he would respond, approach, and offer more of himself.

Such blinding idealization was especially compelling in the case of two therapists: one an exceptionally gifted senior clinician, and the other an eager and talented novice. Theirs was a bond almost as charged as if she had been his patient, and, since the boundaries between a student and a supervisor are not as clearly delineated, more dangerously ambiguous. Adoration and admiration—both of which are compelling—were mutually misinterpreted, causing scenes of intense embarrassment and distress on both sides, and, eventually, irreparable fissures. The divorce of a marriage of true minds—though there was a partial reconciliation later on—was as shattering as the finale of any other passion.

THE HEIRESS UNAPPARENT

It has been two years since forty-nine-year-old psychiatrist Dr. Helen Archer exchanged a word with her former mentor, Dr. Nathan Gold, and twelve years since they worked together in Chicago during her medical and residency training at a top-notch hospital. They met when Helen was a thirty-year-old, third-year medical student and Nate, then in his early fifties, was the storied director of education. Even though she is now married and has a prominent career in another state, their relationship continues to haunt and unsettle her. She still dreams about him, cries over him, and tortures herself about what went wrong between them. Did she ever really matter to him? Could she still?

The first time she watched Nate conduct a psychiatric

interview with a patient of hers, Helen was smitten. His remarkable clinical sensitivity awed and thrilled her; she vowed to become his disciple. "I was in my first psych rotation, and my first patient, who was having his first psychotic break, was in a locked unit. Nate was the teacher," she recalled. So compelling is her memory of their first encounter that she switched to the present tense to describe it. "In the space of a few minutes, he manages to get this guy talking from his heart about his struggles, his hopes, his fears—something I always wanted to be able to do. He demonstrated how truly profound a psych history can be. This is beautiful, so gracious, so human. He's a genius! It undid me." She used the language of desire to describe her passionate reaction to his skill and her longing to make it her own, though she meant it intellectually and emotionally, not erotically.

Helen's ecstatic admiration only grew over time, as she continued to marvel at the depth and breadth of her designated mentor's art. "For the next two years, I watched miraculous things in that hospital—liver transplants, open-heart surgery— but nothing compared to this. He was so intuitive. He asked questions out of left field, and patients would feel so deeply seen, and they were. He welcomed them back into the human community, and before my eyes, they became people I could identify with. I wept. I hated to leave every session. Seeing this changed my life and became my mission in life." She had found her vocation and the master to emulate.

At first, Helen's dream seemed to be coming true. "He became a major mentor; I worked with him and for him. I was his adoring other, his deeply worshipful audience, and it was very intense." One day, he finally said the words she was longing to hear: "Would you like to be my assistant?" But troubling, even maddening, ambiguities were already creeping into their mutual admiration society. Why, she wondered, hadn't he asked her directly, rather than leaving it up to her? He never seemed to declare himself, to definitively single her out, as mentors often do. There was something elusive, something hesitant, in his personality that made him avoid ever embracing their relationship wholeheartedly.

The master clinician turned out to also be a master of self-protection, and his young devotee threatened his equilibrium even as she fascinated him. "Once I asked him to make the psychotherapy class more than an hour and leave room for discussion, but he refused, with the explanation that 'you should always leave them wanting more,'" she recalled. It seemed as if he was expressing his philosophy of life, not just of pedagogy—what Nate himself would have called "ambivalence" or "withholding" in anybody else.

A pattern emerged that would bedevil the young doctor for the next decade, as long as she was under his aegis. "He kept turning down my requests to be my official clinical supervisor, but then he would advise me informally, as though he was giving me a consolation prize," she said. Things between them were far too vaguely defined, and she never felt secure that she had a special place in Nate's mind and heart, as he had in hers. Even when he seemed to be offering her the keys to the kingdom, it was always at arm's length. Was she pushing him away, or was he backing off?

When Helen later became a psychiatric resident, Nate, true to form, made her two major offers in the most confusing way imaginable. First, he informed her offhandedly that he was "going to let [her] teach the psychotherapy class," and then, in an equally casual tone, he asked her to go to the next departmental meeting of the psychiatry faculty in his stead. But the way he expressed the second, more personal request made her feel defeated rather than victorious. "He warned me that there was terrible backbiting in these meetings and seemed dumbfounded when I asked playfully whether he was setting me up to fail." Her teasing remark was actually a bid for reassurance, but it had the opposite effect on the highly sensitive recipient. "He looked like I had stabbed him when I said that," she said. "He was deeply hurt by my not immediately accepting his offer. It was as though he was grooming me for his job and I was refusing to take over for him. He acted as if he was handing me the most precious achievement of his life and I threw it back in his face. But he never *said*, 'I want to hand over my legacy to you.'" She needed words, not just deeds, a straightforward declaration that she was his chosen one, which was something he could never do. To her chagrin, he rescinded the offer that she attend the meeting as his surrogate, although he did "let" her teach the class.

Helen reacted to Nate's ambivalence with some ambivalence of her own by refusing to go into psychoanalytic therapy as he had hoped she would. This would have been a prerequisite for becoming an analyst herself. "I objected on feminist grounds," she explained, alluding to the misogyny and general befuddlement about female psychology that was a feature of the classical Freudian approach in vogue at the time. But she was also asserting her independence from him, the analyst extraordinaire, and punishing him for his refusal to declare her his heir. Why should she unilaterally expose her soul to a therapist when her mentor refused to examine his own conduct? Nate's poetic term for Freud's Oedipus complex, the passionate desire a young boy or girl feels for the opposite-sex parent, was "doomed longing." At the time, this was considered the fundamental predicament of childhood, a major theme that analysis unmasks. But Helen had had enough doomed longing with him (though her passion was emotional rather than physical) to go looking for more on the analytic couch.

Why did these two people, who were obviously simpatico in many fundamental ways and shared a rare professional rapport, keep frustrating and misinterpreting each other? They both had larger-than-life personalities, a knack for showmanship, and a need for an appreciative audience, but she wanted everything verbalized and out in the open, and he was far less forthcoming in his personal relationships—particularly one with an ardent young woman—than he was on the ward. Outside the safe confines of his professional role, the more she pressed him, the less he gave her. The best of him, she said with a sardonic laugh, "appeared only with patients and strangers." Mixed messages were his forte, and he only "gave" at the office. Mentor and protégé did a decades-long dance that a colleague of mine has dubbed "come-away closer": he made ambiguous and seductive offers, she demurred, he retreated, she implored, and then he promised the coveted prize she hungered for, only to withdraw both himself and his offer. Their back-and-forth was simultaneously over the top, as one or the other of them was sure to be "dumbfounded," "shocked," "deeply hurt," "disappointed," and so on in every interaction they had. The two psychiatrists were driving each other crazy.

Helen was unable to access her own clinical skills to understand what was going on or recognize the impact of her own behavior on the man she idolized. She did not see that she threatened and overwhelmed Nate as much as she impressed him. Her desperate desire to break through to him was driven by an unconscious need to be acknowledged by him as her own father had never done. "There were many ways in which my father seemed not to be interested in me, and he never told me he loved me," she said. "I can't believe a feeling is real unless it's put into words." She could not endure being Nate's heiress unapparent; she had to have it spelled out.

Nate, for his part, could not approach Helen directly and declare his intention that she should succeed him because that would have been a frightening admission of what she meant to him. Reticence and avoidance of intimacy characterized all his relationships—"*Everybody* has a fucked-up relationship with Nate," a more experienced colleague told her, to her great relief—but the unacknowledged physical attraction that he felt for her* made it worse. (Nate was married with children.) He inconsistently kept her at arm's length to fight the urge to take her in his arms.

Only in retrospect was Helen able to understand what each party contributed to their excruciating union. "It took me years to realize that watching him tune in to patients made me long not just to learn to do that myself but to be understood by him as he understood them," she said. The girl who had never seen "the gleam in her father's eye"†—the delighted, loving sense of specialness every child needs—longed for her mentor to bestow it upon her as an adult. "I wanted to say, 'Turn your high beams on me.'" Her raw desire for his undivided attention terrified Nate and made him flee, lest he be unable to resist.

In her fourth year of residency, Helen was appointed a chief resident and given a title that coincidentally resembled Nate's, and she no longer reported to him. He let her know that he was shocked that she took the job, as though she was usurping his position. (Of course, she intended no such thing, but he

---

* This is my speculation, based on his behavior, the comments Helen's colleagues made about Nate to her later on, and her own subliminal awareness at the time, which became clearer to her in retrospect.
† Kohut's resonant phrase is "the gleam in the mother's eye," but of course this refers to either parent.

could not see that.) Helen took the risk of going to his home office to discuss it. "For the first time, I broached the subject of us, but he immediately shut down the conversation by saying, 'We have no context or form to work on this.'" Nate deflected her by hiding behind the administrative hierarchy—he couldn't stand the thought of more personal contact between them—and Helen felt so rejected she did not think to say, *No context? How about the context of two people who have a long, complicated history?* She left and wrote Nate a letter—what she called "the most courageously honest letter of my life"—addressing their folie à deux. "'I see you as man of great integrity and great reserve, but I'm in this transference vortex and I'm having trouble coming out.'" Of course, he never answered, by post or in person.

At the end of her psychiatric training, Helen finally separated from Nate by falling in love, getting engaged, and following her fiancé to Wisconsin. This move, and the reason she made it, did not please her mentor; she could tell by his demeanor that he was crushed that she was leaving. A colleague jocularly warned her, "Tell your husband to watch out. Don't be surprised if a courtly gentleman sneaks into your bedroom and tries to stab him."

When they were 150 miles apart, Nate became slightly less distant. He came to Helen's new hometown to attend a professional meeting, and she called him. "I said, 'Nate, I miss you,' and he took me to dinner at this unbelievable restaurant, the best in the state. I decided to talk about ideas, and we had a wonderful evening, although he repeatedly mentioned his wife." But Helen finally mentioned her and Nate. "I told him that I had realized things about our relationship, that I was ashamed of my longing, which had made me behave in confusing ways, and he actually said, 'Are there things that I did that made this hard for you?'

"'I wanted you to love me and care about me,' I said."

His explanation was convoluted. He said, "I didn't want the group to punish you for being my favorite, so I protected you against being special to me. I never assumed we'd stay in touch—we don't know each other that well." Helen did not buy this. "Although I felt like a kicked puppy, I said, 'You were of singular importance to me—how could we not have a lifelong relationship?'" To this, he had no reply. Denial is a powerful force that even the most seasoned psychoanalyst can fail to recognize when he is in its throes himself.

The last time they met was an unexpected encounter at the funeral of a mutual colleague. His guard was down, and his behavior, perhaps because of the occasion, was considerably more revealing than usual. "Nate saw me, seemed shocked, collected himself, and then greeted me. We shook hands, and he kept holding mine." She told him what he meant to her. "I want you to know that everything I do is your legacy. Watching you all those years changed me. You taught me to return the outcast into the circle of humanity." Her guard was down too, so she also told him how trying he was. "You never meet *me*. I make myself so vulnerable and you never show up—you've been crazy too." But the moment passed, and he retreated once more into silence. This time, she was fully prepared never to hear from him again. Their exchange, she assumed, would trail off, as in a Henry James short story, never to be fulfilled.

But she was wrong. Two years later, Helen got an unexpected "Friend" request on Facebook. It was from Nate. "I almost fell off my chair," she told me. A little research revealed that he had opened his account just hours earlier and that she had been one of the first people he contacted. She accepted, with the old anticipation but with more insight than she had when they were working so closely together at the same hospital. Time, distance, and maturity have sharpened her perceptions but not severed her tie to him or diminished the intensity of her distress over his elusiveness. Maybe, she hopes, she will finally see the real Nate—Facebook to Facebook, even if not face to face. Or has she already seen all that there is? Has age—he is now seventy-five—mellowed him? Will the protective shield of the Internet allow him to reveal more of himself to his former acolyte? The jury is still out. Sometimes the second act between mentors and protégés is every bit as curious, compelling, and unpredictable as the first.

In Greek mythology, the bandit Procrustes had an iron bed in which he forced every passerby to spend the night. If the victim was too short, Procrustes stretched him to fit, and if he was too tall, Procrustes chopped off his legs to make him fit; everyone who slept in his bed was killed because nobody fit exactly. Many mentors—particularly narcissistic ones—have procrustean standards, requiring their protégés to be exact replicas of themselves. They fall in love with what they believe is their own reincarnation. When that reincarnation turns out to be a different person, the mentor feels betrayed and enraged and can turn childish, cowardly, and vengeful. While such a mentor does not literally murder the offending protégé, he punishes, banishes, or disowns him, arbitrarily blaming the former favorite for being himself.

One of the most embarrassing examples of a mentor-protégé relationship gone horribly wrong occurred between the founding titans in my own field, Sigmund Freud and Carl Gustav Jung. Their passionate friendship and collaboration began in 1906 and ended in very public grief and rage six years later.

At the start, Freud was a renowned fifty-year-old Jewish Viennese neurologist and psychiatrist who was in the midst of founding psychoanalysis, and Jung, a Swiss Christian, was a brilliant thirty-one-year-old psychiatrist on his way up, with a knack for treating psychotic patients and a taste for the occult. Their love affair began when Jung sent Freud a book he had written in which he praised Freud's insights. Freud, who had a lifelong hunger for adulation and whose ideas were still being scoffed at in orthodox psychiatric circles, was delighted, grateful, and impressed. It did not hurt that Jung was one of the very few non-Jewish friends of psychoanalysis, which its founder desperately wanted to be more widely accepted and not hobbled by the medical establishment's anti-Semitic prejudice. They talked for thirteen hours the first time they met. Very soon, Freud was referring to Jung as his "adopted son," "crown prince," and "successor." With his adoptive "father's" backing, Jung was made editor of the psychoanalytic society's annual publication and then became chairman for life of the International Psychoanalytic Association—an appointment that was fated to last only two years.

After the first thrill of mutual discovery died down, each began to notice worrisome differences from the other, among them the utility of religion, the centrality of sexuality, and the nature of the unconscious. Jung, a minister's son, wrote that "human nature is by nature religious." Freud, an atheist and rationalist, thought that religion was an infantile delusion. Repressed sexual desire and incestuous wishes, along with aggression, were the central causes of neurotic suffering for Freud, and he believed that "sublimating" these impulses ("Where id was, there ego shall be" was his later formulation of this idea) was the way to freedom. Jung thought that "individuating" and integrating opposing aspects of the "self" was the proper goal.

He discerned a "collective unconscious" of "archetypes" beneath the "personal unconscious" where repressed impulses resided; Freud never accepted this. In addition to their theoretical differences, Jung was already chafing at his role as acolyte by 1912. Both were strong and exceptionally gifted personalities and original thinkers who needed to be in charge.

The growing tension between them reached the breaking point when Jung published *The Psychology of the Unconscious*— an unconscious that was nothing like Freud's. Freud dealt with his disciple's apostasy by writing him cold, wounded letters and pointedly avoiding seeing Jung when he took a trip to Switzerland to visit another colleague in a nearby town. Jung responded by writing enraged, infantile letters of his own to Freud, in one of which he said he would "pluck the Prophet by the beard." Hell hath no fury like two analysts scorned.

The bitterness of their estrangement and mutual sense of personal betrayal made it impossible to keep their inevitable parting of the ways from disintegrating into name-calling. They detested each other for the rest of their lives, and many of their followers continue to do so to this day. Freud was deeply pained by their break, but Jung suffered a near-psychotic episode. In later years, the former crown prince diverged radically from his mentor's ideas and became renowned as the founder of what he called "analytical psychology." Ultimately, the only person who could succeed Freud was one whose loyalty was unassailable, with whom he did not need to compete because her mind was shaped by him in his own image,* and she was his designated and self-designated keeper of the flame: his daughter Anna.

---

* She had also been her father's patient.

THE ENFANT TERRIBLE AND THE BOY GENIUS

When Jung parted ways with Freud, he at least had a large practice, a growing reputation in his own right, and a position at a famous clinic. He and his former mentor and now nemesis also lived in different countries. Deposed protégés whose mentors are their bosses don't have it so easy.

The protégé, who began writing for his idol, the editor in chief, when he was fourteen, went to work for him and his journal of opinion as soon as he graduated from college. A year later, when the protégé was only twenty-three, his new boss took him to lunch at the fancy Italian restaurant that served as his cafeteria. As soon as they raised their first glass of wine, the famous journalist announced his verdict. "I have decided that you are going to succeed me."

The recipient of this declaration was beyond astonishment. "The best word to describe what he did was 'breathtaking,'" he recollected thirty-six years later in far more tranquility than he had felt at the time. "It was completely unexpected; I had no hint. I was the most junior member of the staff, just out of school. First I was to be made the youngest senior editor in the history of the magazine"—this was announced with due pomp soon afterward—"and later I would become managing editor so I could learn how to run it." He was also informed that he would own the magazine outright when his mentor stepped down and that, along with the title, he was inheriting 100 percent of the stock. The current owner had a son of his own who was also a writer, though not a political one; since he did not aspire to the post, the arrangement would not be contested.

Why did the editor in chief, who was fifty-two at the time, at the height of his renown and influence and with no plans to retire, drop this bombshell when he did and the way he did? "I was thinking of going to law school, and he wanted to head off my leaving with a grand gesture; he specialized in grand gestures," said the protégé. "A good way to keep somebody in the building is to offer him the keys to the building."

The building and its contents would be the least of it, he realized with apprehension at the time. To inherit this mantle was to become the spokesman of the political movement of which the magazine was the bible and the editor in chief the messiah, with the attendant duties (defining the mission of the magazine and representing it in the media), responsibilities (endlessly finding and feting donors to the cause), and perks (a glamorous public life) of the role, all of which were utterly alien to the heir's temperament and experience and nothing he had aspired to in his wildest dreams. A gifted writer he already was, but becoming a pundit, celebrity, bon vivant, and media star by fiat seemed inconceivable. How would he ever fill his mentor's shoes? He was so overwhelmed by the job he was summarily informed that he was being groomed for and so in thrall to the man who currently held it—who had, in fact, created it in his own larger-than-life image—that he never dared ask himself whether he wanted to do it, let alone express any doubts about his similarity to the personage whose identity he was slated to assume.

The protégé's precocity clinched the deal for his patron because it reminded him of his own. How could the man who had written a bestselling polemic at age twenty-one fail to see himself in the eloquent recent graduate of the same university he had attended, who as a high school freshman had sent in an article that he himself could have written, particularly since its cheeky, contrarian style had been inspired by the editor in chief's own prose? Overjoyed to find a mirror that reflected so well on himself, he had scrawled "This kid is a *genius*!" on the typescript when a staff member gave it to him for comment, and he published the piece as a cover story with the author's age prominently displayed. He might as well have added, "This Just In: I've Found the Next Me!" In fact, although their writing had a similar sparkle and punch, their personalities were worlds apart. The editor in chief never took into consideration or even noticed that the original "me" was an extrovert and the new "me" an introvert, that the first edition was wealthy and worldly and the second was a naive child of the middle class, or that he himself was supremely confident and self-directed and his successor self-conscious and anxious to please. Talent in a kindred spirit was the only thing he saw.

Beyond literary style and a common political philosophy, what created such intoxicating synergy between them? The protégé's father, a self-contained, unexpressive man, felt little affinity for his younger son and preferred his elder son. The mentor had an intermittently contentious relationship with his own son, who was slightly older than his protégé and considerably more rebellious. The younger man sought an appreciative and inspiring father; the elder one wanted a responsive son who shared his vision. Each seemed to be a perfect match for what the other needed.

This was a once-in-a-lifetime offer the heir apparent could not—dare not—refuse or even consider the implications of too closely. To question his idol's judgment at all would be to risk displeasing the man to whom he owed everything. "He was the most exciting person in the world to me," he said. "I'd been reading his work and watching his TV show for years. He perfectly expressed my own thoughts and beliefs and championed the political cause that mattered most to me. I'd corresponded with him; he'd recognized my talent and given me national prominence as a teenager." He feared, with justification, that he risked losing his unique position if he demurred. Raising any question at all might well be interpreted as ingratitude and cast doubt on his aptness as his mentor's chosen one.

I recall being at least as astonished as my boyfriend (to whom I became engaged the next year and married the following one) when he told me the news the night he received it, looking as much dazed as dazzled. As exciting as it was in the abstract for our future together, I felt queasy about the proposition. Was this, I wondered from the start, what he really wanted? And yet, how could he refuse? To these misgivings in his behalf were added my wondering how on earth I was going to become the official hostess for this small but potent empire, a position I was at least as ill suited for. How could we sponsor private classical music concerts by famous artists in our two-bedroom apartment, as the editor in chief regularly did in his palatial East Side duplex? My own future was in the balance too. Just as the wizard Merlin had revealed the future to his protégé Arthur before his coronation, including Arthur's demise, I had vague fears that there was something ominous in the fate that this modern-day magician was revealing to his crown prince.

Everything seemed to be going as planned when, a year later, the editor in chief made another grand gesture, this one inauspicious in retrospect. "He said, 'I want to talk to you,' and I figured we'd go to lunch again, but instead he took me to Mexico for the weekend; it was a piece of performance art. He insisted that we stay in the same hotel and the same suite he and his son had stayed in, but once we got there, he didn't tell me anything." Being forthright, particularly with criticism, was not among his boss's gifts. "Finally, on the last night, he said that he wanted me to 'step up' to the role he'd assigned me. In essence, he was saying, 'I've decided you're me. You have to be more like me than you are.'" He did not elaborate, and of course his heir apparent was afraid to ask for details or advice; it might have broken the charm.

The editor in chief made another telling gesture on that trip. He bought a turquoise-encrusted silver plate for his protégé to deliver to me when they returned. So sumptuous a gift was far beyond my fiancé's—we had become engaged by then—means to buy for me himself; that it wasn't at all my taste was beside the point. Was this showing off, pulling rank, competing with a younger man who didn't have the resources to be a challenger? Even now, my husband remembers the sting that having to present me with his boss's purchase epitomized and what it stirred up in him. "I felt humiliated and inadequate," he said. "I thought, 'I can't do this. I've got to tell him I have serious doubts about this; what should we do?' But I couldn't take him into my confidence because I couldn't face it myself. 'If I'm not going to accept the offer, can we continue to have a relationship? If I don't become the next him, will he need me at all? What will I do?'" He was still bowled over by the honor, but the weight of expectation that had been placed upon him, with no guidance on how to fulfill it—since they were the same person in his boss's eyes, none should be needed—felt crushing. No one, he was vaguely beginning to realize, can step effortlessly into a ready-made identity. A paralyzing paradox faced him: if he became his own true self, he would lose his special role in the life of the man he adored, longed to emulate, and depended on for his livelihood.

For the next eight years, there were no more subtle complaints from headquarters, and the plan seemed to be going swimmingly. The protégé was given all manner of plum assignments designed to showcase his talents and to initiate him into the position that would someday—though it was never made clear exactly when—be his. He edited a book of his patron's columns, ghostwrote the most challenging parts of his volu-minous correspondence ("I could impersonate him on paper," he observed), produced portraits of all the presidential candi-dates, oversaw the magazine's thirtieth anniversary edition, and became its managing editor. He also wrote his own first book—the editor in chief arranged for his own editor to take it on. Any misgivings he had about this poisoned proposition went underground. "'Is this right for me?' is more formulated than the doubts I let myself have," he said. "To even ask the question meant either risking his displeasure or failing, both awful alternatives."

Then, as swiftly and shockingly as the keys were proffered, they were snatched away. The protégé, now thirty-two, went out to lunch one day and came back to find a letter from his mentor on his desk, marked "Confidential." The deposing was done with more elaborately defensive eloquence than the orig-inal anointing. "It is now plain to me that you are not suited to serve as editor-in-chief after my retirement. This sentence will no doubt have for a while a heavy, heavy effect on your morale, and therefore I must at once tell you that I have reached the conclusion irrevocably. You have no executive flair. . . . You do not have executive habits [or] an executive turn of mind, and I would do you no service, nor the magazine, by imposing it on you." After lowering the boom, he bestowed honest praise. "What you have is a very rare talent, so rare that I found it not only noticeable but striking when you were very young. You will go down in history as a very fine writer, perhaps even a great writer." Writing, he said, was what the recipient naturally inclined to, whereas editing would be "asphyxiative" to his true gift—perhaps as he thought it had been to his own. The mes-sage could be summed up as "do what you're actually good at, and not what I wanted you to be good at just because I was good at it." This turned out to be excellent advice, although the delivery left something to be desired. The editor in chief wanted his soon-to-be-ex-protégé to stay on as a senior editor, and of course to continue to write for him, but at a 60 percent pay cut. To avoid dealing with the fallout, the editor in chief conveniently, if cravenly, left the country before his letter was delivered.

In addition to coping with a blow of gargantuan proportions to his ego, the still-young man, who was no longer as young as he was when his future was mapped out for him, now had to figure out what to do for himself, all the while coping with shame, rage, and the devastation of having been treated abominably by the person he most esteemed. He went from precocious to superannuated in one day. "I had no idea what else I could do," he recalled. "This had been my world since I was fourteen. I'd never written for anybody else—the magazine was an enchanted cave. I was paranoid, sure that everybody knew what had happened, but in fact nobody did until I wrote about it myself decades later. I crafted a cover story that I was cutting back to leave myself more time to write, and I learned to be a freelance journalist; I proceeded to do what I should have been doing all along." He never stopped writing for the magazine, and still does so, but it was no longer the center of his universe.

Eventually, he discovered that being a biographer and chronicler of American history used all the political, psychological, and literary acumen he had been accumulating in the cave. His first historical biography—not surprisingly of George Washington, a father figure who did not disappoint and whose motto was, unlike the editor in chief's, "We must take men as we find them"—made the front page of *The New York Times Book Review*. From then on, he defined his own future, lecturing, making documentaries, and fulfilling his early promise in his own way.

It took longer to mend the tie with his former mentor than it did to create a professional identity for himself. "Of course the relationship chilled," he said. "We were never rude, but when he complimented articles of mine, it felt sour." The elder man never apologized, and they never directly discussed what had happened, but their relationship reconstituted itself with new warmth and less of a power differential over time through efforts on both their parts. Theirs was a slow, but authentic, rapprochement. "The first thing that impressed me later was the concern he showed when I got ill," the ex-protégé said. "In the manner typical of him, he had a piano delivered to me, knowing that I, like him, loved the instrument, and remembering that we had played duets together." This was another grand gesture, to be sure, but it also revealed another side of the man: genuine affection, generosity, and sympathy for people who mattered to him. He even put his money where his mouth was, giving his former surrogate son a large sum, as you would to a family member, to refurbish "your dream house," the country place we had recently bought, where many years later we entertained him. He also gave us a handsome old shotgun to defend ourselves against human and animal intruders—a far more practical gift than the turquoise-encrusted plate.

Then, as swiftly and shockingly as the keys were snatched away, they were proffered a second time.

The person the editor in chief picked to take his place when he finally did decide to retire, a seasoned British journalist who was nothing like him, naturally failed to please him. "It turned out nobody could succeed him—he was unique," said his older and wiser former heir. He was astonished all over again when the man who had concluded decisively that he lacked executive flair thought he saw some that he had missed the first time around and approached him once more. This time, though, the editor in chief made a request, as if to a peer, rather than presenting a fait accompli to a novice, saying, "If you don't want to succeed me, I want to hear it from you formally." Was this a sincere desire to redo history, an authentic reconsideration, or simply a matter of what he considered courtesy? His motivation was never clear. But this time, his former protégé was absolutely clear, because he had found his own voice and his own vocation. He said no.

Only then could the once and almost-future protégé realize that his mentor had done him a favor by firing him in advance from a position he had never aspired to. "He must have had an inchoate sense that becoming him 2.0 would be more, but also less, than what I ought to have been doing. It really would have cut into my writing time." Ultimately, another, even younger, man was chosen to be the successor. He too was nothing like the editor in chief, and the magazine, as is natural, metamorphosed into something quite different in his hands, suited to a different time and an unrecognizably altered media climate, in which political pundits were of a radically different type than they once had been.

The former protégé had an opportunity to pay a formal tribute to the man who had catapulted him into the world in which he ultimately made his mark in his own way. "My symbolic kiss of peace was when he stepped down in 1990," he recalled. "An important statesman threw him a dinner to which he invited me. I planned a toast, since I knew I would be called on for one. I quoted Yeats's poem 'Beautiful Lofty Things,' which talks about his own father's 'beautiful, mischievous head'"—for the editor in chief's head was truly both beautiful and mischievous, and his only real protégé wanted him to know he knew it. "He was moved and asked for a copy of my remarks. But I didn't give it to him. I said I didn't have one. I did that because I knew if I gave one to him he would have printed it in the magazine. This was for him and that audience only; I didn't want him broadcasting it to the world. I was through being his trophy. I did, however, print it in the book I wrote about our relationship after he died. I was man enough finally to print a loving tribute myself, but also man enough not to let *him* print it." The *enfant terrible* stayed an *enfant*, if a less terrible one, all his life, but the boy genius became a man—his own man.

MY MENTOR, MY SELF: MENTORS IN MATURITY

Mentors are not just for the young. They can be found at any age if you seek them, although what you need and what you get from them changes later in life. Since your own character is no longer unformed and your identity is more secure, you are no longer so naive, impressionable, or adoring. As a result, you are more conscious of personality quirks, more attuned to the dynamics between you, and freer to know and to speak your mind. Since these late editions of the mentor-protégé relationship are usually voluntary, you are not beholden to the mentor as an employer or a professor or as a professional role model. You don't have to be as careful because less is at stake. At last, there is no discrepancy of experience, only of expertise in a particular area.

I learned all manner of things from my panoply of mentors, but my current one gave me something unexpected, which turned out to be even more potent and profound than the skill—a new way of swimming—that I came to him to learn. He never consciously sought to teach it to me, and I never sought to learn it from him, and yet it sustained me through the most terrifying experience of my life and continues to unfold its riches. In addition to making a sleek and speedy swimmer out of me, he taught me the uses of adversity.

At age fifty-seven, I decided I wanted to relearn to swim and went looking for a coach. Orthopedic injuries had made it impossible for me to continue studying Middle Eastern dance, and I felt the need for some of that same expressiveness and whole-body involvement that swimming alone could safely provide. I'd loved the water all my life and had swum since childhood, but I wanted to delve deeper. I saw an ad for his technique—it said "Discover your inner fish"—and I was hooked.

Thus began a decade-long and still ongoing dialogue between my coach and me that metamorphosed from focusing on the technique of moving joyfully and expertly through the water (or, as he would say, "with the water") to considering the psychological and philosophical implications of his innovative approach. He told me early on that I had the combination of strength and endurance that constituted "the makings of a long-distance swimmer"—an aptitude of which I was completely unaware, a skill I had certainly never aspired to acquire—but that I subsequently discovered suited both my body type and my emotional constitution. His approach, painstaking, patient, and passionate, transformed me into an athlete for the first time in my life, and I became what I called the "guinea fish" on which he tried out his constantly evolving ideas. I worked with him practically every week, and the lessons were a highlight of those weeks. The water became both my refuge and a source of intellectual stimulation.

At first, I felt intimidated by his prowess—was I good enough to study with such a teacher? But I need not have been, because I have never known a more accessible or generous expert in anything. The thing that particularly suited him to his vocation was that the sport he revolutionized never came easily to him; he wasn't a naturally gifted athlete. He hadn't even been good enough to make the sixth-grade team at his Catholic school. And yet he became, in middle age, a champion distance swimmer and an attuned and inspiring coach with an international reputation, whose mission was to illuminate the sensual and spiritual joys of being in the water by reimagining how human bodies, with their inconvenient appendages, move most efficiently in that alien element.

My coach's motto, based on his life experience as well as his unusually optimistic temperament, was "Injury Is Opportunity," and he took it seriously both in and out of the pool. He himself was no stranger to pain and suffering, since he had sustained many injuries as an athlete and had to contend daily with a congenital tremor that caused his hands to shake uncontrollably at times. He didn't just profess this attitude; he embodied it, never complaining or feeling victimized by something that would have seriously frustrated or depressed most people. He swam through it with remarkable panache and approached his students' physical limitations and psychological struggles the same way he handled his own.

I had an unexpected opportunity to discover the uses of injury and to put my coach's philosophy into practice. One day eight years into our partnership, I showed up for a lesson with a number of unaccountable bruises in strange places. Within a week, I was admitted to the hospital with a rare form of dangerously acute leukemia whose only virtue was that it was curable. The cure entailed daily infusions of arsenic for a month as an inpatient, followed by another nine months of the same treatment as an outpatient. It was as awful as it sounds.

The night before I had to start the outpatient regimen, I had an extraordinary dream that defined the task before me. My coach and I were standing on the shore of a forbidding body of water. We could dimly see the other shore far off in the distance. This was clearly the course for a very long, treacherous open-water swim that I was about to undertake, finding my way and conserving my strength all alone, through darkness, undertow, jellyfish, and dread. It reminded me of the English Channel, the Everest of swimming, which my coach had swum as part of a relay team at age sixty, an exceptional feat. On both shores there were massive, rocky, precipitous hills, which I saw that I would have to navigate both going down to the water and coming back up from it—a reference to the treacherous physical and psychological experiences ahead. As much as I dreaded the treatment, I had not consciously realized that it would be as difficult to clamber back up to the normal world at the end of the ordeal as it was to submerge myself in that dangerous, uncharted "ocean" of pain and fear at the beginning; the two struggles were of a piece. The scene was a physical representation of, and a psychic preparation for, what lay before me.

But I was not alone. My coach turned to me and said in his calm, direct manner, "There is much to be learned from these daunting cliffs."

I awoke deeply relieved, confident, with a mission—to be a student of my own experience, just as I was in my swim lessons—rather than a victim. I knew what I was facing, and that, arduous as the labor would be, it would offer me something priceless.

I clung to the dream image and to my coach's voice throughout my ordeal. For the next nine months, I returned repeatedly to this dream. My coach's pronouncement reminded me that I could, and I would, convert suffering into knowledge. He was telling me that this "race" was, blessedly, finite and that I had the will and the expertise not just to endure it but to win it.

There's much to be learned from these daunting mentors, from the worst to the best of them. They immeasurably enrich your fund of knowledge of the world, of human nature, and of yourself.

8

TRAUMATIC FRIENDSHIP

FRIENDSHIP'S END

There is no term to describe the breakup of a passionate friendship, no ritual or legal proceeding to mark its end, the way divorce does for marriage, even though it often leaves just as large a hole in the psyche. Lost friends are as haunting as lost lovers and just as hard to replace. The more abrupt and inexplicable their behavior, the more troubling and insidious the toll. The fallout from betrayal by friends begins early on and can resonate for decades.

The longing to belong and to be prized by one's peers permeates childhood and adolescence and can be compelling and anxiety provoking at any time in life, as the common dread of cocktail parties in adulthood attests. This need—as old and as potent as erotic desire—is a fundamental part of being human;

according to object relations theory,* we become ourselves by being recognized and loved by others, originally by our parents; their role is later assumed (at least to some extent) by our contemporaries. Therefore, narcissistic injury, the humiliating recognition that you mean less to another than he or she means to you, looms large. It is a common feature of the primordial rifts with childhood "friends"—typically playmates with whom the connection is based as much on proximity as on compatibility—that are an inevitable part of learning to negotiate peer relationships. Occasionally, these accidental companions have the qualities we later seek in genuine soul mates, but usually more superficial commonalities (being in the same class, living on the same block, riding on the same bus) cause us to be thrown together with them, and at first they are the only contemporaries other than family members whom we know.

Some of these early rejections are simply acts of casual thoughtlessness that are not even intentional, as when the playmate to whom I offered to lend my favorite Nancy Drew mystery when we were both eight years old casually remarked that a copy was already circulating in her group of close friends. It's

---

* Along with Heinz Kohut's self psychology, the British object relations perspective is probably the most potent influence on contemporary psychoanalytic theory and practice. This approach is based on the premise that human beings do not develop in isolation and that their relations with their original "objects" (parents) and the meanings they attribute to these experiences create the self. From the very beginning, contrary to Freudian orthodoxy, the people we love influence every aspect of our lives; inner conflicts and drives are not simply projected onto the outside world. Hence, parent-child and sibling-sibling relationships are the template for all subsequent ties—for good and for ill. Freudian orthodoxy in its original form held that inner conflicts and drives are innate, that they unfold autonomously and are then projected onto other people whose special characteristics are essentially irrelevant.

nothing personal; we are simply not on their radar, but we experience the slight of not being invited to the birthday party or picked for the baseball team as devastating because of our own vulnerability and the intensity of our hunger to be recognized and chosen by others we deem valuable companions as much for their social status as their personal charms.

Very few people navigate childhood, let alone adolescence and adulthood, without experiencing several such splits. It is striking that the sting of these early exclusions often lasts longer and embeds itself deeper than the tie to the actual person who does the excluding and that we tend to remember the circumstances long after we have ceased to have the slightest interest in the perpetrators; the only things I remember about the girl who spurned my offer is her name and my reaction. Along with the serious psychic wounds inevitably inflicted by parents and siblings, these rejections become the prelude to the deeper and darker ones that follow.

Crushes on friends (which often include crushes on what particular idealized people and groups represent) happen as early as we have friends, but the most tumultuous ones occur simultaneously with first loves, of which they are a variation. Many people date their initial experience with the ecstasies and torments of their intense nonsexual romances from around the same time they first fell in love and their early lovers fell out of love with them.

It is disturbingly easy to be catapulted back to the high school cafeteria, where, I vividly recall, there was a table of "popular" girls, among whose number I longed to be counted, whom I vainly attempted to emulate by dressing like they did and taking off my glasses as I waited in line, since none of them seemed to need corrective lenses. I could hardly see without mine, but I felt I looked better to those looking at me, and that was what counted. I admired one of these girls in particular from afar, who epitomized everything I wanted to be. She seemed so cool and confident (she was a pert cheerleader as well as a decent student, her hair was perfect, and her flirtation skills flawless) at a time when I considered myself too shy and serious, my hair hopelessly lank, and my manner never clever enough. Once or twice she and her retinue deigned to make room for me, and I was jubilant to be invited into their charmed circle. But I soon realized that though I was not actually spurned, a seat was never saved for me as it was for the anointed ones, and I never seemed to be sought after or missed. No confidences were whispered to me, which would have been a real sign of membership. Since I hadn't done anything egregious or obnoxious or alienating that I knew of, I concluded that I was excluded because of who I was, and that was the one thing I was helpless to change. This experience had such a potent impact on me that when I attended a high school reunion in my hometown at the age of forty-seven, I avoided that cafeteria like the plague. But I did make it my business to go to the library, to which I donated a copy of my latest book; that was my revenge and compensation.

For a thrilling instant, I felt I had vaulted one of life's most daunting gaps and safely landed in with the in crowd and its flawless leader. The memory of my moment of belonging and its evanescence is actually more viscerally alive and more unmooring than my concurrent recollection of the "popular" boy with the green eyes and the red convertible—he would have been considered a catch by anyone at that table in the cafeteria—the first one to kiss me and to take me out for New Year's Eve, who three months later stopped calling and pursued somebody else for no apparent reason. Both seemed heavenly gifts that were snatched away, leaving me helpless and bereft.

Along with the deeply etched woes of family life, these are the twin precedents of every subsequent rejection, including my first serious betrayal by an intimate friend several years thereafter. The need to be accepted is no less compelling than the need to be embraced; they are siblings.

Contrary to what most people assume, hormones are not the prime—and certainly not the sole—motivator of relationships, even in adolescence. To be admired and desired are merged in all our important connections. Our choice of friends—especially the friends we idolize—is influenced by the same life events and family dynamics that lead us to particular lovers; how we deal with abandonment by these special ones comes from the same sources. The qualities we seek in bosom companions change with experience—for me at this time in my life, psychological mindedness, generosity, steadfastness, and a kindred sense of humor have trumped what passed for sophistication in 1963—but the desolation of losing them is strikingly similar at fifteen and sixty-five.

One of the most devastating aspects of being spurned by a beloved friend, whenever in life it happens and on whatever pretext, is the sense of unreality it induces; you think, can this actually be happening between *us*? To lose someone who is still physically present yet suddenly psychically absent or altered seems unbelievable. No one can be prepared for such a sudden, shattering rupture. Dramatic departures or screaming denouements are less common than the uncanny experience of the person simply slipping out of reach or causing you to disappear from her consciousness. A rejecting friend, like the Boojum in Lewis Carroll's nightmarish poem "The Hunting of the Snark," makes you "softly and suddenly vanish away" when you approach her, and you fall into the void. Knowing you will never laugh together again, sharing confidences with reckless ease, causes its own brand of helpless longing. The explanation, if any is offered, can never fully explain, because the motivation to rebuff a former confidante comes from deeply unconscious sources, such as envy, jealousy, fear of merger with a disavowed aspect of the self, and revisiting unresolved conflicts with parents (usually mothers for women friends) or siblings.

The development director of a large corporation, whom I have known for years, told me recently that her best friend in high school had accosted her after class one day and said, "I've just realized that you are everything I don't want to be"—and avoided her forever after. Her voice trembled when she recalled the incident. A Web designer recalled how an attractive and cosmopolitan woman she had met twelve years earlier when they were both new mothers precipitously stopped returning her phone calls and began making excuses to avoid lunch dates two years into their close relationship. "I run into her occasionally, and it really throws me," she confessed. "I still mourn. I have a day of being disrupted when I see her."

I was in my third year of college when I experienced my first major, frighteningly slow-motion abandonment by an intimate friend, one that still baffles me. She and I, randomly assigned and wary freshman roommates in a tiny cell of a dorm room, discovered that we were soul mates the day we moved in. We became inseparable and resembled each other so much physically as well as psychically that people assumed we were sisters. There had been an older girl in high school that I'd loved and idolized (I chose my college because she went there) and maintained contact with for years until we grew apart, but I had never before known anyone who was as deliciously, naturally intimate as my roommate. We bought each other perfectly apt gifts, had similar quirky tastes—she introduced me to the short stories of Thomas Mann that I still love, and I showed her ancient Greek poetry. The ease of our comradeship was unprecedented for both of us; we looked at the world the same way. We both did not suffer fools, disdained hippies because they weren't as intellectually serious as the Beats, visited each other's parents, and exchanged notes in class that I copied into my diary, so full of her arch, pointed observations that I can still hear her voice when I read them. I was overjoyed to find by sheer luck someone who spoke my language and even added to my vocabulary when I had felt so alienated. At a critical time in the formation of my character, I heard my own voice more clearly because she was listening. Never had I opened myself so deeply or felt so intuitively understood and prized by a peer; my own mother once had this role in my life, but bitter adolescent struggles for independence had interfered with our communion.

I was heartbroken when my roommate took a leave of absence to travel to Europe in our sophomore year (she never told me exactly why she went and may not have known herself), but we maintained our dialogue by letter. I kept nothing from her; describing my experiences in detail to her—mostly about passion and loss—was the way I understood them best. Her responses were comforting, empathic, and astute. When she came back to school in our third year, to my relief and delight, we decided to share an apartment. I could hardly wait.

But, to my horror, she had changed. After only a few months, she turned distant, bitter, and cold, and then utterly silent. Even the expression on her face went from animated to sullen; it was as if an alien being had taken up residence in a familiar body. She would disappear for days without telling me where she had been and responded to any request of mine for explanation or conversation with contempt and hostility. I thought I knew everything about her, and now I knew nothing.

Meals together, which had been such a pleasure, became monosyllabic and then ceased altogether. She hadn't replaced me with anybody but retreated into a solitary world that she barred me from entirely. The only clue, which I failed to read at the time, was that she'd made it clear that she detested my new boyfriend, even though he liked her. I kept hoping that she was going through a phase and was too shocked and hurt to ask her to leave. It was bizarre and bewildering to go from virtually perfect accord when we lived five feet apart to excruciating enmity in a cavernous apartment, from shared lives to an armed camp. I was certain that I was the same, but she had become unrecognizable, unapproachable, a different species. Had she gotten a personality transplant? In the middle of our second semester, she precipitously moved out and left town for good, never saying good-bye, telling me where she was going, or paying her share of the rent. By then, her exit relieved me more than it grieved me; I never heard from her again.

One can only speculate on the motivation for rejections like these. My corporate friend's chum, I assume, turned on her after she came to project qualities she feared or disdained in herself onto her. Underground envy probably destroyed the relationship of the young mothers; their rupture happened after the Web designer had a second child (which she conceived effortlessly) and her sophisticated friend was unable to do the same. After my roommate's departure, I spent a long time speculating on possible reasons she turned on me. Could she have felt abandoned or replaced in my affections, especially since her replacement was a man she considered beneath her, and rejected me in revenge? Did this situation evoke some trauma from earlier in her life that we had never discussed, such as her older sister's—they also resembled each other physically and psychically—preferring a new boyfriend to her, thus ruining their special bond? Only in recent years have I considered that the real reason my doppelgänger repudiated me so cruelly might have been that she was in love with me. Such experiences are close to universal and do not fade but are rarely discussed.

One of life's most powerful illusions is that real friendships—at least after the tumult of adolescence and early adulthood quiets down—last forever. Sentiments asserting this supposition adorn countless T-shirts, inspirational plaques, and greeting cards, which suggests how much we need to assert it because we want to believe it. A close friend is the latter-day representative and reedition of the unconditionally loving parent—always available, unchanging, all-forgiving—who never existed, and we have the same fantasies about the one as we do about the other; our lifelong quest for this unattainable ideal confirms one of Freud's most profound observations: "The finding of an object is in fact a re-finding of it."* Losing such a life companion evokes the earliest losses of trust. Like the models on which they are based, these bonds are more ambivalent and far less permanent and guaranteed than they seem; while lifelong bonds with friends do exist, for most people, there is a disconcerting rate of friend turnover over a lifetime.

The wearing away, discarding, and creation of new friendships is a natural and continuous process, but when the fundamental ones, those that have become woven into your psyche, are severed, part of yourself is ripped away. When a lover leaves, the world empties of meaning; when a best friend does, you are diminished—at least temporarily—because the person who heard

---

* Freud, *Three Essays on the Theory of Sexuality* (1905). Paraphrasing him, I also believe, for good or ill, that every seeking is a re-seeking.

your true voice is no longer listening, and you can no longer see your undistorted reflection in the mirror of the other's eyes.

Later life experience provides opportunities to recover from these ruptures even if it does not insulate us from the pain they cause. At least after the first few times, you have more resilience and a more solid sense of self that allows you to find others after your own heart; after every lost friendship in my life, I have found a new, unexpected friend—sometimes sooner, sometimes later—to sustain me in ways that are both similar to my erstwhile one and completely unique. Along the way, you also realize that you were probably not your former friend's only casualty. This, and the recognition that the other person or the relationship has changed irreparably, allows the mourning process to begin.

It is the false friends of adulthood—those who start off as true friends and then inexplicably convert—who shock us the most and grieve us most deeply, as deeply as lovers and spouses. Such relationships can implode mysteriously, even after decades of intimacy. These are the ones who are supposed to stand by you when all else fails; when your beloved, your family, even your health, abandon you, they sustain you. They are an unassailable bastion in an unpredictable world. Their desertion dashes the myth of permanence, of guaranteed trust—forever, for some people. The details of the endgame burn into memory—the last conversation that cannot be unsaid, the coldness that replaced the warmth you counted on, the power to make you laugh on a day you had rued. When such a confidante forsakes you, it undermines your hope that there is always some comfort to be had. It is easier to accept the death of love—even death itself— than that such a friend can turn away forever and no longer wish you well. Even if you eventually find another truer and more stable companion, the original one can have no exact replacement, because people are not fungible.

These ruptures are different from the fading of shallower ties based primarily on proximity in school or jobs or stages of life, which end as interests and experiences diverge—one moves away or marries or has a child or a successful career, and the other doesn't. Those endings seem natural; the traumatic ones are against nature, cut off even though we expect them to continue as long as we do.

What underlies the death of serious friendships? Subtle envy and competition (always underground elements in even the more enduring bonds) eat away at trust; changes in fortune that could not be anticipated create barriers that eventually become unbroachable. The causes may never be known, but they shake one's emotional foundation and undermine a cherished and tenacious assumption: that there are at least a few people whom you can always count on no matter what, that their love transcends any conflict, that you can always talk it over, that you are as indispensable to them as they are to you. Such a friend is more than a latter-day parent or manifestation of an ideal self; he or she becomes an auxiliary self. Part of you is destroyed when the other leaves you.

Even in maturity, we maintain the fantasy that we have fewer fantasies about friends, whom we expect to be more akin, than we do about lovers, which makes it more excruciating when we are proved wrong. Their role is to accompany us throughout life, and we think we know that we will never be alone as long as they are in the world. Even when it happens, it still seems inconceivable that someone who can finish your sentences and elevate your mood, who has been at your side for decades, suddenly cannot or will not understand you. How can it be that your lives will go on, and end, without each other? I still find it hard to accept that the most intimate friend I shall ever have, my soul mate for a quarter century, is lost to me forever, our bond severed irreparably. We cherish the notion that we choose our friends more rationally than our lovers, without the pressure of desire. No longer being able to reach them makes us doubt that we can count on anything, including our own judgment.

ONCE BURNED, FOREVER SHY

The lure of friendship and its rewards are too great for most people to resist seeking replacements, even after grievous injury. But returning to the fray means accepting vulnerability and taking another chance, typically multiple times, which not everyone is willing to do. After I lost my beloved roommate at twenty, I longed for new friends and found several, never as inseparable as she and I had been, but warm and sustaining; additional intimacies and betrayals—by friends of both sexes—came later and also left me wounded but not inaccessible. The woman who was dismissed so viciously in high school by the girl who suddenly wanted to be nothing like her did not retreat from seeking and finding others who appreciated her afterward. However, the mother who was dropped when she had a second child essentially swore off making new friends because the rebuff resonated so deeply for her and exposed fault lines in her self-esteem. "I had a sense I didn't measure up—she was somebody I wanted to be like," she said. "I mourned it for a long time." With a mixture of bravado and self-doubt, she added, "I don't have a best friend now; is that really what everybody needs? I'm very extroverted and have a wide circle of acquaintances, but they're kind of secondary. I'm close to my sisters, but they live across the country. I have my husband. I keep other people at arm's length." Not all rejections are created equal, and they do not all have equivalent effects on the victim.

Abandonment by a soul mate brings out extremes in people; some rush out to replace a lost friend just as they do a lost lover, and others retreat to lick their wounds before venturing forth again. But a few rare people seem remarkably exempt from the anguish of losing this kind of love and the urgency to re-place it—at least on the surface. They decide that the best way to prevent a recurrence is never again to get deeply involved, never to show too much or need too much from a friend. Such people differ from those who are genuinely unable to experi-ence closeness; they have done it, gotten burned, and retreated for good into a simulacrum of autonomy that becomes a badge of courage. Emotional self-sufficiency doesn't feel like a prison to them but a wise and rational choice. Is it possible—is it ever desirable—to swear off friendship? Who does this? What is lost and what, if anything, is gained?

Rachel Carlson, a fifty-eight-year-old reporter for a prestigious magazine, looks like excellent friend material—smart, attentive, reliable, and warm. She has a devoted husband and two sane grown children, as well as colleagues whom she admires and whose company she enjoys. But there is something held back and inaccessible about her; a relationship with her does not sig-nificantly deepen over time, a fact she acknowledges uneasily. She rarely initiates contact or shares confidences. By her own admission, Rachel has not had a "real" close woman friend for forty-two years and wants none now. This, she asserts, is a matter of choice and a point of pride, even with its pitfalls.

It was not always so. The daughter of a pioneering woman journalist, Rachel naturally gravitated to working on her high school newspaper. By her senior year, she had become editor in chief, and she selected her two dearest friends as her news and feature editors. But in the middle of the fall semester, they simply stopped showing up for duty, offering no explanation and leaving her to put out the paper single-handedly. Her erstwhile deputies also stopped speaking to her for the rest of the year. "My best friends stabbed me in the back; it was horrifyingly lonely," she said—quite an admission for someone not given to hyperbole. She attributes their abrupt decampment to her inexperience as a leader. "It's hard when you have nobody to teach you how to lead your peers," she said, and, judging herself as harshly as she judged them, added, "I'm sure I was really bad at it, and they must have resented me." They said nothing, and she noticed nothing, until the damage was irreparable.

After that, Rachel rejected friendship (at least the kind in which you confide in and rely on others) but continued to pursue journalism with gusto for the rest of her life. "The experience made me wary. Even at the time, I saw that I was okay by myself, and since then, I've never counted on friends emotionally; I don't trust them, and I don't need them, and I'm too afraid to get hurt again. But when I went to college and worked on a paper with a real organization to back me up, it was nirvana." A well-functioning institution proved more reliable than other people.

Now she is sociable but guarded. She maintains strict limits on what she seeks and what she gives; her connections with colleagues sound more like arm's-length acquaintanceships. "I do more listening and less opening up. I don't want to be dependent on anybody, so I tend to deal with stuff myself," she says. Rachel recognizes that she is missing something and that her self-containment creates barriers. ("When I disclose, I'm vulnerable, so I avoid being intimate. It makes relationships one-way—I fear I'm a lousy friend as a result.") Still, she never questions the need for such drastic measures. Her reticence extends even to her "unemotional" husband, whom she turns to only for advice, not consolation.

Rachel understands that the perfectionism that has served

her well professionally also makes her prey to depression and insecurity and that she has forfeited forever the antidote to self-criticism that a real friend can offer. "I'm my own worst critic, and not having anybody to temper that can get really difficult," she admits. "I can get pretty depressed, and I don't see a way to accept help, so I really try not to be needy. The prospect of hanging hopes on another person and not getting enough, or any, help back just seems awful to me. I wouldn't trust anybody else with my happiness, even though the loss makes me feel empty. It's much safer to cultivate inner strength instead." The deepest part of a loving friendship is never to be hers, a price she willingly pays for self-protection.

It is as though she became, at an early age, a fervent adherent of the principles Ralph Waldo Emerson enunciated in his 1841 essay *Self-Reliance*: "Trust thyself," "Live wholly from within," "The voices which we hear in solitude . . . grow faint and inaudible as we enter into the world," "Nothing can bring you peace but yourself." I found that essay thrilling when I read it as a seventeen-year-old, but I interpreted it as a paean to individualism, not solipsism—charting your own course rather than traveling alone.

Assertions of self-sufficiency aside, Rachel never forgot the dark days at her high school newspaper and was gratified when the opportunity arose to show the culprits that she was beyond caring. "One of my nemeses came up to me at our twenty-fifth reunion and apologized, and I just laughed it off," she told me proudly. It reminded me of someone having to demonstrate to a former boyfriend who had left her that she was perfectly happy without him.

Why did Rachel view her wretched experience with the other budding journalists not as a result of immaturity, bad luck, or poor judgment but as a defining moment, a calamity

to be avoided forever after, even at the risk of a lifetime of un-
assuageable loneliness and self-doubt? Such an abandonment
would haunt anyone, but most people her age eventually take
another chance on friendship, just as they do after an excruciating early love affair and accept the loss as a natural and inevitable part of growing up, not a peril so devastating that it
should never be risked again. Most of the women and the men
I have known have endured things like this and worse, but
they all have rebounded rather than retreated. For her, however, eschewing friendship was the only possible conclusion. It
seemed automatic—almost predestined by her character—as
though she had forearmed herself by embracing a tough, fundamental truth. "It was soul crushing, but it really doesn't hurt
anymore," she claimed. "I made it not hurt even then; walls
went up. A door closed. I'll never let anybody get through that
door again. Even though I know it's a little sad, I'm really glad
to know I learned the lesson that friends are crutches, the en-
emies of my autonomy."

I had a sense from the unshakable ring of conviction with
which she described her self-imposed isolation that her swearing off the support of others was actually the endpoint of a process that had begun before her friends deserted her—that it
was a confirmation rather than a revelation, with roots in her
experiences of intimacy and its dangers to the self.

Two sources, one inspiring, the other tragic, predated
Rachel's decisive retreat from friendship after her journalistic
debacle. She saw in her own family both a positive example of
the rewards of self-sufficiency and a negative one of the dangers of craving companionship. Her mother was proudly inde-
pendent. "She was a loner, busy all the time, and the housewives
in the neighborhood couldn't relate to her." But her older
brother had slid into addiction and death. "He was a golden

boy in high school, the student council president. It was the seventies, when everybody started taking drugs. He couldn't stand
being all by himself, so he became a drug user and went rapidly
downhill; a lot of people who do that right themselves later, but
he never did. His death convinced me that I needed my friends
too badly and that I had to change and rely only on myself."

She clung to the conviction that she could protect herself
from becoming her brother by emulating her mother and never
needing another peer. Her brother, she believed, was destroyed
by his hunger to belong, not by his inner demons. Resisting her
own similar desire for companionship was her way to inoculate
herself against sharing his downfall; she would be strong
where he was weak. While the logic may be suspect, taking
these stringent steps fortifies her and gives her the illusion that
he too might have been saved by self-sufficiency and will-
power. It is a calculation that has paid off for her even as it has
limited her ability to be comforted.

There is no simple explanation why anyone turns away for good
after betrayal by a friend, but a tragic end to an admired sibling,
as well as an exacting nature, a dread of dependency, and un-
willingness to take the risks of engagement can make intense
human bonds seem too dangerous. Someone who associates
emotional connection with mortal danger cuts off the possibility of proving her pessimistic notions of friendship false and
makes it impossible ever to have a corrective experience. Sup-
pressing her wish for companionship, she keeps inviolate space
around her innermost self, asserting all the while that "if I had
to do it over, I'd do it the same way."

To seek friendship anew after a violation of trust, you must
be willing to expose yourself once again to unpredictable losses,
to take another chance on strangers who are not under your

control, to accept new influences that might cloud your judgment, or even subjugate your will. These were risks that Rachel dared not take, so she retreated, proud and alone, forever more.

I CAN'T STOP LOVING YOU

Rachel's reaction to unfriendly friends was extreme. Equally radical is the opposite response: clinging to the perpetrator ever more tightly the more outrageously you are treated. Friendship can feel like a trap to be avoided at all costs or a haven worth any price.

Why would an appealing, vivacious fourteen-year-old allow herself to be brutally humiliated and violated by a charismatic classmate and her cronies, never resisting or processing what they did to her, continuing to crave her tormentor's company, adoring her, living for their moments together, for years afterward? Because it was the only time she had ever felt loved.

There are many unconscious layers lurking beneath the functions that a friend, particularly a thrilling one encountered at an impressionable age, fulfills, and these go well beyond somebody to talk to, hang out with, or emulate. Such a person can provide—very much like a beloved does—a reason for living or be a substitute for parental care or for a sense of self. Miriam Higgins came from the wrong side of the wrong side of the tracks in rural Indiana. "My parents were the 'crazy people' in town," this forthright forty-five-year-old woman recalled. "Mostly, we ate the game my father shot; there's no way you can make squirrel taste good." It was a background of destitution and emotional squalor that could have turned her into the kind of kid who gets sent to reform school (her brother is a career criminal) or becomes a porn star, but instead she became a psychiatrist and, not surprisingly, a vegetarian. From an early age, her allure was her most dangerous asset, which she used but which also caused her suffering, because her father desired her and her mother hated and envied her. There was nowhere to turn. "My father molested me when I was five years old," she told me. "My mother sacrificed me to stay married to him." She is one of the very few people I have known, including my patients, who have ever described her parents so starkly.

Miriam needed somebody to look up to, and Donna—"athletic, competent, rich, manic, and popular"—filled the bill. In addition to offering the trappings of affection, Donna gratified that most potent of desires and provided a commodity as precious and compelling as passion: "gilt"—prestige, reflected glory—by association. "She was it to me, my first love," said Miriam. "She thought I was smart and deep. I developed an intense attachment to her, and we became best friends." Hers was an early adolescent crush based on idealization, not sex. "She was always the first pick for teams, and I was the last," Miriam recalled, that common gym class humiliation of the clumsy still rankling. "Donna knew how to get ahead, and she could do whatever she wanted; I couldn't do anything, and she could do everything. I wanted to be her."

This self-described "lost kid" basked in the warmth of her idol's attention and appreciation, things she was starved for and that no one else had ever given her. Donna—who, unbeknownst to her acolyte, had serious problems of her own—hungered for adoration as much as Miriam needed someone to adore. Miriam describes, still rapturous, the dawn of their passionate friendship. "Her family had a huge house with land and horses. We'd get up early and ride together and then watch the sun rise as we ate chicken soup with buttered crackers, the most delicious food in the world to me"—particularly after a diet of squirrel. "My need to have her love was so intense; when we were getting along, it was the best high I'd ever experienced. She was my sun, the center of my world, and everything revolved around her." The comparison with her own wretched home life made Donna's charms especially compelling. "She was just so much better than my family that I clung to her, or the idea of her, for many years."

But there was a horrific dark side that emerged early in their courtship. When the girls were in eighth grade, Donna gave a slumber party and deigned to invite Miriam, who was ecstatic. "I was very excited to go. There were six of us in her finished basement—it was not a dank one like ours." All of a sudden, the atmosphere changed from delightful to ominous, and Miriam found herself pinned down and stripped naked by Donna and her posse. "They started making fun of my flat chest and laughed at how small my breasts were—I developed late. They called my nipples 'chocolate chips.' They poked and touched me everywhere." Because she had everything to lose, she kept silent and stayed rooted to the spot, and the party continued as though nothing untoward had occurred. "Then we watched movies, ate popcorn, and went to sleep," she said, her voice now flat. "It was clear in my mind that she had abused me. I think of it as rape, really. I don't remember a lot of things from that period—I dissociated—but this I remember. She took advantage of me. It was a classic sadomasochistic relationship, and I think it was sexual for her, but not for me." Much of her childhood suffering became a self-protective blur, but the excruciating details of this episode she could not obliterate.

I was appalled and incredulous when Miriam told me that they remained best friends throughout high school, but her explanation of her ongoing attraction to Donna made sense. "It was having the attention of a very exciting object; I was like a dog chasing a car. I really needed her. Everything that seemed important to me she had and she was. Of course, I knew that all the sadistic stuff was bad, but she cared about me, and my parents hated me, and I couldn't do better than that. I was focused on the addictive drug of her affection, and I would do anything to get it—like a crack addict. When Donna's with me and she's telling me, 'I love you; you're so stunning'—that's my fix."

The power of her longing is still so potent that she switches to the present tense when she describes it. She got something essential that she needed—the authentic, even if inconsistent and unpredictable, loving appreciation of someone she admired, and it sustained her; unlike Rachel, she did not consider the price exorbitant.

Miriam's description reminded me not so much of a compulsively car-chasing dog but of a desperately clinging baby rhesus monkey, the kind psychologist Harry Harlow studied in the 1950s in a series of experiments* on the effects of maternal deprivation that were both compelling and controversial because they were so cruel. I have never forgotten the photographs of these little creatures with their despairing humanlike faces holding tightly to the awful wire surrogate mothers Harlow fashioned and that he named "Iron Maidens." They provided milk but shot out sharp spikes, administered electric shocks, and blasted the babies with cold air. No matter how they were tortured, the babies would not let go, because these mothers were all they had.

The dynamics between the troubled teenage friends changed dramatically when Miriam finally no longer had a flat chest and became popular with boys. She also acquired another considerable asset: a driver's license. "By the time I was

---

* Harlow summarized his results in "The Nature of Love," his 1958 presidential address to the American Psychological Association.

sixteen, I had more capital—I looked older than I was, so I could buy liquor, and I had a car. I developed new confidence," she said. Her final victory, which reveals the sadistic streak in every masochist, was to leave town at age seventeen with Donna's former boyfriend. She soon ditched the boyfriend but never went back. Donna became seriously depressed for some time after her departure, demonstrating that their needs were more enmeshed than they appeared on the surface.

Miriam's tie to her beloved tormentor did not dissipate quickly, even after years passed and she completed a lengthy psychotherapeutic treatment, became a physician, married a caring if self-contained man, and established her psychiatric practice in another state. Even when her identity was far more solid than it had been in adolescence and she had friendships not based exclusively on desperate neediness, the old tie to her wire-mother-surrogate still had a hold on her. She felt compelled to impress Donna by sending her copies of the two books she published, but she never got a response.

Then, years later, Donna, now married with four children, friended her on Facebook. Miriam forwarded the request to me:

> I know, in the past, that you have tried to get in touch with me. The reason I didn't respond was selfish on my part. I just felt too busy with life to really invest in a friendship with you. Let's just be friends on a "Christmas Card" level. I am very happy with my busy busy life. I hope you understand.

The thrill was not entirely gone, but this time, at last, Miriam's response was not masochistic enthrallment:

I don't want to be "friends" with someone who won't actually talk with me. If you want to have a real conversation, let me know. I am readily available. To be honest, I feel that you have been really cruel to me. For us to even interact socially, I would need to talk with you about it. I realize that I had my own issues in becoming attached to people who did not treat me well, and certainly I had my own problems with aggression. But some of the things that you did, some of the things that I allowed, make it really hard for me to think of you as a superficial friend. For me, history is not so erasable.

Now that she finally has a sense of self, Miriam no longer needs to cling to Donna or tolerate her cruelty. She also sees through her former friend's self-promoting attempts to make her feel inferior; a person with a genuinely full and productive life is no longer awed by someone who touts her own "busy busy" one. Now she has nonsadistic sources of sustenance, when before there had been only Donna. Miriam can finally think and speak clearly, confront the truth, and demand to be treated with respect. Her eyes are open, and she is fully awake. "I see my relationship with Donna as a distant but important dream," she said. "My attachment to her was irrational." Is there any love—even one with far fewer sinister elements—that is not?

Unlike Rachel, Miriam craves intimacy and is not totally satisfied with her current friendships, which, not surprisingly, tend to be with people who are "safe" rather than seductive. "Since Donna, I have been careful," she says. "I usually choose passive-aggressive people who don't express anger directly." Considering how the actively angry person treated her, this is a step up. Her desperate quest for love once led her to accept victimization and never protest, protect herself, or reject her tormentor. Now that she has an identity of her own, she has freed herself from bondage. Remarkably, she continues to acknowledge, and to prize, the love and admiration that was priceless amid the pathology.

THE OCNOPHIL AND THE PHILOBAT

Why did Miriam's tumultuous affair with Donna not make her phobic about friendship? Objectively, humiliation and sexual molestation seem far worse than being left by your friends to publish the high school newspaper by yourself. But trauma is as subjective as desire, and the meanings we attribute to experiences, as well as the context in which they occur, determine their ultimate effect on our lives.

Miriam craves loving companionship. "I appreciate friendships a lot," she told me. The misery of her childhood (and lots of hard emotional work) made her resilient and taught her to seek the positive even in dreadful situations. She cultivates a talent for intimacy, while Rachel mistrusts and rejects it; the solipsistic journalist feels more in control, and more herself, when she is by herself. Paradoxically, Rachel's tragic and talented brother proved a worse example than Miriam's criminal sibling; since Miriam never looked up to him or identified with him, his fate was not something she worried that she would share. She never imagined that he was led astray by his desire for human contact.

Miriam concluded—and I agree—that Donna did her more good than harm. Their passionate attachment was a source of real love, not just torment. Donna, with all her dangerous flaws, buoyed Miriam up at a critical time in her youth when she had nothing else, when her parents rejected and exploited her. Now she has learned to seek sustenance from safer sources.

It is counterintuitive but true that you can get precious things from someone who treats you badly, that the wonderful is often mixed with the terrible in human relationships.

Michael Balint,* a founder of the British object relations school of psychoanalysis and an innovative and profound clinician with a quirky mind, invented two cumbersome—even comical—words to describe the opposite temperaments exemplified by Rachel and Miriam: "ocnophil" and "philobat." These terms never caught on—they do not trip off the tongue like other Latin-based neologisms like *id, ego,* and *superego*—but they perfectly describe basic attitudes toward intimacy central to the way people experience friendship and its discontents. Philobats are loners who retreat when anxious. They consider relationships more dangerous than comforting. The close-binding ocnophils cling when they are anxious and seek human contact to assuage their fears. Relationships are comforting and safe for the ocnophil, but the lonely space between them and others is fraught with danger; the self-sufficient philobat prefers to cope with danger and uncertainty alone.

For every ocnophil and philobat—as well as for those of us who are an amalgam of both or who vacillate between the two extremes—friendship's end is shattering. It leaves us differently bereft than passion does, but just as bereft. How we re-

---

* Balint, who worked in Britain, was a disciple and patient of the remarkable analyst Sandor Ferenczi, a fellow Hungarian, one of the most gifted, empathic therapists of all time. Freud, whom Ferenczi revered even though he disagreed radically with him, was reputed to have said, "If you send a sick horse to Ferenczi, it will get well."

  Balint elaborated on his mentor's work with two unusual and influential books, *Thrills and Regressions* and *The Basic Fault*. He taught that therapy works by offering the patient "a new beginning," an opportunity to repair fundamental deficits in the self caused by damaged bonds with the original caretakers.

cover, and what course our lives take after such a loss, may differ depending on life circumstances, history, and personality, but there is no avoiding the anguish of losing a precious companion at any age.

No matter whether we seek it or flee from it, friendship has its dark side, like every other kind of love. But I believe, as Miriam does, that you still get more from friends than you lose, even when you factor in the emotional devastation and self-doubt that their leaving causes. Trauma, like so much else, is in the eye of the beholder. Despite the pain I have experienced as well as any pain from betrayal still in my future, I'm not canceling my ocnophil membership anytime soon.

PART III

FULFILLED LOVE

9

LATE FIRST MARRIAGE

The Triumph of Hope over Resignation

AT LONG LAST, LOVE

Mieczyslaw Horszowski, last of the great romantic Polish piano virtuosos in the tradition of Chopin and Arthur Rubinstein, married for the first time in 1981 at the age of eighty-nine. He wed Bice Costa, an Italian concert pianist (a fan and first-time bride) forty years his junior. Why did he wait so long? "I didn't find the right girl until then," he explained wryly, adding, "It only goes to prove that there is no such thing as a confirmed bachelor." They had twelve satisfying years together until he died a month before his 101st birthday.

Whenever it happens, late first marriage is qualitatively different from second marriage. It is not, as the renowned eighteenth-century English author Samuel Johnson quipped about second marriage, "the triumph of hope over experience." It is the triumph of hope over resignation, a resignation fraught with bitterness, envy, shame, sorrow, and—occasionally—relief. Marrying for the first time later in life means defying the verdict—false, as it turns out—that you are destined to live out your days alone. This requires overcoming the inner obstacles to identifying, let alone pursuing, a partner capable of lasting love. Becoming authentically emotionally available, which involves expressing feelings and responding to other people's, is a prerequisite, and it is often an arduous, time-consuming job. Self-created impediments and unconscious residual wounds from the past are far more daunting than the outer obstacles (such as the absence of available partners within a fifty-mile radius) that I have frequently heard patients and acquaintances cite for remaining single.

Older first-time brides and grooms feel a depth of emotion that contradicts jaundiced assumptions about matrimony, spouses, and themselves. Most can hardly believe their good fortune. Vanished is the cynical bravado and seeming indifference to their singlehood that masked the anxiety and despair they can only acknowledge fully in retrospect. "I was spectacularly lucky," a still-astonished fifty-seven-year-old recent bride told me, "but I helped myself to become lucky. I had come to the conclusion long ago that there might not be anyone out there for me. There was a huge amount of emptiness and loneliness. When you're in it, it's almost an addiction and a drug; you can't let it go."

"He has my back; nobody ever had it before," a forty-seven-year-old woman celebrating her first anniversary told me, still amazed that it was so.

Quietly, with deep emotion, a sixty-one-year-old man in the ninth year of his first marriage said, "This relationship allows me to give of myself, and I can receive now—things come in, they resonate."

And a forty-year-old bride-to-be said simply, "He's home."

I have never before conducted interviews in which every one of my subjects was joyous.

One prerequisite to finding a mate in midlife and beyond is admitting to yourself that you want one, that you need lasting intimacy to feel fulfilled. Many people are too afraid to say so because they cannot bear their own longing or have shut themselves off from it altogether. When you are shut off, you are blind to possibilities, no matter how numerous or fetching they may be.

A sharp thirty-five-year-old woman architect whom I saw in therapy for two years had only had a few relationships, and these were exclusively with men who were not really interested in intimacy; the previous one had lived in a distant city and had expected her to do all the traveling, and the current one, whom she clung to despite ample evidence of his ambivalence, was a guilt-ridden divorced father who insisted on arranging their time together entirely around his children's schedules. She complained with contempt and bitterness that no man she had ever known wanted a woman who was his intellectual or professional equal, and she doubted whether such paragons even existed. She insisted that her only options were men who were either beneath her or otherwise engaged, and she refused to consider that anything she might be communicating unconsciously contributed to her predicament; the male ego and sexism in society were the sources of her solitude, and she was convinced that these problems were insurmountable. In fact, her entire childhood and much of her adulthood had been spent trying to get her parents' attention—an impossible task, since they were completely absorbed in caring for her younger brother, who had been paralyzed by a fall when he was an infant, an accident for which they held themselves responsible and spent their lives trying to remedy. She had learned early on to fend for herself and to neither ask for nor expect help from anyone, hoping in vain that her hard work and professional success would someday earn appreciation, but nothing she did was ever enough. She never could acknowledge that being intimate with a man and wanting him to prize her made her feel more threatened than being alone made her feel bereft.

The willingness to take emotional risks—humiliation, rejection, disillusionment, revealing your needs, and letting yourself be vulnerable when you cannot control the outcome—can make all the difference, as it did for another patient of mine, who began seeing me when she was twenty-eight and stayed for the next twenty years. For the first five of those years, it certainly looked like she, too, was destined for a solitary life. But she hungered for love and was determined to seek it even though she initially despaired of ever finding it. Intense shame about her own neediness and fear of rejection inhibited her; she kept herself more aloof than she realized lest she reveal her naked longing for closeness, which caused her to exude a false aura of self-sufficiency and unapproachability.

She, too, had been forced from childhood to rely only on herself. Her shockingly neglectful, childish mother envied the bond between her capable daughter and the charming, workaholic father who doted on her but never protected her or compensated for his wife's deficiencies. Although the family was prosperous, the house was dark and dirty, there was never food in the refrigerator, and her mother was always late to pick her up from the deserted suburban train platform, leaving her to wait in the dark alone. Somehow, despite her upbringing, she managed to avoid cynicism if not depression and was less rigid and more open than my patient the architect was. Even as hope ebbed, through multiple disappointments with self-involved men, she persisted.

We never discussed it directly, but witnessing her misery and seeing the opportunities she was too blind or paralyzed to pursue made me decide to become her relationship coach as well as her therapist. I felt that a woman with a mother as inadequate—and a father as enticing but limited—as hers needed hands-on instruction about how to navigate the world as much as she needed insight into herself.

Although "life coaching" has now become ubiquitous, offering direct guidance was an unusual role at the time for someone who had been trained, as I had been, in the classic psychoanalytic tradition of not giving advice or talking very much in order to keep the focus on the patient's experience. Fortunately, my own analyst had violated both these directives, and I naturally emulated his hands-on style.

Therefore, while my lonely patient and I were investigating her history and her current struggles to express herself and to feel she deserved to be heard in her professional life—she was a lawyer who was afraid to speak up even when arguing a case before a judge—we also discussed in detail the rudiments of how to interact with men. I showed her how she came across to the opposite sex in social situations. I pointed out how she communicated, what she concealed, and what she had to learn to reveal. I detected that male colleagues and acquaintances were attracted to her long before she did and made sure it did not escape her notice. I advised her explicitly about how to converse with men who intrigued her, translating or interpreting nuances that were initially lost on her. I showed her how to recognize and return subtle advances no matter how much she wanted to bolt and even if she assumed, incorrectly, that someone was not interested romantically and wanted only her companionship. Afraid and hesitant as she was, she drank it all in.

"Take the initiative," I told her once when she described a bashful but thoughtful and charming man she had met tango dancing and whom she had written off because he had never unequivocally approached her. "Suggest going out for coffee. He's as shy as you are. I think he likes you and is waiting for a sign." He was. They married three years later, when she was thirty-eight, and are married still. She is now a judge herself, as well as a popular tango teacher.

Why did I feel compelled to intervene? I saw in her situation what could have easily been my own fate. She once told me that she was so ashamed of being single that she felt she had no right to walk down the street alone or have a meal in a restaurant by herself on Saturday night, and that sometimes, especially on weekends, she forced herself to stay up until she could justify going to bed, knowing she would feel as empty and alone when she arose as when she lay down. I had felt all these things myself.

I was thirty years old when I met the man I would marry at thirty-three, so I just squeaked under the age limit that would have qualified me as a late marrier, according to demographers. The thirty-year marker would be made infamous by a 1986 *Newsweek* cover story ("The Marriage Crunch"). Citing seemingly impeccable scientific evidence, *Newsweek* proclaimed that virtually all women over age thirty were condemned to what used to be called spinsterhood. The chances of a thirty-year-old woman marrying were 20 percent, declining by age thirty-five to 5 percent and then dropping precipitously until by age forty, the likelihood of her becoming a first-time bride hit 2.5 percent—lower, so the story notoriously intoned, than her chances of being attacked by a terrorist.* These statistics, which turned out to be seriously flawed, were taken as gospel by the media and by terrified women and were not recanted by the magazine until twenty years later.

I didn't need a magazine to tell me that nobody I wanted would ever want to marry me. This was an old and deeply held conviction of mine, rooted in my childhood experience, that persisted despite the fact that someone I cared about had actually proposed to me when I was graduating from college and I had been the one to refuse; I was lucky enough to realize at the time that neither his personality nor the life he envisioned were right for me. My dark presumption was catastrophically confirmed even more compellingly when the man I lived with for five years while in graduate school, who did seem right for me, left me abruptly on the verge of our being engaged, announcing at the door that he had ended a long affair with a mutual friend of ours the year before. I only realized in retrospect how blind I had been to aspects of his character that should have disqualified him. It took me the rest of my twenties to recover, during which I loved a series of men who were uncommunicative, ambivalent, distant, troubled, or inaccessible and whom I desperately tried to convert into real prospects, lamenting all the while that there was no one to truly love me. The only man

---

* It is particularly dismaying that this ghastly oft-quoted comparison was not in the original research on which the story was based (D. E. Bloom and N. G. Bennett, "Marriage Patterns in the United States," *Journal of Family Issues* [April 1985]) but was intended as a joke inserted into the article by the woman who wrote it—a baby boomer herself—who claimed that she assumed nobody would take it seriously. Of course, people did, because it fit their own pessimistic assumptions. Follow-up has demolished these dismal statistics; 68 percent of women who were forty years old when the original story ran have since married. The magazine's tardy and unapologetic recantation, "Rethinking the Marriage Crunch," was published in 2006.

to hug me on my twenty-eighth birthday was my unorthodox analyst.

It took intensive work in therapy—which in my case meant seven years, four times a week—to unearth the real reasons I gravitated to men who could not cherish me: my father, my mother, my parents' relationship, and my sense of myself. As a direct result of these labors, I eventually ceased trying to convert unresponsive people, both male and female, into responsive ones. Unavailable men lost much of their luster, and I began to feel I deserved requited love. At thirty, I finally met my future husband in a singing group that performed Renaissance religious music on street corners in New York City. He was a sweet-voiced journalist eight years younger than I, whose politics were diametrically opposed to mine, and he chose me despite the adamant disapproval of his family, which I dared not believe he would defy until he actually proposed to me. Thirty-five years later, I can hardly believe I found him.

ROCKY ROADS TO LOVE

There are many routes to finding a mate later in life, and few of them run smoothly. Therapy facilitates the search by alleviating anxiety and diminishing unconscious impediments to recognizing or responding to a soul mate, should one appear. Some people resolve to defy the odds and actively seek a spouse; the less sanguine cast fate to chance and hope a prospective spouse will seek them, putting themselves at least passively in the way of opportunity. And sometimes a lover finds a beloved by finding himself.

Anna Schneider, a fifty-seven-year-old television producer-director, would never admit that she longed to be loved; she kept herself so busy that she hadn't let herself think about it for years, and she revealed her feelings hesitantly. No casual observer would notice that this dashing, intense woman had a reclusive streak, that she had spent the limited time she allotted to her private life painfully lonely, or that she had quietly given up on marriage decades earlier. "I put my career first," she explained. "I've been highly successful and very well known in my field." Even though many people find time for both a career and a relationship, she certainly picked the right profession to confirm her rationalization; her job was so demanding and she immersed herself so deeply in it that she found little time to think about what was missing emotionally, or why.

Secretly, Anna feared that her being alone forever was "not an unlikely possibility," since most of her friends were single or divorced. "I know that desperate feeling many women get," she said, uneasily including herself in their number. "You think only short term: how will I get through this holiday or weekend?" So, like others in her situation, she focused instead on achievements as the basis for her identity. But unlike my two patients the architect and the lawyer, who vocally resented or worried about the dearth of men in their lives, she had made strenuous efforts to suppress any desire for intimacy, because she felt she did not have a knack for it, and she was a self-critical perfectionist. "I'm not that good at relationships," she admitted. "I don't like to be too analytical about my emotions; there are all kinds of ways I feel inadequate. I'd rather think about work." Her confidence was confined to her professional acumen, for which she had to rely only on herself; as long as she was successful, nobody needed to know about her private anxieties.

For someone who had so painstakingly cultivated both her friendships and her career, it was surprising that Anna described her two previous ten-year relationships (the last one twenty years earlier) as "happenstance." Even when she was younger, she had never actively pursued a man. "My default was to be involved with people who were not available," she said. For years, she had prevented herself from acknowledging that there was a hole in her life; she almost obsessively avoided thinking about it because she felt helpless to fill it.

Though Anna comes across as warm and engaging, there is something guarded and closed off about her. "I'm not intimate with my own family," she admitted. "My father is thoughtful and knowledgeable, but I'm not emotionally close with him." She does not share much of herself, even with herself; activity, rather than introspection, is her métier. I got the feeling that beneath the energetic, stylish façade there was something untouchable that she broadcast to men. Her bright exterior masked sadness within.

Then, eight years ago, her life began to change profoundly as a result of a whirlwind courtship by a colleague whom she never expected to pursue her, let alone want ardently to wed her.

Anna was not looking for a mate when she met Dan, a senior television executive, at one of the countless conferences she was always attending. They had an enormous amount in common, and he was an excellent, enthusiastic mentor. Although his intelligence and expertise impressed her and she enjoyed his company, she never considered him a real prospect because he was fourteen years older and married, although unhappily. "I was a little surprised that he was so keen to stay in touch with me," she said. And the honorable way he behaved, declaring himself early on and soon thereafter getting separated and divorced, impressed her. ("He was thoroughly serious, completely clean, and pure.") For him, courting her was anything but happenstance. He was the one who had to convince her to marry. "The idea came from him," she said. "He was keen to do it; he felt it was important." And, like the shy creature she was, it took quite a while for her to consent.

Getting engaged was exciting ("I thought it would be really fun because I'd never done it, and there's so much promise around it," she told me, as though she were describing a challenging new TV series she was creating), but she had continuing doubts about whether she was marriage material. "I like a little space around me; I may not want to be truly, truly intimate with anyone," she worried. As is often the case with someone who has arranged her entire adult life to her own specifications, she felt resistant to the change and compromise living with another person always involves—even though they managed to slow down the pace of acclimation by living in different cities during the week and seeing each other only on weekends. "People think it's very odd, but it works for us," she declared.

On a deeper level, she was terrified to rely on anybody, to let down a guard that had long been in place. She didn't want to have to reveal herself, something she never had to do before; she knew that marriage would require more openness than she was comfortable with, but Dan was confident and willing to wait. Since Dan's wife had demanded and required constant caretaking, Anna's self-containment and competence must have felt refreshing; looking after someone who, as an equal, looks after herself, feels like a choice—even a privilege—not a demand. After a lengthy engagement, they married when she was fifty-six, eighteen months before we spoke. Only now are they starting to look for a place to live together.

How did this confirmed loner, well into middle age, feel safe enough to go through with it? She had attended conferences for years and never met anyone before. The difference this time was that Dan, a man she admired, made all the moves and

took all the risks. He was the one to seek her out, to recognize
that she was what he was looking for, and to act decisively to
win her. Being chosen and seriously pursued meant everything
to her. It made her feel worthwhile, as being loved does when
you have not had enough of true devotion.

Like many first marriages in maturity, theirs is unconventional;
the relationship is about the two of them and the world they
share, not family life—she is childless by choice—of which he
has had his fill. Slowly she is starting to let herself need him.
Anna's eyes shine as she talks about Dan, and she shyly begins
to smile. "I was willing to take the leap," she said. "I was finally
old enough." Marriage is always a leap of faith; she was finally
brave enough. She does not mention it, and perhaps doesn't
even realize it, but there is something retroactively curative in
the way he cares for her that was probably absent in her childhood.

　　Love and marriage are a brave new world for Anna, and
she is still adjusting, anxiety mingling with her delight. "I've
had a hard time figuring out what a relationship really is," she
acknowledged. "I don't do a lot of caretaking. I don't do traditional things like cooking. I had built a lifestyle and work life
for myself. There's a lot you don't know about a real relationship until you're in one, until you finally say, 'I'm committed,
I'm here.'" She finds herself wanting to be alone with Dan much
more than she imagined she would. "Now that we're married,
I don't feel as compelled to be out and about all the time," she
observed. She likes having someone to come home to, at least
on weekends.

　　Mortality has a new meaning too. Considering their age
discrepancy, I asked her if she was afraid of his dying. She answered decisively, if probably unrealistically. "Yes, but I think

I'll go first; he's much healthier than I am." Then, recalling her solitary years, she acknowledged that she might well face aloneness again, even if it would be a different aloneness. "I've learned what it's like to have a real sense of security with someone who is always there, but I haven't forgotten what it's like to have to be on my own and resourceful. I think I might be less able to do it than when I was young, and that would be my fear." This legitimate fear does not faze her, however, because she is secure in Dan's love. "I have real comfort—I know he's there. I count on him a lot, actually for more and more. I get a lot of guidance from him; he's good at figuring out problems and helping me."

There is relief in her voice about not having to do everything herself anymore. "He is really steadfast. I can absolutely rely on him, not like most of the male persuasion I've known. He knows that slowly things are changing between us as I come to relax with him."

One perk of a good marriage is that your spouse can tolerate things about you that you find hard to tolerate about yourself. "I've become much more confident and accepting of myself because he's 100 percent accepting of me and does not judge, even as I grow older," she says—a great comfort for a woman who has been so exacting. His tolerance of her wariness ("He knows our relationship is evolving") soothes her.

For a woman who never felt in control of her relationships with men, she knows she was "spectacularly lucky" to find him, and she is proud of her intentional self-restraint. "Although I could have, I never pushed him to say when he would be free. It was entirely his own decision, and I was excited that he made it."

He truly loves and appreciates her just as she is, quirks and all. He lets her be herself and waits patiently as she slowly opens to him. As Robert Frost said in his poem "Hyla Brook" about appreciating beauty all the more because of its uniqueness and fragility, "We love the things we love for what they are."

It was essential for Anna Schneider that a man seek her out. Forty-year-old Lisa Deutsch took the opposite approach to finding a mate: she needed to be the one to do the choosing. For this born entrepreneur who recently started her own company, the product she is proudest of—the one that had the longest, most difficult launch and required the most intensive marketing efforts to make successful—is herself. She is the female Horatio Alger of the altar.

Pleasure and enthusiasm, tempered with a tough-minded assessment of what she had to overcome within herself to be genuinely receptive to marriage, emanate from her as she describes how she mounted a campaign that was a triumph of will, insight, diligence, and nerve. In Churchill's words, she never, never, never gave up.

Lisa's career, like Anna's, came first in her twenties, and she, too, found professional success easier to achieve than a lasting relationship. "I was part of corporate America. I only had three boyfriends in the whole decade, and every one broke my heart." These rejections devastated her. "It took me forever to get over them," she told me. "I was not interested in dating for a year after the last breakup—it was really hard; I'm a loyal person."

It was not until she turned thirty that she began to consider that she herself might be the problem. She discovered that she was gun-shy and more demoralized by these failures than she had let herself know. "I would brush off opportunities. Once I was at the airport with a colleague, and she said, 'Did you see that hot guy checking you out?' and I hadn't noticed. I was just not aware. I needed to do something about this." Unlike my patient the cynical architect, Lisa did not conclude that men were the problem; her own blindness was.

Characteristically, she took matters into her own hands. She joined the Internet dating site Match.com "and started doing two dates a day"—a slightly manic solution, but one that certainly beat feeling like a victim or sitting at home alone. Lisa also cleverly arranged to protect herself from rejection and to manage the disappointments inevitable in such a project. When a candidate did not work out, she went right back on the computer, where, she announced gleefully, "there would always be at least four other men waiting to ask me out; it helped with the heartbreak." Even though she never did find the right match in seven years of online searching, she met two appealing men, one who was her old type ("Fascinating, but ultimately unavailable") and another who was a real possibility ("Successful, my own age, so nice") but whom she wrote off at the time because he was divorced—one of her arbitrary negative criteria.

Eventually, with help from a therapist, she figured out what was really going on. "I was afraid of real intimacy; I passed up some really good guys because I was looking for the wrong things." She had been energetically pursuing external solutions to an internal problem, with roots in her past that had not yet been explored. This was the beginning of wisdom.

The sources of Lisa's fear turned out to be, as they usually do, her relationship with her father ("He was successful, but I couldn't feel comfortable or confident in his consistency. Trying to get his attention and approval led me to be attracted to unreliable older men. It was easier to be with someone mysterious and intriguing.") and her parents' marriage ("I was afraid of repeating their relationship and divorce—they enjoyed common interests but didn't really connect."). She saw that she had spent years seeking men like her father and trying to transform them into real partners—a popular but thankless project, even for somebody as hardworking as she.

Although Lisa had close male friendships, she put lovers in a different category. "I did not believe that I could confide in a person I was dating—I always discounted that," she said. She was never at ease with her boyfriends because she had to work so hard to win and keep them, and she could never speak her mind for fear of the consequences. "I never had to put that much effort into friendships," she observed. "I didn't believe it was possible to have a comfortable, deep friendship with a man I loved until I met Jerry, and then *OMIGOD!*" I asked her if Jerry, her fiancé, whom she finally met when she was thirty-eight, was different from the other men she knew. "Very," she said with joyful relief.

Finding Jerry, a fifty-two-year-old divorced father of three—the divorce taboo evaporated when she met him—was no lucky accident. In addition to her therapy, a TED Talk entitled "Thirty Is Not the New Twenty," which Lisa heard when she was thirty-seven ("It explained everything I did wrong with men") galvanized her to reconsider her dating strategy and get serious about finding a mate. She identified with the deluded twentysomethings in the talk who rationalized killing time in relationships that were going nowhere, and she decided to try a different, more focused approach, very old but new again: she went to a matchmaker. "I was open to any way to meet people," she said. And she went with the top of the line, hiring the equivalent of an executive spouse-search firm that charged male clients $35,000 a year for introductions. This, she concluded, was an indication of their seriousness, as well as their net worth.

"I met him at a networking event—I didn't put much weight on it because everybody they had set me up with was nice and successful, but I felt no connection. I was seeing somebody else when I was introduced to Jerry. I decided just to have a drink, because he could be a good business contact; I was feeling jaded at that point. This happened two years ago, and we fell in love in a few months." Lightning often strikes when least expected, even when you are on the verge of giving up hope after trying everything you can think of. But when you are ready—at thirty-nine or eighty-nine—a mate may suddenly appear with the very qualities you ignored or overlooked or wrote off before and have now come to prize.

Even after Lisa found her soul mate, obstacles to their union remained; in this case, it was he who was gun-shy. They went to counseling together. "He realized he was holding back because of a bad divorce, and he wanted to be really careful," she said. "He cried in a session. 'Why am I holding back?' he said." His emotion moved her; in every other relationship, she had been the one to cry, and only in private. "We worked through our fears. It freed us. We've been engaged for eight months."

Late marriers, especially if they are women in early middle age marrying men who are considerably older, often have to accept that they are forfeiting having children. If the man is not a first-time groom, he often does not want another family. I asked Lisa whether this was an issue for her. "I was more interested in finding a soul mate," she replied, "and my fiancé's children are grown, so I had to mourn the decision I didn't realize I was making." But she feels amply compensated by the ease of their intimacy, something she never imagined would be possible with a man and that her parents never had together.

How does their thirteen-year age difference affect her, since this had been a deal breaker earlier in her quest? "I have a fear of him dying, even though he's very healthy and he has more energy than I do," she admitted. "I'm afraid of losing him now that I've found him." The fact that it took so long and that she worked so hard to do it makes him even more precious. "I finally chose the right person—that's why it feels so good. If my radar had been better earlier, it's possible that I could have found somebody else, but I'm glad I didn't because I wouldn't have met Jerry." For someone who has "worked hard for everything in my life," the effortlessness of their rapport is a huge relief. "I'd always heard that relationships are work, but living with Jerry does not feel like work at all; when something feels like too much work, then maybe it is. I love caring for him, and he for me. We get each other. He's mine," said the corporate cat that ate the canary. "And he paid $35,000 to meet me!"

She was worth every penny.

A problematic father—like Anna Schneider's distant one or Lisa Deutsch's inconsistent one—makes it difficult for his daughter to find a man who can love her wisely, but a father whose child calls him a "cockroach" would seem to make it almost impossible. How can anything sustaining be built around such an image of maleness? And yet, Wendy Myers overcame her treatment at the hands of a father as repulsive as he was reprehensible to marry a man she esteemed and who made her laugh, at the age of forty-six.

Wendy's cockroach father was no Gregor Samsa, the tragic hero in Kafka's story *Metamorphosis*, who was tormented and neglected by his family; rather, he was the one who tormented, exploited, and ultimately abandoned his family, including Wendy, his youngest and most responsible daughter. Early on, Wendy had been designated—and allowed herself to be designated—as the caretaker of her inadequate, overwhelmed, and selfish parents. By the time her two older sisters were marrying and starting families of their own, this highly organized and competent young woman (she was director of human relations at a major company) took over running their household. When her mother was diagnosed with cancer, Wendy became her nurse and surrogate mother until she died when Wendy was thirty-seven. "I served my parents," she said without self-pity. "I never said no. They couldn't handle themselves, didn't like each other that much, and wanted me to act as a buffer between them; nobody ever took care of me."

Wendy started to have suspicions about her father's character during her mother's illness, but she could not have imagined that he would shamelessly flirt with women at her mother's wake until she witnessed it. Three weeks later, announcing that he'd "started a new chapter," he moved in with one of them and sold the family home, leaving only a box of mementos for her. "I was dumbfounded," she said. "He dropped the whole family. The last straw was when I overheard a conversation he had accidentally recorded on his phone in which he said that we meant nothing to him, that we were worthless, and that he never wanted to see us again."

He was a man of his word. Over the next several years, Wendy discovered that her father had never even made a living—her mother's parents had surreptitiously paid their bills—and that he had squandered the inheritance her mother had bequeathed to her and her sisters. Then, in his final act of abandonment, hatred, and self-hatred, he committed suicide in his girlfriend's bedroom, "leaving a huge mess, as usual." Wendy had cut herself off from him so completely by then that when I asked if she had any reactions to his death, she replied coolly that she was shocked that he died, "because I viewed him as a cockroach, and I thought cockroaches lived forever." She added, "I considered him dead long before."

Despite everything, this tall, striking, and tart-tongued

woman never became sour or depressed. She kept busy with her career and her friends. There was never a lack of male attention—when I met her at a mutual friend's wedding a decade ago, she was surrounded by a bevy of admirers—but although she attracted many men, she never got close to any of them.

Soon after she was freed from family obligations, Wendy realized that taking care of her parents as a young, single woman had served another purpose for her than simply doing her duty. It had provided her with an excuse to avoid involvement with a man, which she implicitly feared would be a reprise of her parents' relationship. To make up for lost time, she, too, joined Match.com, and, like Lisa Deutsch, searched it avidly with an adventuresome spirit and a head for business. "I was a big dater in my late thirties," Wendy recalled. "If you asked me out, I went out. I had three first dates in one weekend—it was fun! I'd go into interview mode; it helped being in HR and having a recruiting mentality. I got a gem from everyone I met—either he said something clever or he took me to a new restaurant. I tried to be open and optimistic and think, 'Let me see if this works.'" But for years nothing ever did, because her father stood in the way.

During her speed-dating days, Wendy did make one deep and enduring commitment: she began seeing a therapist right after her mother died and stayed through her midforties. Her father, though still alive, had already become a "nonentity" to her. "I needed to figure out what I did and did not want," Wendy said. "I had no male role model."

In fact, she had a very potent but poisonous one: her father was a perfect negative role model, an ideal counterexample of what a loving man should be. Conventional wisdom says that positive role models of parents—or parent-surrogates—are critical in making good choices in relationships, but it is possible to make judicious use of a terrible one. Of course, much more mental effort is involved in learning from a father for whom you have only contempt than from one who, though flawed, loves and cares for you. To come to terms with a despicable parent, you also have to grieve for what you never had, make some sense of his personality, and recognize that you did not cause or deserve mistreatment. And even if you do not forgive such a man—a legitimate choice—nursing hatred for him exacts a toll. The relationship lives on inside you, so hating a parent always involves hating a part of yourself. Years of intensive therapy were necessary for Wendy to accomplish these feats.

Wendy learned how to extrapolate from her father's repugnant character and shocking behavior; she discovered what to flee in a man, and, conversely, what to seek. "Not all men treat women the way my father did. I had to look for his opposite," she said. "I had to make comparisons: this is what a crappy man does, and this is how a good man acts."

However, seeking a mirror image is not enough. By itself, it is a reflexive, behavioral solution that addresses only the overt part of the problem. In order to create inner receptivity to loving and being loved in the aftermath of being exploited and discarded, you also have to change how you feel about yourself. "Therapy gave me self-esteem and belief in myself," she said. Once she knew she had a right to be cherished, she could seek somebody who could cherish her, and only then could she recognize and respond to such a man.

Wendy's priorities, and what she was looking for and projecting, changed over time. "I finally started getting my act together at forty," she told me. "I've always been a late bloomer. I worked at dating; I wanted a partner and a companion. What I used to believe was important in a man—the superficials of how he looks and what he does and his finances—has evolved. Now I need compatibility and comfort, generosity and loyalty, someone who keeps me intellectually challenged and entertained. Relationships take more thought when you're older, and you're able to give it." Why did she focus more on the external attributes of potential mates when she was younger? "When I was insecure in myself, I was looking for qualities I wanted to emulate," she explained; she could hardly have looked to her father for examples. "Now I know what I value and what I bring to the table." Ever the realist, she also accepted that marriage might not be in the cards at her age, even though that was what she really wanted.

By the time Wendy was forty-five and a longtime therapy veteran, her father's grip on her psyche had loosened. She finally found what she was looking for on Match.com. Mark was a fifty-two-year-old lawyer—"funny as hell, smart as a whip, loyal, and handsome," and she became his wife when she was forty-seven. "It took a year before I moved in with him—I needed a large closet of my own; a girl has shoes," she announced, making a joke of her anxiety. Then she added quietly, "I'm still surprised I'm actually married. I had given up the dream of ever doing it."

Wendy had to give up one of her dreams in order to fulfill the most important one, however: she had also wanted to have a family. "We talked about it," she told me, "but I don't think it's fair to be an older parent." She also sees the advantages, emotionally and financially, of being just a couple, because it involves one less adjustment to make at a time in life when flexibility does not come easily. "Children would have brought different wonders, but it would be a big change," she admitted. Echoing Lisa Deutsch, she said, "If we had met ten years earlier, we would have done it, but we couldn't have met then. I needed to go through a lot to find him."

Her husband, whom she talks about with unabashed delight, gives her what neither her mother nor her father ever did. "He respects me, appreciates me, puts me on top—I never had that before," she said. And marriage brings out the best in her. "It makes me generous and genuine. I didn't use to compromise, but now I don't get as picky about things, like losing my cool over emptying the dishwasher. When you're single for a long time, it's all about yourself." Now she is part of "we."

When you finally find happiness, you are loath to lose it, and the older a spouse is, the more likely the loss. What if Mark died first? She answered with a wisecrack. "He can't. I don't know how to use the remote control or open the safe." Then she said seriously, "We've had the practical conversations; you have to talk about these things realistically. We made sure we have the financials in order." Even though she has told him "I've lost too many people, and I'm going to go first," she is prepared for the alternative; she bought "a Cadillac premium long-term care policy in case I'm alone."

Determined not to repeat her mother's mistakes, Wendy approached marriage with clear-eyed practicality as well as passion. "Mark is the first man I've known who was as practical as I am," she said appreciatively. "I'm a romantic, but I also believe that a marriage has to be a business. My HR experience makes me view it as two companies doing a merger; I've been around."

Wendy's commitment to Mark led her to make radical changes in the way she lived, which she did willingly. "I used to travel every weekday for my job—I used my house as a hotel. It was an excellent distraction; I did very well in airport lounges, where I met lots of men. I took a demotion and made a conscious choice to be home so we could live together, so I could build a relationship with him. And I wanted to be there."

She believes that a marriage between two mature people tends to be more civilized and less tumultuous. "We don't fight as much as younger couples do," she said. "We talk things out more, and we don't have children to fight over. We have just the two of us and a nice lifestyle with no money problems." This is a very different scenario from the family she grew up in.

Despite her love and belief in Mark, it took time for Wendy to trust him completely. "Is he going to do what he says he is going to do? I used to worry about this, and he was afraid about the same thing with me. I've had so much tragedy and so much betrayal, but I've been able to free myself. I have no more chains around my neck."

Paradoxically, Mark's two previous failed marriages turned out to be one of the most compelling proofs that he was the right mate for her, the key that unlocked the chains that bound her. "His first wife cheated on him, and he caught them; it was ugly. His second marriage lasted only three weeks, and he left because he realized it would never work," she said. Wendy's husband suffered because of his wife's infidelity, while Wendy's father's behavior showed that he had cared nothing for his wife. It is a curious coincidence that three weeks figured in both men's second relationships, but her father's hasty hookup was cold and selfish, while her husband's hasty divorce was thoughtful and moral. Wendy could make the comparison: this is what a crappy man does, and this is how a good man acts.

BUILD IT, THEY WILL COME

Anna Schneider, Lisa Deutsch, and Wendy Myers all faced emotional obstacles stemming from their family relationships, some almost insurmountably severe, before they were able to seek and find lasting love. But Ted Thomas was a foundling who started life cast adrift in the world with no family relationships at all—no parents, no siblings, no known relatives—and who lived in various foster homes for the first three years of his life. However difficult it was for them to find intimacy with a beloved, he had never experienced a full, authentic connection with another living soul and, by his own admission, had none with the deepest parts of himself well into adulthood. His passionate pursuit of therapy and music finally opened his inner reservoirs and taught him how to give and receive love. The ability to trust others and to express himself, which he nurtured through relentless commitment to these twin pursuits, allowed him to marry for the first time at age fifty-two. He was a sixty-one-year-old father of two children, with dual careers as a violin maker / string orchestra leader and a psychotherapist, when we spoke.

Ted talked about his life with quiet intensity, frankness, and a sense of wonder. "I've always wanted to have real relationships," he said, "but I had to work out parts of my own story and defuse my emotional land mines before I could do it."

"I was moved around as a kid," he said, emphasizing the enforced passivity that was part of the trauma he was born into. Given up at birth, he lived in five different foster homes before the age of three; nine months was the longest time he spent in any of them. Then he was adopted and spent the rest of his childhood with new parents and siblings, but he never felt completely secure and withheld a part of himself even from them. When he grew up, he searched for his birth parents but discovered that his mother, who "had a lot of issues," had died, although he did eventually track down members of her family in England. "I don't know who my father is and never will," he said starkly.

Ted was fully aware of how profoundly the repeated losses he had endured in his most vulnerable years affected his ability to rely on anyone. "It was a question of risky attachment," he said, using a psychological term to describe his style of relating.*

He recognized in his adult self the deep-seated and lifelong wariness of a young child who, having been passed through a revolving door of caretakers, shuts down and withdraws out of self-protection against yet another abandonment. This pattern became his fundamental mode of relating to everyone—friends, lovers, and himself. "It was predetermined that I would play it out in relationships. I was terrified of letting my guard down. I remember this strongly; even as a kid, people could feel me holding myself back."

---

* As a psychologist, Ted was familiar with attachment theory, the perspective articulated by British psychiatrist/psychoanalyst and child development researcher John Bowlby (1907–1990). Bowlby studied the way children (and the adults they become) relate to those they love and need based on the level of security in their earliest relationships. Ted saw that he was a textbook case of a subtype of what Bowlby called "insecure attachment." The insecurely attached have difficulty forming deep bonds because they had no consistent source of solace available when they were anxious as children. Of course, Bowlby had experienced intense separation anxiety and its aftermath in his own childhood.

Bowlby was an iconoclast who demonstrated the centrality of human connections in development from the very beginning of life. He coined the term "separation anxiety" and defined four types of attachment styles: secure attachment; and three types of insecure attachment—anxious-ambivalent (Ted's), anxious-avoidant, and disorganized. His seminal works are the trilogy *Attachment* (London: Hogarth, 1969), *Separation* (London: Hogarth, 1973), and *Loss* (London: Hogarth, 1980) and *A Secure Base: Clinical Applications of Attachment Theory* (London: Routledge, 1988).

The contributions of this innovative thinker, who was himself insecurely attached to the psychoanalytic movement and was often at odds with his colleagues, have influence far beyond the immediate focus of his work. Trauma studies, the psychology of mourning, and the relational approach to therapy that dominate current contemporary psychodynamic thinking owe much to him.

Of necessity, Ted had taught himself to be friendly and charming, as those who have to live in other people's homes often do. He had developed a cheerful persona but kept his real feelings to himself. Ted felt his own restrictions acutely without having any idea how to change them. He had anesthetized himself to the pain of loss so successfully that it was simply the way he was.

His one emotional outlet was music. After college, he turned his lifelong love of playing the violin—the instrument most like the human voice—into a profession and became a violin maker in New York.

Still feeling "a little bit lost" at age thirty-two and seeking an additional source of the self-expression he so deeply craved yet found elusive, Ted changed direction and went to art school to study painting. He also began psychotherapy with a Jungian* therapist, "an older guy" who symbolically replaced the unknown father he craved. Just when he won a third-year competition that offered him free tuition, the remark of a fellow student galvanized him to make a decision that changed the course of his life.

---

* Swiss psychiatrist C. G. Jung (1875–1961), Freud's most famous disciple and heir apparent who became his bitter opponent, called his own method analytical psychology. Instead of sex and aggression, he emphasized spiritual development and the study of "archetypes" manifested in myths and dreams to put people in touch with the "Self" and tap into the human legacy of wisdom he called "the Collective Unconscious." His most accessible works are *Man and His Symbols* (New York: Random House, 1989), and the autobiographical *Memories, Dreams, Reflections* (New York: Doubleday, 1964). Jungian thought has had profound influence on the humanities; Joseph Campbell and Thomas Moore are among his popularizers. Ted was undoubtedly attracted to Jungian therapy because he was seeking a narrative of his life and an understanding of the compelling—Jungians would describe them as "numinous"—dreams that had always symbolically expressed emotions he could never verbalize.

"A Japanese friend in my class said, 'I've known you a couple of years, but I actually don't know you at all.' His comment seemed to come out of left field, but it helped me at a pivotal moment by making it clear to me how hard it was for me to risk giving my heart. You wouldn't know it about me because I'm very social, but there are times I've felt some very intense aloneness—not just loneliness but a profound sense of separation and isolation. My therapist was moving to Vermont, and I decided to turn the scholarship down and follow him. I was in the process of discovering my role in all the things I had to sort out. I had to get to the bottom to go on."

For the first time, although somebody Ted loved and needed was leaving him, he had the option to follow. Turning passivity into activity, he chose that option. This uprooting, intentional and self-initiated, was actually a replanting. He finally had a secure attachment, and he wanted to keep it; it was the most precious thing to him, his lifeline to being fully human.

"So I came up here to Brattleboro," he said. "Being able to work at discovering myself was like waking from a dream." This move was also a symbolic homecoming. "It made sense because I wanted to come back to New England, where I had been raised."

I had particular empathy for Ted's seemingly radical act, because I had done a similar thing myself. I began my analysis at twenty-one, before I began my analytic training. My analyst, who was a seasoned graduate of the same institute I attended, had not yet reached the exalted rank of "training analyst," so I was told I had to leave him and begin treatment with someone on the approved list. I decided instead to leave the institute and stay with him because I knew that he was what I needed, my route to a healthy relationship with a man. The only reason I returned to the institute was that he died, suddenly, at age fifty, in our seventh year together. I eventually went into treatment with my supervisor, who was on the officially sanctioned list, and completed my training. She was of great help to me, but I never felt as deeply loved or understood.

Following his analyst was a smart move indeed for Ted. "I worked with him for twelve years and developed a profound trust in him," he told me. "It really awakened a part of myself. I had an awareness that my dreams were speaking." Symbolic exploration was only part of what Ted needed and accomplished. "I learned to tolerate the difficult feelings, the deep sadness I'd been carrying around. Being able to feel things in myself allowed me to feel things in the presence of others; it let me make the space for a relationship."

His relationship with his beloved analyst was the first one in his life that not only lasted but changed the way he related to himself. Being loved and understood in the unique way that analysis provides can heal the past. You internalize the intimacy and feel free to open parts of yourself that were too dangerous to express. Having someone reliable to count on, as Bowlby showed, develops the capacity to count on yourself. As Ted explained it, "My relationship was not just with him but with aspects of myself. I came to recognize that I had the capacity to love; I could trust that. It was a constant. Nobody could take it away." Ted became free to grow from within. "My ability to feel was evolving, and it still is," he said. Identifying with his symbolic father, he became a therapist himself, one who is "very tuned in to these issues in my work with patients." Words joined music as a means of communication.

Ted learned to relate first to his analyst and then to himself, and from the synergy of the two, he turned to the world. Women had not been immune to his charms earlier in his life; he had been immune to forging a lasting bond with any of them. "I had five relationships before I was fifty," he said. "Several of them wanted to marry me, but I just couldn't risk it. I didn't have the capacity to believe that a relationship could last."

While Ted was learning to feel, he experienced another traumatic loss, but he handled it very differently. One of his adoptive sisters fought a three-year battle with pancreatic cancer, and he sustained her through it, loving and grieving as he never had done before. "You have to really be open to go on this journey with someone who's dying," he said. "Maintaining a really real connection in the presence of losing somebody helped me find the courage—I think it was courage—to take the risk of committing myself to another human being."

Six months after his sister's death, he rekindled a relationship with a woman he had met a year before when she was newly divorced. "We didn't strike it up right away because neither of us was ready, but then another opportunity came when we crossed paths again." Even so, it took Ted almost two years more to act on his newfound courage and propose. "She was willing long before I was," he noted. His bride, who is thirteen years younger, happens by chance (or, as the Jungians would say, "synchronicity"*) to be a violin-playing psychotherapist.

Before the marriage took place, Ted had a dream of extraordinary power and beauty:

> I was going into a neutral country. The border guards wouldn't let me in, but marched me instead into the customs house, marching me back through a series of rooms until I got to one without a window. It was completely black in there except for a light shining on a

---

* A term Jung created to describe phenomena that occur by coincidence but are meaningfully connected.

table. A guy motioned me to the table, where I saw a violin. He gestured to me to pick it up—and on the back was the image of a small boy crying.

"Before I had language, the violin was the way of giving voice to a part of myself, the vehicle I had created," Ted observed about his dream.

The "neutral country" he was about to enter was marriage—a clean slate, ready for his imprint, like a canvas prepared for a painting. The "border" guards—his defenses of his boundaries that had kept him from passionate intimacy—did not give him immediate permission to enter this strange new land without first stopping at the "customs house"—the repository of his past. In the dark, windowless room in its deepest recesses, the place inside him where the light of the outside world could not penetrate and only inner light illuminated, the "guy"—his beloved analyst—pointed out the precious, lifesaving violin embodying the disconsolate child he had been. He had to take it with him to the place he was going, where he could speak as well as play and laugh as well as cry, no longer alone. Naturally, there was lots of violin music at their wedding, and his analyst was present to share their joy.

Secure attachment has brought Ted both joy and ease. "I can relax at a much deeper level," he said. "I had stress constantly eating away at me in different ways; now I've let go of it."

Ted and his wife, who have two children, perform together in the multigenerational string orchestra he founded in 1986. The ensemble plays instruments Ted has handcrafted.

"Being able to create a family together is a spectacular, amazing gift," he told me exuberantly. "It represents commitment in an even bigger way than marriage alone." Watching his children grow up from the beginning in the stable home he made for them has repaired many wounds. "Not only did I get to see what the early years were like, but that connection with a child is amazing; it feels eternal." As Tom Robbins said, "It's never too late to have a happy childhood."

"I've always been caring," Ted said, "but the depths of my caring now, having the trust of a partner and having children, make me freer to give of myself. This was the gift of marriage."

The world is full of men and women; why is it so hard to find one to love later in life? There are fewer effortless opportunities, to be sure, no constant supply of new prospects as in college or your twenties when most people cycle through jobs and friends; you have to actively seek them at a time when your character and habits have become entrenched and accommodation to another person is hard work. It is easy to lose heart and become convinced that, because of your looks or your personality or a lack of opportunity, there is no one in the world who will want you. Yet these four people, with their assorted pathologies, prejudices, and imperfections, defied the odds and married. How did they do it? Anna was lucky and ready; Lisa and Wendy resolved enough of their problems and made finding husbands literally their business; and Ted knew what he was up against in himself and went to extraordinary lengths to change it.

One element that their stories have in common is that soul mates come in more different sizes and shapes than you imagine. They often bear little resemblance to the numbingly upbeat self-promotions, complete with lists of beguiling but entirely external and often irrelevant qualifications that fill dating Web sites and personal ads. They can be divorced—sometimes multiple times—considerably older or younger, inconveniently located. They can have a different religion (or none at all) or vote for the other political party. Each of these people learned to overlook what looked like compelling disqualifications that became unimportant when they fell in love. They each knew enough to realize that what matters most is tenderness and steadfastness.

Despite what Maestro Horszowski said, the "right girl" does not just come along. You have to be able to recognize her in whatever guise she presents herself. You have to tolerate the embarrassment of being on the market at this late date, acknowledge that you want someone, let the world know it, and kiss a lot of frogs. Clearing out the detritus of the past, with or without the help of a therapist, makes all the difference. You can't find love if you don't look for it—or at the very least know how to recognize it when you see it.

Happiness is earned.

10

LOVE IS STRONGER THAN THE GRAVE

The self-contained, austerely elegant woman who walked into my office certainly didn't look like a prostitute. Her manner was so self-effacing that she hardly seemed to be present. Her voice was so quiet that she was almost inaudible, like someone unused to conversation, and yet there was a held-in intensity about her. She had come, she said, because she was so shy that she could hardly utter a word.

It wasn't until our second session that she told me about her past. She had grown up in a family with parents who were professionally successful but silent and strange, incapable of giving attention or the most rudimentary sense of direction to any of their six children, of whom she was the eldest. Their world was virtually mute; family members barely spoke to one another. Their self-containment was so extreme that when a brain tumor caused her mother to lose the ability to speak, the level of conversation in the household barely changed at all.

My patient felt so deprived of emotional sustenance that she fled across the country at twenty with a much older man, the first person to take an interest in her. Like many self-absorbed people with artistic aspirations ungrounded in actual talent, he felt that working for a living was beneath his dignity; pimping struck him as an ideal occupation, and he readily recognized that his attractive, compliant new girlfriend would provide a convenient source of income. "I could walk into any hotel at any hour, and nobody would stop me," she explained. She longed for even a perverse facsimile of relatedness so intensely that she forced herself to comply. "For the first time in my life," she said, "someone was telling me what to do, even if it was to jump off a cliff." All her johns quickly became regulars because she seemed so hungry for love and so eager to mold herself to their desires.

After two years of self-abasement, she could take no more and packed a suitcase and fled, leaving her master no forwarding address. Within ten years, she was working successfully as an assistant to an interior designer and was living with a man who genuinely cared for her but knew nothing of her former profession; I was the only one who did.

I told her that if she wanted a future with this man—which she longed for—she had to reveal her past to him. With surprisingly little hesitation, she did so (it must have been a burden to harbor such a secret), and his response proved him worthy: he hated what her life had been, but he knew she was a different person now and that she was his.

They lived together for five more years when she finally admitted to herself that being his companion wasn't enough to satisfy her; she wanted to be his wife. The sanctity and legitimacy of marriage were essential for her in order to neutralize the furtive unreality she had once vanished into. She had never before recognized, let alone verbalized, that she wanted to be uniquely special to anybody—you have to have a sense of self to do that—but she wanted it now, even though she was deathly afraid to reveal her desire. I told her she had to inform him, directly and unequivocally; she had to feel she deserved and then to hear herself ask for him to make a lifelong commitment to her. Just as her first act of selfhood was to flee one man, her second would be to embrace another. And to do that, she had to speak.

Ironically, it was far more torturous for her to tell him that she wanted to marry him than it had been to reveal her shame. She was giving him power over her fate and opening herself to the possibility of being rejected. He had been unhappily married before and was reluctant to go through the formalities again, but after a two-year struggle, she managed through force of will to make herself clear. Finally, he bought her a ring—she proudly showed me the sleek and unusual one that she had selected—and they set a date.

Her success had an unexpected consequence. To my astonishment, she came to her next session in a state of terror, weeping, almost hiding, and more silent than I had seen her in all the years I had known her. She was getting the thing that mattered most to her: being seen, heard, and chosen. She was loved and honored for the first time in her life—why was she quaking? She looked at me with frightened eyes and said in a passionate whisper, as if saying it any louder would make it magically come true, "What if he dies?"

I told her that loss is built into love. When someone becomes precious and you let yourself need him and tell him you want him, there is no way to avoid this eventuality. You are putting yourself in his hands, and he becomes irreplaceable. When you give yourself that way, the real way—neither embodying another's fantasy nor disconnected from your authentic self—an essential part of yourself is forever bound up with the other's fragile life. You merge your destinies. Only the whole person she had now become could join her beloved so completely. When you have someone, you have someone to lose.

Since risk hangs over shared lives, ardor and anxiety are inextricable. You never know how the loss will come—whether he will lose you or you him, but it is a certainty that there will be a shattering involuntary separation. Death is the abandonment caused not by betrayal but by fidelity. Even so, a relationship this deep lives on as part of you. It becomes inextricable from your identity; it cannot be wrested from you utterly. Could she dare to take the chance? She steadied herself and proclaimed, "I will."

Half a century earlier, another young woman was also paralyzed by shyness and unable to speak. Since she lived in Vienna in Freud's heyday, she decided to seek therapy after more than one young man bewitched by her soulful beauty but put off by her silence had declared, "For such a pretty girl, why are you so arrogant?"

She told me this anecdote as a seventy-five-year-old matron the first time she invited me to a dinner of wiener schnitzel and apple strudel in her rambling apartment on Central Park West when I was a twenty-six-year-old graduate student. We had met working in the research department of a psychoanalytic institute, where she, a social worker in her youth, edited a newsletter.

All I really knew about her then was that she was the widow of a psychiatrist and founder of the institute (its library was named for him), who had been the protégé of Wilhelm Stekel, one of Freud's earliest and most radical adherents,* and that he had died years earlier. But the real story went far deeper.

I had never been anywhere like Lilly's apartment. The place was a time warp, furnished entirely with perfectly preserved artifacts from the late 1930s. The old concert grand was in the living room, where the couple and their musical friends had played quintets on Sundays, with Lilly on piano and her husband, Emil, on viola, which his mentor had decreed that he had to learn so they would always have the requisite string parts. She had lost him suddenly from a heart attack when she was sixty-three and he was seventy, but his consulting room, a book-filled oval space behind the living room—complete with an archetypical oriental carpet–draped analytic couch and walls covered with old photographs of the Freudian elite—seemed untouched and still ready to hear secrets. She showed me a calling card of Freud's and the handwritten file where Emil had transcribed and organized by theme all the dreams of his patients, which became the basis for his book on the subject. There was an entire shelf of copies of this book—one of many he wrote—in numerous languages, and she gave it to me. That night, she also opened her wardrobe and displayed the hand-embroidered linens from her trousseau, carefully folded and perfumed, which her mother had begun stitching at her birth.

I asked her the identity of the ravishing woman whose full-length portrait hung in her dining room, and she replied with downcast eyes, "It is myself." Her husband, she said, had accepted it in lieu of payment from the artist, who had been his patient—one of his countless acts of generosity. Her admira-

---

* Stekel, whom Freud expelled from the psychoanalytic movement in 1912, advocated "active analysis," a briefer form of therapy in which the analyst interacted more with the patient than in classical Freudian (known as "orthodox") technique.

tion of him was boundless; it was because of his clearheaded judgment that her entire family had escaped to America before the Anschluss.

I was curious to know how they had met. Only then she told me that at the end of her last session, her analysis success-fully concluded by mutual consent, she sat up on the couch to bid a grateful farewell to the compelling young psychiatrist who had helped her overcome her anxiety and find her voice. But instead of showing her to the door, he turned to face her and asked a question engraved on her memory: "And when may I see you?" They married within the year. "He was my analyst. Now it can be told," she said shyly, almost blushing to reveal at last what had been a transgressive secret, a taboo-breaking risk, for decades; sexual relationships—even marital ones—between therapists and their erstwhile patients were then considered ver-boten because of the Oedipal implications and boundary viola-tions involved.

Soon after her revelation, we went to a concert of chamber music together. It was a program of string quartets by Schubert, her favorite composer, and she idolized the dashing young first violinist. At the end, moved to tears, she said with quiet inten-sity, "That was too beautiful to bear. It was like analysis"—an analogy that would be absurd uttered by anyone else, but was the simple truth from her. Analysis, music, and falling in love were ecstatically intermingled for her in an inimitable way. No ordinary suitor could compare, then or now.

Lilly didn't exactly lower her voice when she spoke her hus-band's name, but it brightened, and her eyes softened, every time she did so, and the many circumstances in which she evoked him suggested that he was a constant point of reference; her inner monologue was dialogue and communion. She often referred to him both obliquely and directly, and yet it was never morbid or off-putting, because he was so alive for her. For example, when I told her I was marrying a man who was eight years younger than I, she replied, "Ah yes, the perfect age difference," since it was the interval between hers and Emil's age, even though in reverse.

Was she just living in a bygone era, obsessed with lost love, immersing herself in it to avoid her present loneliness yet afraid to move on? I think not. She seemed not so much clinging to her past as buoyed up by it; she saw life through the lens of their relationship and the power of his personality. Her solitude was not lonely. Hers was a quietly intense, self-contained world, infused with memories that were living presences, into which others were welcomed. Freud said that "neurotics suffer from reminiscences," but Lilly was consoled by hers.

Psychoanalytic theory, from Freud's day to the present, has not had nearly as much to say about healthy passion as about the more grotesque pathological kind. What would it make of hers? Self psychology, the modern theoretical approach founded by Heinz Kohut, would recognize Emil as Lilly's "self-object," her internal touchstone of sustenance, solace, and self-esteem. Making use of another in this way is a sign of mental health and a source of stability. But Otto Kernberg,* who has written extensively about the prerequisites for long-term erotic fulfillment, might be wary of an all-consuming romance after death like hers and question her unassailable fidelity. According to him, an earmark of mature love is the ability to grieve fully for the dead beloved, to retain the relationship within

---

* Kohut focused on the development and maintenance of a person's sense of self; his rival Kernberg, who remained in the more traditional psychoanalytic camp, emphasized the role of conflicts between love and aggression and how significant relationships are internalized.

oneself, and then to accept (and to seek) a new partner "without guilt or insecurity."

In Lilly's case, giving herself to another would have been sacrilegious, because she felt that she had the ultimate experience of marriage, and it sufficed for her. Their relationship was so unique and precious and so vividly present that it could never be superseded. Emil's love for her, and hers for him, continued to fulfill her. To seek another love would be an unthinkable act of infidelity not only to him but to herself and to the woman she had become, the life she had had, because of him. It was choice, not fear or limitation in her ability to relate, that bound her eternally to him.

I was always struck by the remarkable contentment, the lack of bitterness, that Lilly exuded as she faced old age and death alone; she had two grown sons and several grandchildren, but they had their own lives at some remove from her. Of all the American institutions she admired, she loved Thanksgiving the most, because, she said, "I have so much to be thankful for." She took joy in small things and seemed utterly devoid of the envy that many in her situation are corroded by (with one glaring exception: "The only thing I've ever envied," this fine musician confessed without a trace of irony, "is my brother's perfect pitch"). Other than a severe mouse phobia—Emil once found her in their hotel room after a traumatic sighting, standing on one leg on the bed, trying to read a book while she waited for him to rescue her—I never saw a sign of psychopathology such as depression, intense anxiety, or withdrawal in her.

A birthday card she sent me, one of the few I have ever saved or whose message I've remembered, epitomized her attitude: "Life itself is life's great treasure." And she did not hoard her treasures; her wedding gift to me was an exquisite set of sleek red-and-gold-banded art deco demitasse cups from her trousseau. The gesture brought to mind "Hello, Young Lovers" from *The King and I,* one of the most generous love songs ever written, in which the middle-aged heroine Anna exhorts a pair of furtive lovers not to pity her, because their passion recalls her own. Lilly was overjoyed for me.

The risk that my silent patient daringly embraced, my formerly shy Viennese friend had actually endured: the loss of the man who had given her a voice and saved her—my patient, from a life of degradation, Lilly, from literal death in the Holocaust. Like Pygmalion, each man was irreplaceable to the woman he had rescued—with her active participation—from silence and enlivened through love. At the beginning, my patient did not know that she could sustain herself through him even if he died, but I knew that she could, as Lilly had done; he was hers forever.

Lilly, the most romantic, fulfilled soul I have ever known, was alone but not lonely. My patient had been lonely as only a person without a center, who had never known comfort or been prized before, can be. Thanks to her husband, she could never feel that way again; even his death could not take away what she had become. Kohut would say that she, like Lilly, used her husband as her selfobject.

I say they are both true lovers, sustained from within, and mated, like swans, for life.

Both my patient and my friend clearly idealized their husbands; they found fathers and mothers and saviors in them. This was realistic on their parts; the personalities and actions of both men made them highly idealizable. But the way these women looked up to and needed their husbands did not make them dependent or infantile; they functioned as professionals in their own right and as friends and soul mates to the men they admired, and they were admired in turn by their husbands. Their attitude was an essential part of their fully adult appreciation of how remarkable their mates and their marriages genuinely were.

Psychoanalytic theorists are ambivalent about whether idealization is a sign of mature love or a regression to childish reliance on a parental stand-in who cannot be seen as realistically flawed because the fantasy of the loved one's perfection shores up an immature sense of self. Michael Balint, one of the original members of the British object relations school of thought, believes that idealization "is not absolutely necessary for a good love relation" and agrees with Freud's observation that idealizing a beloved can actually hinder the development of fulfilling love as an adult; perhaps Freud was speaking from personal experience, since his adoring letters to his fiancée, Martha Bernays, are full of idealization, and there are questions about how ultimately satisfying that union was. But Otto Kernberg claims—and I agree with him—that "a mature form of idealization" is fundamental to a marriage of true minds. I believe that this type of adulation must not just be one-sided, and, unlike Kernberg, I think it can outlast death. Not every marriage is like my patient's or Lilly's, but the deepest ones are. They are like the halves of the reunited primordial egg that Aristophanes refers to in Plato's *Symposium*: "And when one of them meets the other half, the actual half of himself . . . the pair are lost in an amazement of love and friendship and intimacy and one will not be out of the other's sight . . . even for a moment: These are the people who pass their whole lives together. . . ."

When I went to see Lilly in the hospital during her last illness, she was welcoming, overjoyed to have company, full of praise for the care she was getting, thankful for the first solid food she was able to eat. She gently corrected my husband's German accent when he wished her a gallant farewell. There on the table next to her bed, where she could gaze at it until the last, was Emil's photograph. It was as though her favorite Schubert song, "Du bist die Ruh," was silently surrounding her, bearing her back to him:

> You are my peace, my joy and rest,
> You are the yearning in my breast
> I pledge to you, my sacred place,
> all pain and joy.
> Towards me now face
> and softly close the door behind . . .
> My eye's whole sight, so much in thrall
> in your own light—
> oh, fill it all!

11

LOVE HIM, HATE HIS POLITICS
How a Liberal and a Conservative Stay Married

Next Election Day, like every Election Day for the last three decades, I'll show up faithfully at my polling place, rain or shine. I'll make it my business to get there even if there's a blizzard, a hurricane, or a tsunami, and if I can't go in person, I'll use an absentee ballot. Once again, I'll be pulling the levers (or tapping the screen) for some people I actually agree with, for some I'm not crazy about, and for others I've never heard of. Of course I'm planning to participate in every future presidential election, but I'll be sure not to miss the midterms, either. On the first Tuesday after the first Monday of every November, for the rest of my life, I'll register my choices for senators, congressmen, governors, state senators, assemblymen, mayors, city council members, and judges. As long as they're Democrats, they can count on my support.

It's a matter of moral obligation, not just civic duty: I've got to cancel out my husband's vote.

For thirty-five years, I, a card-carrying liberal, have been married to a conservative Republican. My husband is not just a fervently committed conservative Republican; he is a *professional* fervently committed conservative Republican—a senior editor of the leading right-wing journal in America.

My husband and I violently disagree on every conceivable political issue, including abortion, gun control, and assisted suicide, as well as on the necessity of an impregnable wall of separation between church and state—all of which he opposes and I passionately support and consider sacred. The only public issues we agree about are that both parties in New York State government are riddled with corruption and that increasing the number of gambling casinos here is a terrible idea. His deepest convictions haven't budged in the thirty-eight years I have known him, and mine haven't, either. Nonetheless, I can say unequivocally that marrying him was the best decision I ever made and that he is probably the only man I could ever live with.

I've long been aware that our mixed marriage is unusual (until recently, I knew of no other among my acquaintances), but I didn't realize just how exotic—bordering on extinct—it actually was until I saw a study from Stanford University* stating that the ferocity of political partisanship in the United States is so intense that marriages across party lines are "exceedingly rare"—9 percent—and that the prejudices that each side feels about the other are even more deeply ingrained and

---

* S. Iyengar and S. J. Westwood, "Fear and Loathing across Party Lines: New Evidence on Group Polarization," *American Journal of Political Science* (2014), doi:10.1111/ajps.12152.

virulent than racism. Parents now worry about their children marrying outside party affiliations, and, to my astonishment and dismay, many single people consider political orientation a more important criterion in a potential mate than physical or personality attributes.* Our prejudices haven't changed, but antagonism in the rest of the country toward the other side has escalated ominously since we wed in 1980, thanks in part to the Internet and ever more rabidly partisan radio and television.

How did we find each other? So insular was I in my youth that I was not even conscious of knowing any Republicans other than my father and certainly never imagined having one as a boyfriend. I equated conservatism with the fanatical, paranoid John Birch Society. But in my late twenties, I joined a Renaissance singing group, and there he was—tall, clever, with intense blue eyes and a lyrical baritone. I was delighted to discover that he was a professional writer, although I was taken aback when I learned where he worked. It didn't stop me, though; I'd been treated abominably by too many men who shared all my opinions to let his convictions get in the way.

My future husband was considerably more open-minded about love across party lines than I. Even though his parents were both committed conservatives, he grew up in the era when liberalism was the dominant ideology, which gave him much more exposure to the opposition at an early age. He even dated a former Communist in college.

Our wedding was a bipartisan affair. My mentor, one of the early victims of the McCarthyite purges, gave me away, and my husband's publisher, one of McCarthy's most avid enforcers, gave a reading. A knowing friend quipped, "Bedfellows make

---

* J. R. Alford, P. K. Hatemi, J. R. Hibbing, N. G. Martin, and L. J. Eames, "The Politics of Mate Choice," *Journal of Politics* 73(2): 36279.

strange politics." Somehow everyone behaved, setting a trend that we have emulated—and worked at—with only a few painful exceptions ever since.

The most bruising of those exceptions occurred in 1989, the only time we had our version of a knock-down, drag-out confrontation, and it was so unnerving that I remember all the particulars. It was initiated by me; my husband knew better than to broach so radioactive a topic. One morning, I picked up *The New York Times* and read the front-page headline about the Supreme Court's *Webster* decision, which allowed states to place significant restrictions on abortion rights. I knew that this would open the door to massive efforts by conservatives to dismantle *Roe v. Wade*, and I was beside myself. I said, half under my breath but audible all the same, "This is the end. I'm going to have to join a protest march." He uncharacteristically rose to the bait and countered, with grim determination, "If you march, I march." Fortunately, I knew not to respond to his counterpunch and let the tension escalate into real warfare; this was a fight neither he nor I could win, with the potential to destroy everything we had carefully built and that we both cherished, without accomplishing anything. We kept our distance for the rest of the day. It was torture. I felt lonely and bereft, and so did he. That night, we agreed to disagree and drop the subject. We pulled ourselves back from the precipice and have made sure never to approach it again.

Even after I learned to inhibit such outbursts, it took our first decade together for me to fully accept how yawning our ideological divide really was, despite how much we were in harmony about virtually everything else. Slowly, I became reconciled to the fact that not even my considerable powers of persuasion—not to mention the self-evident correctness of my positions—would make him change his mind, but, alas, it is so; he never even tried to change mine.

It is a pernicious fantasy that you can alter your spouse's political opinions any more than you can transform his other habits, character traits, or ways of seeing the world. Persuasion doesn't work, and showing him the error of his ways doesn't work because he doesn't think his ways are in error even if you do.

Does our marriage endure because we have both mellowed and become so serene and levelheaded that we have found a civilized way to rise above the fray and debate matters politic? No. Absolutely not. Experience has taught us that there are times when avoidance alone, enforced by self-control and silence aggressively and consistently applied, is the key to forestalling painful and hopeless arguments, extended icy silences, and sinking feelings in the night. It's like learning to forcibly restrain yourself from telling your spouse "You're just like your mother" when he has done something infuriating, even if it's horribly true. It does not erode our integrity or prevent us from supporting whatever causes we wish without provocatively announcing our beliefs or our actions to each other; the moral high ground is dangerous territory in any marriage. This limitation on my freedom of expression in my own home is a price I willingly pay. Why is it worth it? Because the companionship of the other resident is the greatest joy in my life.

Twenty-five years after the *Webster* affair, I read another front-page *Times* headline announcing that most of the abortion clinics in Texas were being forced to close. I felt exactly the same way about the issue in 2014 as I had in 1989, but I behaved differently: I simply said that it disturbed me deeply, with no

threat attached. My husband said nothing. I dealt with my outrage by making an unannounced contribution and commiser-
ating privately with people who agree with me; I assume he did
the same, although I wouldn't think to ask. We don't have to
share everything; we just don't rub each other's faces in it. I
don't feel untrue to my convictions because I cannot make the
slightest dent in his.

These days, we rarely fight, at least about public policy, and
we never begin sentences when discussing the news with "Do
you *really* believe [fill in the blank]?" We have learned to resort
to nonincendiary inquiries like "What does your side think
about X?" or "Who will you nominate?" My husband's years as
a journalist have made him a savvy political analyst, and I find
his insights fascinating. I am much better informed and more
sophisticated—and more liberal—as a result of being married
to him than I otherwise would be. My opinions, however, are
reserved for my fellow liberal colleagues and friends, and if they
ask me, as they often do, how my charming and sensitive husband can possibly hold the opinions he does, I suggest they
ask him directly. It takes tact and dexterity, but doesn't marriage require these things of everybody? Doesn't every couple
have profound, fundamental disagreements, even if they vote
the same ticket at the polls?

Living together so long has taught us that it is possible to
tolerate our opposition on serious issues because we agree on
what matters most, which is that the camaraderie we have created in every other sphere is more basic, and far more precious,
than ideology. Nobody makes me think, makes me laugh, or
comforts me when I cry, the way he does. We both have reason
to know that, when you're lying in a hospital bed receiving
chemotherapy, you don't check the party registration of the
person by your side faithfully getting you through it.

It also helps that we have an enormous amount in common in every other arena. Both of us are psychologically minded nature lovers who prefer each other's company to almost anybody else's. We both write books; I'm delighted that his recent ones are historical rather than polemical, so I can enjoy them wholeheartedly. Our temperaments are at once similar and complementary, and we enjoy a rare degree of mutual appreciation, lack of envy, and delight in each other's company. He expresses his political views in writing or with his colleagues, not in conversation with me. Over the years, I have also come to know many of these colleagues—who disagree with me as much as he does—and count them as friends. It stretches the mind.

The things that bring us together are deeper than the things that could have torn us apart; we can finish each other's sentences on every subject but politics. He loves me for what I am, which includes the ways I am maddeningly different from him.

Living with someone who profoundly disagrees makes you think about what you really believe and why. Paradoxically, it broadens and deepens your convictions. Agreement in the political sphere, however, is no shortcut to compatibility in any other, and a life partner's convictions, even the most passionately held ones, are only as important as the character of which they are a part.

So why don't we both agree to stay home on Election Day? The reason that we don't is one of the keys to why our marriage endures: even though I trust him with my life, I don't trust him, and would never ask him, not to vote his conscience. I respect his right to his opinions, even though they seem dangerously benighted to me; this, we both believe, is the American Way. I also respect them because they are an integral part of him—just like mine are part of me. I married the whole man; he would not be who he is without them.

I'm sorry for the growing number of people who look for love only on dating Web sites that are segregated, like radio or television networks, by redness or blueness. It's really no better than a match by astrological sign or any other external criteria, because the political beliefs people subscribe to say surprisingly little about who they really are. They will never discover, as I did, that it's possible to find a soul mate with whom the only thing you don't have in common is politics.

I know only one other couple who are married across the ideological divide. They make our differences appear slight, but the underlying dynamics of their forty-year union are the same. They had more to overcome than we did, because when they met in graduate school, back in the Nixon administration, they agreed with each other more or less, but he changed allegiances radically later on. She has been a socialist and an activist since her student days. "He used to be two steps to the left of center," she told me a little wistfully. "I just didn't know yet that I really was a neoconservative," he countered.

Politics is too ingrained in each of their identities for an avoidance strategy like ours to work for them. He, too, is a political journalist, with a more combative style than my husband's, although it is tempered by his fundamentally sweet disposition and his reverence for his wife's intellect. She, with all her quiet intensity, is a formidable opponent, both persistent and well informed about their numerous hot-button issues. Unlike my husband and me, these two go head-to-head about politics regularly. "She's hard to fight with because she always has her facts and dates right," he complained. She didn't say so, but I know that he's hard to fight with because he never concedes and revisits old battles as a point of honor.

Outside the political arena, however, their rapport is touching to behold. The way they look at each other and talk of and to each other, after so many years together, shows that lasting love is an ongoing achievement, not a happy accident. Their amity is profound, and it has seen them through differences that would seem irreconcilable. Their goodwill transcends the ideas that divide them; their fundamental values—loyalty, honesty, kindness—unite them. This has allowed them to face numerous tragedies and reversals of fortune over the years and never to fail each other.

The pilot-philosopher Antoine de Saint-Exupéry said, "Love does not consist in gazing at each other, but in looking outward together in the same direction." That direction is neither to the right nor to the left but straight to the heart of things.

12

RECOVERING THE GOOD FROM
A LOVE GONE BAD

It took me a year to wear her earrings again, the ones she had bought me in Paris. She had bought them long before her failure to visit me in the hospital and our awkward, painful breakup. Those wonderful earrings were purple carved acrylic crystals resembling quartz, and only she would have recognized them as my taste. I'd let them languish in my drawer, intentionally overlooked, because they forced upon me the stark reality of losing her—the intimate friend who had witnessed and participated in all the vicissitudes of my life for twenty-five years, with whom I would create no more memories and get, or give, no more special gifts.

Putting them back on for the first time was an act of defiance: I don't miss you. I don't need you. I refuse to deprive myself of these charming baubles any longer just because you've deprived me of yourself.

Soon I put them away again. Try as I might, I found I could not yet separate the gift from the giver; the shock of her ill treatment still hurt too much to be neutralized by an act of will. So back they went into the drawer after their brief foray on my ears—out of sight and out of mind once more.

Another year went by. I'd almost forgotten about their existence, but I found myself reaching for her earrings again, just as I began to write about her. Seeking them out was a palpable part of the process of reconsidering and working through the meaning of our relationship, of not just filing it bitterly away but letting it live again, if only in my own mind.

What I felt when I put on her earrings again was unexpected. The pain, the anger, and the sorrow had not completely dissipated, but another emotion had now joined them, welcome but unbidden: appreciation. This time, the earrings rekindled the memory of having been loved and understood in a unique way by a person the likes of whom I would never find again. I wasn't cutting off hope for other intimate friendships in the future, but I knew that no one could ever replace her, because relationships are not interchangeable. Even if her gift was the only artifact left of her love for me, even if I could never forgive her, that love was real, precious, and indestructible. She had changed, but I retained what she had given me, the good she had done me—and her later unloving actions could not wrest it from me. I had no illusions about rekindling our relationship, but I began to recall it with pleasure and gratitude, despite its shocking, inexplicable denouement.

Only grieving—reengaging with every feeling and looking away from none of them—allows you to begin the process of recovering love. Mourning a loss acknowledges there was something to lose. It ultimately restores to you what was valuable (if anything was), burns off some of the devastation without entirely erasing it. You find that you are left with more than ashes in your mouth.

I faced a related but different predicament trying to come to terms with Michael, the golden-haired faithless lover of my youth: was there anything worth retrieving from that tormented relationship? At least I had my friend's earrings and two decades of devotion before she abandoned me. But he had been in my life for a much shorter time and caused me more harm than good. I had no photograph, nothing concrete but my own words in a tattered diary left to remind me of him. I myself had destroyed his letters almost fifty years ago and had tried my best to bury my memories of the sorrow and unquenchable longing I felt in order not to be crushed by them.

Then I remembered the one "gift" that had passed between us. It was the golden condom I had created and sent him when he had written to me to ask advice on how to seduce another woman. Gilding and mailing that condom was a flamboyant gesture that had the unexpected, paradoxical effect of impressing and re-seducing him. Although the occasion was one of the worst rejections of my life and the aftermath was bitter, the memory of my action and the impact it had was sweet indeed.

For all the grief he caused me, I cannot say that I wished we'd never met or that I'd never loved him; this meant that there was good to be recovered. We had shared episodes of passionate delight, even though they were interlaced with pain for me almost from the beginning. I certainly did not love wisely, and part of my love was desperate and blind, but it was never mere masochistic submission; the joy I felt with him was precious and real, worthy of being remembered—unique, indelible, mine forever.

Rediscovering good things among the ruins does not mean

denying the bad ones, but it requires a rigorous effort of excavation and a willingness to relive experiences that felt unbearable at the time; you have to spread the whole relationship before you, and to hold all its contradictions in consciousness simultaneously, in order to judge it accurately. When I no longer had to wall off the worst of him, the best of him became accessible to me again—a parallel experience to my rediscovering my friend's value.

I will always carry a scar as well as a spark of the eternal desire I felt for him. All this is part of me, and I welcome it all, without bitterness or hatred. My beloved, like my lost woman friend, is woven into the fabric of my self, where delight and damage intermingle. Now my memories of both of them are real, three-dimensional, bright as well as dark.

Harry Guntrip, one of the major figures of the British object relations school of modern psychoanalysis, reported in a starkly revealing and moving autobiographical essay* a life changing observation that his analyst, the profoundly gifted D. W. Winnicott, made to him. This observation ultimately consoled him and cured him of a despair so deep that it had almost fatally undermined his health numerous times. It has always resonated for me. Winnicott asserted that even though Guntrip's mother had become shockingly violent and abandoned him early on, she had been a naturally good mother for the first few months

---

* Harry Guntrip, "My Experience of Analysis with Fairbairn and Winnicott," *International Journal of Psycho-Analysis* 77 (1996): 739–754. Here, in his own words, is how Guntrip (1901–1975) recalls the revelation: "He [Winnicott] enabled me to reach extraordinarily clear understanding that my mother had almost certainly had an initial period of natural maternalism with me as her first baby, for perhaps a couple of months, before her personality problems robbed me of that 'good mother.'"

of his life. The recognition that he had once been loved by her, Guntrip realized, became a source of inner sustenance for him and had permitted him to refind that primordial loving mother again in his nurturing male analyst.

I believe that it is one of the most important things in life not to lose anything of value that you have ever gotten, from the living or the dead, even from those who later forsook you, betrayed you, or bitterly disappointed you. Love, joy, and meaning can be resurrected from the most unlikely sources, from relationships saturated with sorrow, shame—even hatred. While it is impossible to predict what will emerge as meaningful when you choose to search it out, the very effort creates the potential for discovery and gives you more of a say in your own life. I don't think it's possible or necessary to recover appreciation for everyone who has violated your trust, but when there is something meaningful to retrieve, celebrating it is a genuine compensation for loss. It sustains you from within.

If anything in your love was real—imperfect, ambivalent, obsessive, or selfish in part but tender and true at the core—it is yours forever, even though the one you loved loves you no longer or never fully returned your devotion. The authentic core of love is eternal, even if the person who inspired it will never return to you. But you have to hold fast to it and fight through your despair, your disappointment, and your bitterness to find it, to resurrect it, to claim it. With work and with will, the consoling promise of Dylan Thomas's words comes true: "Though lovers be lost love shall not."

ACKNOWLEDGMENTS

Everyone I interviewed for *The Golden Condom* deserves my gratitude for the generosity and candor with which they shared their intimate experiences. I am especially indebted to my patients, who for the past forty years have taught me about love in all its guises.

Kaja Perina, the editor in chief of *Psychology Today*, gave me much-needed wise counsel in the initial stages of this daunting enterprise. Dr. Douglas Mock, evolutionary biologist and emeritus professor at the University of Oklahoma, served as my first science officer, providing a witty and accessible tutorial on the neurological substrate of love. Dr. Anne Hallward, creator and host of Safe Space Radio, introduced me to remarkable people and encouraged them to tell me their stories. She has been an invaluable resource, both personally and professionally. Dr. Nina Smiley and Bernadette Miles were my emotional bulwarks throughout the process.

My heartfelt thanks to my colleague Jennifer Irvin, LCSW, for bringing to my attention revelatory contemporary psychoanalytic work on obsessive love, which greatly deepened my understanding and helped me interpret aspects of my own experience that had been opaque to me.

My husband, Richard Brookhiser, read and heard every word I wrote, often in multiple iterations, and offered his expert, clearheaded advice at every turn. The description of my youthful follies did not faze him.

The enthusiasm and skill of my agent, Michelle Tessler, is precious to me. The help provided by Peter Horoszko, assistant editor at Picador, went far beyond the call of duty.

This book could not have been written without the inspiration and the gimlet eye of Stephen Morrison, my nonpareil editor. His empathy, expertise, and dedication brought out the best in my writing. The experience of working with him has made this, my sixth author-editor marriage, worth the wait.

I am dedicating *The Golden Condom* to my coach, Terry Laughlin, founder of Total Immersion Swimming, who has taught me invaluable lessons about living, both in and out of the water.

ABOUT THE AUTHOR

Jeanne Safer, Ph.D., a psychotherapist in New York City, is the author of five books, including *The Normal One*, *Cain's Legacy*, and *Beyond Motherhood*. Dr. Safer has appeared on *The Daily Show* and *Good Morning America* as well as numerous NPR broadcasts. Her work has been the subject of articles in *The New York Times* and *The Wall Street Journal*. She blogs for *The Huffington Post* and *Psychology Today* and is, most recently, a contributor to *Selfish, Shallow, and Self-Absorbed: Sixteen Writers on the Decision Not to Have Kids* (Picador, 2015).